PRAISE FOR MIC

EXPERIENCING
THE NEXT WORLD NOW

"Grosso is an original thinker whose contributions in the field of human consciousness reflect his deep understanding of the most pressing spiritual questions of our time. He tackles the questions about what lies ahead—and within us—with masterful skill. He is a magnificent writer."

—Caroline M. Myss, author of *Sacred Contracts* and *Anatomy of the Spirit*

"I can't think of anyone who can handle this challenging and all-important material any better. Grosso expresses himself with wonderful clarity, and with humor, and manages at the same time to maintain a proper attitude of skepticism."

—John Cleese

"If anyone can write a book on survival that is both easy to read and true to the research, both exciting and worth reading, it's Grosso."

—Bruce Greyson, Bonner-Lowry Professor of Psychiatry, University of Virginia, and editor of the *Journal of Near-Death Studies*

Experiencing
The
Next World
Now

MICHAEL GROSSO

PARAVIEW POCKET BOOKS

New York London Toronto Sydney Singapore

PARAVIEW
191 Seventh Avenue, New York, NY 10011

POCKET BOOKS, a division of Simon & Schuster, Inc.
1230 Avenue of the Americas, New York, NY 10020

ISBN: 0-7434-7105-9

First Paraview Pocket Books trade paperback edition January 2004

10   9   8   7   6   5   4   3   2   1

POCKET and colophon are registered trademarks of
Simon & Schuster, Inc.

Manufactured in the United States of America

For information regarding special discounts for bulk purchases,
please contact Simon & Schuster Special Sales at 1-800-456-6798
or business@simonandschuster.com.

To my brother, Stephen,
and my sisters, Bella and Anne

Contents

Introduction   *xi*

PART ONE: EXPERIENCES   1
CHAPTER 1: Ecstatic Journeys   *5*
CHAPTER 2: Of Ghostes & Spirites   23
CHAPTER 3: The Medium and the Message   63
CHAPTER 4: One Self, Many Bodies   *103*

PART TWO: CHALLENGES   127
CHAPTER 5: Explanations   *129*
CHAPTER 6: Imagining the Next World   *145*

PART THREE: CONNECTIONS   153
CHAPTER 7: Evolution   *155*
CHAPTER 8: Mental Bridges   *170*
CHAPTER 9: The Otherworld Nearby   *188*

PART FOUR: PRACTICE   221
CHAPTER 10: Flatliner Models   *225*
CHAPTER 11: Changing Our Way of Life   *255*

Epilogue   273
Notes   281
Acknowledgments   293
Index   295

Introduction

I must have been about seventeen years old when I woke up one day and realized I was going to die—not immediately, *but sooner or later*. My main thought, after the first wave of terror passed, was: "No! There's got to be a way out of this!"

The idea of my future extinction *felt* grossly unfair, not to mention *very* annoying. I couldn't stop thinking about it. I walked around, agog, in a kind of trance: streets, storefronts, people walking back and forth, seemed wobbly, unreal, and for days things glowed with a sinister light. The more I thought, the more I protested. And the more I wondered about—everything! Exactly as Dr. Samuel Johnson famously quipped, the thought of death concentrated my mind.

The concentration took the form of a nervous eagerness to get to the bottom of the mystery. Right from the start, I was convinced my ignorance was bottomless. I felt sure there were depths of mind, of life, I couldn't even imagine, no less hope to fathom. So, in this abrupt and stinging way, the discovery of my mortality turned out to be a blessing in disguise. It made *life* more interesting—more edgy and challenging. In the end, it made death interesting. Would my death be a meeting with nothingness or a great opening to the unknown? I felt goaded to explore the supreme mystery—the miracle of consciousness—that allows the world to appear to us in all its glory.

This book is the story of what I've learned so far. I began my search haphazardly in the jungle of ideas and strange emotions we call religion. At seventeen, I wandered into a building in New York City that housed the Vedanta Society, and was struck by what I read on the wall: "Truth is one; men call it variously." (How tolerant that seemed, how friendly and generous!) I met an old man in Central Park whose passion was making religious icons. He surprised me with a story about an out-of-body experience he once had, and was fond of saying that he looked forward to death as "the great adventure."

I discovered there were beings called mystics and shamans and yogis who claimed to be familiar with the exotic outback of human consciousness. I found there were Western scientists who collected facts about the enigmas of human capacity. And I should add that there is something fey that runs in my family, and that I've had a few venturings of my own[1] beyond the enchanted boundary. I've seen with my own eyes how strange the universe can be, and that has made me receptive to the often stranger stories of others.

I soon found that the present scientific zeitgeist is unsympathetic to the idea of life after death; the topic is decidedly off limits. I hope to show in this book that it's very much within the limits of science, for there are facts that suggest we survive the sea change called death. Most educated people sidestep these facts—often called the damned, the excluded.[2] Still, a stubborn if small band of scientifically minded inquirers continue to collect, sift, and weigh the merits of the data. I believe that what they have to say has revolutionary implications for human psychology, and for how we should view the world and live our lives.

In the course of my quest something gradually changed. The more I probed the less I found myself thinking about life *after* death. A more important result was the growing freedom I began to feel to live life more fully here and now. I kept bouncing back into the arms of the present, and I came to see the world with a new freshness of perception. So, without meaning to sound paradoxical, this book is as much about present life as it is about the hereafter.

We will confront stories that point toward a future greater than most of us can imagine. Still, as I hope to show, good evidence for the afterlife may not be enough, not quite the thing we most need, not the soul food we most hunger for. For myself, I want to experience my life-enhancing truths in my body—now—and not just deduce them from isolated anomalies or puzzling observations.

I will begin by presenting evidence, personal testimonials of Otherworld encounters. But no less important are the practical implications of this evidence, which we hope to use as the basis for launching a more *direct* form of afterlife research. Luckily, we don't have to start from scratch. Spiritual seekers and psychic explorers since ancient times have gathered the fruits of their wisdom, and much lore exists to guide the curious who wish to experiment. Great wisdom traditions have been with us for a long time, have long addressed our metaphysical needs, and we will draw upon them.

Our problem today is that the sacred stories that inspired humanity for thousands of years have been challenged by science, forever changing our mental landscape. It all began when the Greek philosophers got into the habit of quizzing nature, raising doubts about everything, and mocking the religion of Homer. Sacred forms of experience were scorned and disparaged and eventually a certain kind of science came to dominate our thinking; the old wisdom traditions were forced to take a backseat.

Of course, it's easy to tote up the pluses of science, which has freed us from ignorance and superstition, cleared the way to mastering the forces of nature, extended human life, and made things comfortable for the affluent in capitalist societies. On the other hand, according to the official view, consciousness peeps out momentarily, a flickering phosphorescence of nerve tissue, and is destined to vanish forever after death. Materialist science has torn down the ancient myths, and made the implausibility of life after death an article of faith.

Frederic Myers, one of the great founders of psychical research, powerfully felt the disillusionment born of the new scientific materialism. "It must be remembered," Myers wrote toward the end of the nineteenth century, "that this was the very flood-tide of materialism, agnosticism, the mechanical theory of the Universe,[3] the reduction of all spiritual facts to physiological phenomena." Myers wrote that he was left with "a dull pain borne with joyless doggedness, . . . a horror of reality that made the world spin before one's eyes—a shock of nightmare-panic amid the glaring dreariness of day."

Myers and the philosopher Henry Sidgwick were among the English founders of psychical research, which became, in effect, an underground tradition[4] in revolt against the "mechanical theory of the Universe." Provoked by this rabid materialism, a small, dedicated group of Cambridge scholars decided in 1882 to *scientifically* investigate the question of what happens to us after death. As the decades unrolled, they amassed quite a bit of data: reports of ghosts, hauntings, apparitions, mental mediumship, ecstasy, possession, anomalies of hypnotism, and physical mediumship. English, French, German, Italian, American, and Icelandic investigators scrupulously collected this data, which, en masse, I believe, may hold the secret to undreamed of human potential. And yet it languishes, unrecognized, unconfronted by science.

Psychical research attracted many distinguished scientists, including some of the great pioneers of modern psychology: William James, Gustave Flournoy, William McDougall, Sigmund Freud, and Carl Jung; physicists like William Barrett, William Crookes, and Oliver Lodge (who invented a working radio before Marconi); astronomer Camille Flammarion; Nobel Prize–winning physiologist Charles Richet; and Alfred Russel Wallace, coinventor with Charles Darwin, of the theory of natural selection. Their achievements in psychical research have vanished from most history books, and barely left a trace in academe. One reason I have written this book is to remind the public that such a body of work exists and why it's important.

A book should be a partnership, a joint venture on the high seas of thought. So what I've learned, I offer you, the reader, to use, test out, and make your own for personal experiment. The plan is to lay the groundwork for attempting to experience the next world now—an idea whose rationale I hope to clarify as we proceed. I have a hunch we're not meant to know all the answers, but to be kept partly in the dark—always unsatisfied, always a little hungry. What we do have is a feast of possibilities: enough, I hope, to egg us on to explore, to open up to new experiences, perhaps just enough to take the proverbial sting out of death.

An early Gallup poll showed that 67 percent of Americans believe in some form of afterlife. Since then the numbers have gone up. In May 2000, the *New York Times Sunday Magazine* published results of a poll conducted by

Blum & Weprin Associates; 81 percent said they believed in life after death. (The numbers take a nosedive among the scientifically trained; this isn't surprising.) More than once in the past, popular belief has been wrong in matters of great moment, science right. But will mainstream science prove wrong this time and popular belief on the right track?

Billions of people probably accept some form of afterlife, the vast majority because it gives hope, mollifies anxiety, and promises reunion with loved ones. A few dream of high post-mortem adventures, romantic or mystical. Still others disbelieve because the afterlife idea disturbs them, seems scientifically impossible, morally dangerous, or just plain stupid. A psychopathic few use it to justify barbaric acts of terrorism. It seems to me time to get to the bottom of this mystery.

We're in the midst of the greatest period of scientific discovery, the greatest information explosion in history, yet most of us know more about our DVD than we do about the fate of our souls after death. We need to remedy this absurd disconnect. We need to know all the facts; and most of all we need more personal experimentation. Immortality and resurrection are ideas embedded in our consciousness. Neanderthals buried their dead in sleeping postures, as if to symbolize what the prophet Daniel would later say: "Many of those that sleep in the dust of the earth shall awake" (Dan. 12:2). The oldest written tale, the epic of Gilgamesh, is about bereavement and the quest for immortality. According to Renaissance physician, Marsilio Ficino,[5] to believe we are immortal is as natural for us as neighing is for horses.

If it's so natural, is it psychologically unhealthy to repress our yearnings for immortality? Are there insidious dangers we should alert ourselves to? In Plato's *Symposium,* the mysterious Diotima, Socrates' counselor on the mysteries of love, declares: "Think only of the ambition of men and you will wonder at the senselessness of their ways, unless you consider how they are stirred by the love of an immortality of fame. They are ready to run all risks, greater by far than they would have run for their children, and to spend money and undergo any sort of toil, and even to die, for the sake of leaving behind them a name that shall be eternal." Denying and repressing our afterlife yearnings may distort our personalities in profoundly perilous ways. If Diotima is right, it exacerbates the craving for fame, for self-esteem, and for power and recognition at all costs.

So it might be better to acknowledge our yearnings for immortality. Knowledge that we actually survive death might moderate the distortions of personality that Diotima speaks of. We should be frank about the importance of honoring our deep soul needs, not only in theory, but in practice. The human drama calls for a bigger theater of time, wider dimensions of reality to unfold its full potential, and it would be a boon if we could imagine our lives resuming on other tracks of existence, pursuing our stories in new and more favorable circumstances. So let's look at some of the facts, the evidence, the experiences that people have that support a greater vision of human destiny.

PART ONE

EXPERIENCES

As religion and tradition continue to decline as viable options for today's scientifically minded people, we face the emotional question of our mortality with diminished resources. For most of us the instinctive response to the Uncomfortable Fact is repression; for others it may be stoical detachment. Tactically handy moves, as long-range solutions they are unsatisfactory. The strategy in this book is to appeal to facts and evidence. *Evidence,* a word related to the Latin *videre,* means "to see"; in our postreligious, postmythical world, evidence becomes the way to "see" truth.

As far as evidence for life after death, the public is acquainted with the tip of the iceberg. We know about the near-death experience, reports of which have seeped into the culture and reshaped the way movies and fiction represent death. It is not, however, the strongest type of evidence. Stronger and headier stuff has been part of the public record for over a hundred years.

In the end, you will have to make up your own mind; one aim of this book is to give the reader tools and materials to do so. Another equally important aim is to inspire a more practical approach to the question of life after death. As we proceed I'll try to explain what this means. The gist of it is that if others before us became convinced of a greater existence through experience, it should be possible for us, too.

Note that no single case by itself can bear the burden of conviction. Conviction is more likely to come by sifting through patterns of cases and strands of data; truth, if you can catch it, won't be traced in miniature but on a broad tapestry whose design may only slowly come into focus.

People tell four distinct types of story suggesting that consciousness survives death: out-of-body experiences, apparitions of the deceased, mediumistic possession, and reincarnation studies. It appears that we may survive in different ways. We may be reborn, for instance, so that our mental life rolls onward in time through different bodies. Or we may pass on to a separate afterworld. Some evidence suggests that our full personalities survive, some that only fragments of our inner selves persist, perhaps intermittently, in diluted fashion. Afterlife consciousness may occur rarely, dimly, or even unconsciously. The old mythologies of Hades and Sheol described in classical antiquity suggest such scenarios. Still other accounts imply that we enter into a fuller existence in more evolved and realized worlds.

One thing seems sure; the nature of our present life is bound to change if we survive death. It should be obvious why. Gone will be our familiar bodies along with our present environment. This blast of newness may be a blessing to some, a nightmare to others. Survival may resemble our dream life in which we are seldom aware that we're dreaming. We may survive as active individuals or low-level psychic fragments. We may merge with entities greater than our-selves, a popular idea in Eastern thought. The postmortem exodus may be personal, subpersonal, or superpersonal, or some combination of them all. The possibilities are breath-taking.

CHAPTER 1

Ecstatic Journeys

The discovery of the worm in the apple of my existence led, as I said, to my waking up, a heightened savoring of life. And I felt driven to discover something More, something Greater. The discovery of my mortality jolted me to seek enlightenment, to explore the mysteries—it also threw a long shadow on my world. A shadow of "black bile," of *melancholy*—the old term for that ill-humored state that nowadays we call depression.

It's hard to say just how many people suffer from depression. There are all kinds and grades of this affliction, running from occasional bouts of feeling "down in the dumps" to serious clinical depression and all the way to the kind of suicidal madness of depression described so graphically by William Styron in his memoir *Darkness Visible*. The causes of depression, no doubt many, are still hard to pinpoint in any one case, and Styron finds something disturbingly mysterious about it. Neurotransmitters play a role, as may genetics; and of course all sorts of life incidents, mainly centering on loss, could trigger the plunge.

"For the Neo-Platonist," according to classical scholar Charles Boer, "the soul does not want to be in the body, and melancholy is its cry for escape." The cause of melancholy may lie in our embodied human condition. We do not want to be in our bodies, according to the Neoplatonists, because our bodies are the cause of all suffering, pain, and fear, and the root of all our losses, including, it seems, the inevitable loss of our own existence. If so, the only cure for depression is ecstasy—the experience of being out of the body.

An experience I had in my metaphysically agitated twenties may explain what I mean. It was my first out-of-body flight. I woke up one morning and realized I was floating above my bed, hovering before the bedroom window. The sun was streaming through a transparent blue curtain. The "I" I allude to was the same inner self I knew as me, except shorn of its usual bodily baggage. There I was! Ecstatic—"standing outside" myself, a disembodied center of awareness. Exhilarated, self-contained, serenely poised to take off to parts unknown, I knew that I had only to will it, to think the thought, and I'd be off through the window on a galloping trip to Oz. But hold on, I reflected. What if I can't find my way back? The moment I had this thought, I snapped back into my body, like a paddle ball on a rubber string, my heart pounding like a jackhammer.

For a few memorable seconds I had tasted the elation of pure existence. My melancholy, born of being trapped in my body, had completely lifted. Still, something prevented me from going all the way. I held back. What I most needed, it now seems, was what I most feared. If being trapped in a mortal body is the cause of melancholy, leaving the body can cause terrible anxiety. It was an unfortunate paradox, a double bind not easy to escape. Luckily, there are exceptions, and some of us do escape.

Ecstatic Separation

A man was traveling to Damascus to arrest disciples of a Jewish prophet whom the Romans had crucified. Fourteen years later he wrote down an experience he had on the way. He had a vision and heard the voice of the man whose followers he was planning to arrest; he saw a blinding light and a voice said: "Saul, Saul, why are you persecuting me?" He said of himself in a famous letter: "And I know how such a man—whether in the body or out of the body I do not know, God knows—was caught up into Paradise, and heard inexpressible words, which a man is not permitted to speak" (2 Cor. 12:1–4). This is perhaps the most famous out-of-body experience, for it converted Paul of Tarsus to the new Christian faith. It was the turning point in the apostle's life, an experience of ecstasy, which by its aftereffects changed world history.

Consider another, more recent but still well-known example. The Oglala Sioux warrior and medicine man Black Elk[1] had a life-changing ecstatic experience when he was nine years old and very sick. He heard voices calling him. Lying down, and too sick to walk, the boy looked outside the tepee and saw two men descending from the sky toward him. They said: "Come! Your Grandfathers are calling you! Then they turned and left the ground like arrows slanting upward from the bow. When I got up to follow, my legs did not hurt me any more and I was very light. I went outside the tepee, and yonder where the men with flaming spears were going, a little cloud was coming very fast. It came and stooped and took me and turned back to where it came from, flying fast. And when I looked down, I could see my mother and my father."

Black Elk traveled in this visionary world, and met the "Six Grandfathers," wise old men who taught him spiritual secrets and warned of the coming destruction of the Indian way of life. "For the nation's hoop was broken like a ring of smoke that spreads and scatters and the holy tree seemed like dying and all its birds were gone." Returning to his body, Black Elk said: "Then I saw my own tepee, and inside I saw my mother and my father, bending over a sick boy that was myself. And as I entered the tepee, someone was saying: 'The boy is coming to; you had better give him some water.' "

Black Elk's vision differs notably from Saint Paul's. Paul's experience signaled the rise of the new Christian age; the apostle was guided by his dreams to bring the "good news" to Europe. Black Elk's experience was a funeral dirge for the native way of life in North America. Content and context aside, both men experienced an ecstatic separation of consciousness from the body, a journey beyond the melancholy of embodied existence.

A Widespread Experience

Not every out-of-body flight is a world-shaking event. Most are pretty mundane. I've been asking students about their out-of-body adventures for about two decades; in an average class of twenty, about two usually report having the experience. Not every one is as deeply touched as Black Elk and Saint Paul were, but some are sufficiently impressed to feel their customary sense of reality affected. The experience can undermine the belief that our minds are totally wed to our bodies. The implication is obvious: If we can separate from our bodies, maybe we can survive the death of our bodies.

I recall a student in his mid-fifties who had been working himself to the bone with three jobs, trying to make lots of money but not knowing quite why. He never enjoyed what he did and was generally miserable. One night, after a particularly stressful day, he dropped down on his bed, weary with despair: With pain in his chest, he blacked out, and found himself above his body, looking down on his pale, drawn face. (Later it was determined he had a mild heart attack.) In a moment of exaltation he saw what a lethal farce his life had become, and he made up his mind on the spot to reduce his workload and return to school.

Or this: "I was a United States Navy scuba diver at work off the coast of Florida and temporarily lost consciousness while performing an underwater operation. All of a sudden, I found myself out of my body, watching my wife who was at home miles away. I could see what she was cooking, and I heard the phone ring and watched her answer. After I was rescued and rejoined my wife, I told her what she was doing at home. I repeated some bits of conversation she had over the phone. I tried to explain my experience, but she was so upset that I knew what she was doing that she accused me of spying on her. For a while we went through some rough times because she refused to believe my story."

Finally, from a twenty-three-year-old woman: "One morning I was startled from a deep sleep by a loud sound outside my window. I raised my head, looked around, leaned back, and seemed to fall asleep. Suddenly I was floating near the ceiling; I looked down at my body, my face squeezed between two crumpled pillows. My mouth was open and I looked stupid. Feeling totally light, I looked around, and saw on the molding near the ceiling what looked like a small bug. Then I snapped back into my body. I wondered if it was a dream, so I got out of bed and climbed a small ladder to see if anything was on the molding. There was. I saw a small, dead spider."

The last two stories seem to have been, in some informational sense, objectively real.

The Core Phenomenon

In a sense, this experience is the core phenomenon of after-life research: *an experience of what it might feel like to exist without a body—of what it might be like to be a "spirit."* If there is a life after death, the out-of-body experience may give us a foretaste, a dress rehearsal for the final act.

Such experiences have powerfully shaped myth and religion, as we saw from the historic examples of Saint Paul and Black Elk. Ecstasy is also central to shamanism: "The shaman specializes in a trance during which his soul is believed to leave his body and ascend to the sky or descend to the underworld," writes Mircea Eliade, adding, "The ecstasy is only the concrete experience of ritual death." Shamanic ecstasy is a form of ritual death, a way of gaining power and knowledge of the next world by direct communication with the spirits. " 'Seeing spirits,' in a dream or awake, is the determining sign of the shamanic vocation."[2]

So we already have a model for experiencing the next world now. The traditional shaman understood this for whom leaving the body was, as Eliade points out, an experience of "ritual death." In the out-of-body state, you become like a spirit; you see and interact with actual deceased spirits. Figuratively speaking, it's like stepping into the "vestibule" of death. It represents a state of temporary disembodiment—temporary death. In Part Four, we will describe some procedures for inducing this experience of entering the "vestibule" of death.

What's Really Going On Here?

Do people *really* leave their bodies? *Really* know true ecstasy? The consensus of mainstream science today may find this incredible, even meaningless, but in light of the data gathered by psychical research, shamanic claims of ritual death and soul travel acquire an added dimension of truth. Experiencers report changes in their perception of reality. They feel they now "know" that an Otherworld exists. As we explore the different kinds of afterlife evidence, we will keep returning to the idea of direct experience, which I believe is the key to tipping the balance toward resolving the afterlife enigma.

When thousands, if not millions, keep reporting the same kind of experience, it seems wise to pay heed. According to one survey, 95 percent of world cultures believe in out-of-body experiences, which may occur in perfect health, deep relaxation, acute stress, or near-death.[3] Many well-known writers had the experience, for example, Goethe, Ernest Hemingway, and Guy de Maupassant. Jack London wrote a novel called *Star Rover* about a prisoner who learned to consciously induce these psychic voyages. London's star rover defies his cruel jailor to place him in a straitjacket and brags he can leave his body at will. The story was based on the real case of San Franciscan Ed Morell.

It would help to gain a sharper sense of what the experience is like. The main thing is that consciousness seems to become detached and located outside its customary bodily envelope. You might be sound asleep or near death, totally calm or wildly aroused, meditating on your navel or racing a motorbike. In fact, there are so many ways to slip out of our bodies that one wonders how we manage to stay inside them in the first place. The conscious mind certainly hangs around the body, but doesn't seem all that attached or terribly loyal to it. Consciousness, I think it fair to say, likes to wander.

Otherbodied Environments

Sometimes the out-of-body environment is perceived in a realistic way and everything appears perfectly normal. The clock is above the mantelpiece and the moon is shining through the window. But sometimes, on closer inspection, the environment seems more like a dream. Psychical researcher William Roll described his out-of-body experience in a moonlit room.[4] Roll floated out of his body and found himself in a part of the room where moonlight cast shadows on the floor; he memorized the location of the shadows in relationship to the carpet pattern, returned to his body, got out of bed and examined the carpet. No shadows at the location he recalled. Roll concluded he hadn't really left his body; the experience seemed more like a realistic dream. But in a survey conducted by parapsychologist John Palmer, about 15 percent of people claiming to leave their bodies were able to verify their experience.

Otherbodied environments vary. Sometimes things appear transparent or suffused with light. In rare cases, the experiencer senses nothing in the environment, or finds himself afloat in a black void, but most of the time perception is detailed, realistic, and *more* vivid than usual. The environment often consists of the familiar world, but sometimes it takes on the appearance of a vestibule, doorway, or tunnel leading to another world.

The Out-of-Body Body

Most sacred traditions speak of a "subtle" body. Thomas Aquinas describes the speed, lightness, and translucency of the resurrection body, but let's see what modern research has to say. English parapsychologist Celia Green found that subjects may occupy a subtle body, a replica of the physical.[5] The new body isn't bound by laws of physics, but passes through solid matter, is luminous and gravity-free. This sounds like the radiant body that Saint Paul and the Neoplatonists spoke of and that Aquinas made into Catholic doctrine.

Sometimes, the experience is "asomatic"; subjects sense themselves as points of light or luminous vapors. Some observe a so-called astral cord connecting them to their physical body, others don't. Some can control their out-of-body capers. In brief or emotionally disconcerting experiences, control is difficult. Loss of control may stop the experience, as in my first out-of-body transport. Some report being aware of leaving and re-entering. Now and then you hear of a person projecting to some location and appearing to others. A young woman wrote: "I had several out-of-body experiences when I was in my late teens. One night I fell asleep as soon as I hit the pillow and had a vivid dream of being at my girlfriend's house. I was standing outside her room watching her arrange her clothing on the bed. She looked up in my direction. Then the dream ended. The following day my friend phoned me to say she had seen me standing outside her room, looking at her." I have found other cases of people dreaming of places where they were seen. I guess you could call these examples of living ghosts.

Here is a case Saint Augustine described fifteen centuries ago. "I believe that a person has a phantom which in his imagination or in his dreams takes on various forms through the influence of circumstances of innumerable kinds. This phantom is not a material body, and yet with amazing speed it takes on shapes like material bodies; and it is this phantom, I hold, that can in some inexplicable fashion be presented in bodily form to the apprehension of other people, when their physical senses are asleep or in abeyance." And he gives a good example. "Another man reported that in his own house, at night-time, before he went to bed, he saw a philosopher coming to him, a man he knew very well. And this man explained to him a number of points in Plato, which he had formerly refused to explain when asked." Later, the man who saw the vision confronted his philosopher friend, and asked why he came to visit so late at night. The philosopher replied: "I did not do it; I merely dreamed that I did." Augustine concludes: "This shows that what one man saw in his sleep was displayed to the other, while awake, by means of a phantom appearance."[6]

The Traveler's Inner State

What does it feel like to leave your body? In a November 6, 2000, *New York Times* story the English author Philip Pullman commented on the worldview that informs his novels: "I wanted to emphasize the simple physical truth of things . . . rather than the spiritual or the afterlife." He added: "That's why the angels envy our bodies—because our senses are keener, our muscles are stronger. If the angels had our bodies and our nerves, they'd be in a perpetual state of ecstasy." I wonder how Mr. Pullman came to know all this. Fortunately, we do have some evidence from out-of-body experiencers who *can* claim to know what it feels like to be without a body.

Pullman thinks that without bodies and nerves, perception has to be dull and flat. But surveys of out-of-body experiences prove otherwise, revealing them to be vivid, intense, and *ecstatic*. Contrary to Pullman, one could say that being in a body is a drag on experience, and that any angel worth its salt would loathe being forced into one. My point is not to heap gnostic contempt on the body, but that certain facts point to possibilities at least worthy of our curiosity. We should be more open-minded about the possible range of human experience.

J. H. M. Whiteman, a mathematician and physicist who taught at the University of Capetown, besides being a scientist, was a psychic, mystic, and visionary, and was well suited to observe, classify, and analyze his extraordinary experiences. Leaving the body, he thought, is the first step on a scale that leads toward the mystic light and union with the Godhead. Whiteman's experience was triggered by a lucid dream. Lucidity implies something we experience only occasionally even in waking life, and that is *being reflectively aware* of what we're doing or thinking or feeling.

If you can become self-aware while dreaming, you might trigger an out-of-body excursion. "Then," according to Whiteman, "suddenly the dormant faculty of recollection having become stirred, all that up to now had been wrapped in confusion instantly passed away, and a new space burst forth in vivid presence and utter reality, with perception free and pin-pointed as never before; the darkness itself seemed alive. The thought that was then borne in upon me with inescapable conviction was this: 'I have never been awake before.' "[7] Sorry, Mr. Pullman, but the most intense physical experiences seem pretty dull by comparison with these ecstatic journeys.

A Curious Experience

Is there a relationship between heightened self-awareness and the out-of-body state? According to Celia Green, reflecting on your personal identity can induce the experience. I can attest to this. I was a student at Columbia University, at home in bed reading a book by Jean-Paul Sartre, *The Transcendence of the Ego*. The ego is a product of reflection, says Sartre; unless we're reflecting and thinking about ourselves, consciousness is egoless, and lacks all sense of ownership.

Studious even in sleep, I dreamed about Sartre's ideas. In my dream, I began to wonder if I could stop thinking about my ego and experience pure consciousness; the moment I thought this I felt a whirlwindlike sensation of being sucked out of my body. I was drawn out through the nape of my neck into thin air. Shocked by the suddenness of this, I woke to my mundane bedroom, shaken. Again, the experience quit on me, probably because I was violently surprised and my emotions were too much aroused. So the experience takes many forms, and ecstasy comes in many colors. Just thinking very deeply about who you are may produce one of these surprising flights of consciousness.

Verifiable Flight

Can the experience be verified? The scuba diver claimed to have accurately observed his wife while out of his body, and the young woman verified the dead spider on the ceiling molding. Consider a well-known case from the early days of psychical research.[8] In 1863, after eight stormy days, a Mr. S. R. Wilmot was sailing from Liverpool on the steamer, *City of Limerick,* to New York City. On Tuesday, October 13, he finally fell sleep and toward morning dreamed his wife came to his stateroom in her nightdress. After hesitating at the door and looking at the other man in the room, she stood beside him, bent over, and kissed him.

The other man was William Tait, a fifty-year-old librarian from Cleveland, Ohio. In the morning, Mr. Wilmot found Mr. Tait staring quizzically at him. Mr. Tait said: "You're a pretty fellow to have a lady come and visit you in that way." Mr. Tait was a "sedate and very religious man, whose testimony on any subject could be taken unhesitatingly." Wilmot, before leaving the ship, questioned him three times about what he saw; each time Tait repeated the same description of what Wilmot had *dreamed*. Mr. Tait seems to have seen Mrs. Wilmot's dreambody.

Upon arrival Mrs. Wilmot said to her husband: "Did you receive a visit from me a week ago last Tuesday?" She explained that she had heard reports of storms in the Atlantic, and was too anxious to sleep that night; then, at four in the morning, it felt as if she "went out to seek" him, crossed the stormy sea, found a black steamer, and entered her husband's cabin. There she saw another man on an upper berth staring at her, which caused her to hesitate before going to her husband's berth to kiss him. Mrs. Wilmot asked: "Do they ever have state-rooms like the one I saw, where the upper berth extends further back than the under one?" Although she never physically entered the ship, she accurately described the way the berths were arranged.

So here we have an out-of-body experience in which three people are reciprocally involved. The investigator Richard Hodgson interviewed the parties, except Mr. Tait who had in the meantime died. Tait did report what he saw to Mr. Wilmot's sister who was a passenger on the boat. "He said he saw some woman, in white, who went up to my brother." Tait's oral testimony was confirmed indirectly through Wilmot's sister. Researcher Eleanor Sidgwick concluded that the story "tends to show that Mrs. Wilmot was actually there in some sense other than a purely mental one." When three people have mutually confirming experiences of the same events, it's hard to dismiss their accounts as based on mere fantasy or hallucination.

A more recent example from the files of Celia Green:[9] "I was in hospital having had an operation for peritonitis; I developed pneumonia and was very ill. The ward was L-shaped; so that anyone in bed at one part of the ward, could not see round the corner. One morning I felt myself floating upwards, and found I was looking down on the rest of the patients. I could see myself, propped up against pillows, very white and ill. I saw the sister and nurse rush to my bed with oxygen. Then everything went blank. The next I remember was opening my eyes to see the sister bending over me.

"I told her what had happened; but at first she thought I was rambling. Then I said, 'There is a big woman sitting up in bed with her head wrapped in bandages; and she is knitting something with blue wool. She has a very red face.' This certainly shook her, as apparently the lady concerned had a mastoid operation and was just as I described." Verifiable out-of-body experiences like this one are not rare. Since this is an important step in building the argument for postmortem survival, let's also look at some experimental studies.

Experimental Studies

California psychologist Charles Tart conducted a classic experiment.[10] A Ms. Z claimed to have out-of-body experiences twice to four times a week. She typically did this during sleep; she agreed to be tested in Tart's sleep lab. Ms. Z spent four nights in Tart's lab and was closely monitored for physiological changes. She usually found herself floating near the ceiling, wide awake and out of her body; perhaps she could do it under test conditions.

Tart had to determine if her experiences were just fantasies or contained veridical perceptions—crucial to the survival hypothesis. If her experiences proved to be nothing but fantasies, they would have no positive implications for survival. If during her out-of-body state she could identify the target correctly, that would mean she really did somehow exit her body, and would count as a step toward proving postmortem survival.

A target number was set up on a shelf five and a half feet above her head near the ceiling but not visible from where she lay in bed. Electrodes and cables attached to her body recorded brain waves and other physiological variables and prevented her from sitting up in bed more than two feet. If she at any time disconnected herself to sneak a look at the target, it would have been automatically recorded. If she left her body and saw the target number, she was to wake up and report what she saw through the intercom.

The first night was uneventful. The second night Ms. Z called out: "Write down 3:13 A.M. I don't see the number, but I just remember that." Ms. Z had floated out of her body, not high enough to read the target number, but high enough to read the clock. Next evening Ms. Z had a nightmare whose details corresponded to a murder that took place in the city. A suggestive anecdote. Third night, Ms. Z had a flying dream, in which she seemed to converse with her sister. Later, her sister reported that she dreamed of Ms. Z at the time of her flying dream. This incident resembles the reciprocal experience cited in the Wilmot story above.

On the fourth night Ms. Z floated out of her body during sleep and correctly called out the five-digit target number. "I needed to go higher because the number was faceup." Tart comments: "It should be mentioned that Ms. Z had expected me to prop the target number up against the wall on the shelf; actually, I had laid it flat on the shelf, which she correctly perceived." Could this have been a lucky guess? The chance of guessing the correct sequence of five digits is one in ten to the fifth power. So on the fourth night the evidence for a verifiable out-of-body experience was strongest.

What about brain waves and physiological variables? EEG was a mixture of Stage 1 sleep and alphoid activity, without rapid eye movements and cardiovascular and skin resistance changes—a pattern not found in the sleep literature. William Dement, an authority on sleep behavior, confirmed Tart's assessment that Ms. Z's EEG was an unknown pattern, associated neither with waking nor any sleep stages. Alphoid—lower alpha—rhythms have been linked with sensory isolation and Zen states studied in Japanese laboratories. Absence of rapid eye movements shows she wasn't dreaming but in a brain state suggesting Zenlike dissociation from external stimuli. This landmark experiment confirms the reality of verifiable out-of-body experiences.

In 1980, Karlis Osis and his assistant Donna McCormick of the American Society of Psychical Research reported a series of out-of-body experiments.[11] They were lucky enough to find a gifted psychic willing to cooperate. Alex Tanous was a Lebanese with unusually dark and intense eyes that reminded me of photos I've seen of Rasputin. I met Tanous several times and found him a little spooky. He once held out his hands before me. "It's through these," he said, "that I feel things." As a child he experienced the death of many friends and relatives, and his specialty was sensing death. Tanous also had the rare ability to will himself out of his body. The two abilities are most likely connected.

In the Osis experiment, Tanous was to project himself to a specified target area, an enclosed space containing an optical viewing-device that displayed randomly selected visual targets. To see the targets you had to be right in front of the viewing-device. Tanous lay down in the dark in a separate, sound-reduced room, relaxing and meditating as he prepared for projection.

The aim of the experiment was not just to prove out-of-body perception but to test the hypothesis that *something* gets out of the body, perhaps the same *something* that survives bodily death. It was a test for the existence of the "subtle" body. According to Rhine, "psi," or psychic capacity, have two sides, cognitive (ESP) and kinetic (PK), "information gain and kinetic action." In short, if the mind can get out of the body, it should be able to prove it by out-of-body information gain *and* out-of-body kinetic action.

To test for this "body," a device called a strain-gauge sensor was installed near the target. This would detect the slightest movements or vibrations of anything physical in the vicinity—hopefully, Tanous's localized "subtle" body. To see the target in the optical device, Tanous would have to project himself to a point right in front of it. If he viewed the target correctly, the sensor should register his presence. Tanous was told nothing about the strain gauges.

In a series of 197 trials over twenty sessions, he succeeded 114 times. The extra chance factor was modest. What was important was that *when* Tanous correctly guessed the targets the strain gauges acted up, proving some kind of physical presence. Osis concluded that this correlation supported the hypothesis of a localized out-of-body entity, and claims to have caught Tanous's living ghost, so to speak, in a net of objective measurements.

This experiment repeats Tart's, for Tanous, like Ms. Z, correctly identified targets during his excursion. There is a detail in Tart's experiment that seems especially important. Ms. Z had to rise to a certain point near the ceiling to "see" the target number, which Tart laid flat on the shelf. It sounds like Ms. Z, in her out-of-body state, maneuvered her "subtle body" to the correct position above the shelf to observe the target. From her description, she occupied a localized "vehicle" that moved through space. In short, like the Tanous experiment, her experiment bolsters the view that *something leaves the body.*

I think I have said enough to give the reader a sense of the out-of-body experience. It is widespread in time and geography, a recurrent potential of human consciousness. There is reason to believe it has shaped the history of religion, especially the experience of shamanism, but also of mysticism, prophecy, and even philosophy. (Plato once said that philosophy was the practice of leaving one's body.) The experience is stunning for its mental lightness, clarity, and expansiveness, and qualifies for what Abraham Maslow called a "peak" experience. From a practical and emotional stand-point, it gives us a glimpse of what it may feel like to exist without a physical body and therefore of what it may feel like to survive death.

What are the implications of this experience for life after death? In the first place, verifiable out-of-body experiences are inconsistent with materialism, the view that persons are just material objects. If persons were just material objects, verifiable out-of-body perception should be out of court. But such perception doesn't prove survival because the person in the out-of-body state is still very much alive. However, if the consciousness of a living person can function *physically at a distance* from his body, it suggests to me a *latent* potential for survival. For if my consciousness can function *outside* and *at a distance* from my body, why not survive death without *any* body?

It may be objected that verified out-of-body experiences at best prove clairvoyance accompanied by the illusion of being located far from one's body. It has also been argued that the action on the strain gauges was an artifact and not evidence that Tanous got out of his body. Supposing all this were true—and I'm not willing to grant that it is—the sheer fact of clairvoyance would still be a significant step toward showing that consciousness can survive death.

Clairvoyance implies there is something about the mind of a person that can interact, mentally or physically, with things beyond the reach of the body. That is what we *mean* by an action or cognition being paranormal. Paranormal ability, however, by itself proves nothing about any particular person surviving death. At most, we can say it's a necessary but not a sufficient condition for survival. Now let's move on.

CHAPTER 2

Of Ghostes & Spirites

I have to laugh when people ask me, "Do you really believe in ghosts?" My reply, hoping to shock a little: "Believe? I *know* that ghosts exist!"

"Oh—but that's impossible."

"Your question is ambiguous. It could mean: 'Do I believe that people have experiences of things they call ghosts, fetches, spirits, and the lot?' In that sense, I know—having studied the records and talked to all sorts of folk—that ghosts exist."

"OK, but . . ."

"But there's another sense to your question. Do I believe that the ghosts people experience are the conscious remnants of once-living people? That's a more interesting question, and one whose answer we're looking for in this book. The better question is not, Do they exist? but, What are they?"

The next question I'm often asked is: "Have you yourself ever made the acquaintance of a bona fide ghost?"

Again, I seize the opportunity: "Acquaintance? A ghost once attacked me. That's right, physically assaulted me!"

In brief, this was my experience.[1] I had been invited to

spend a night in a haunted house in northern New Jersey. The family reported many haunting oddities, religious pictures disappearing, gas jets going on for no reason, curtains being turned inside out, and the annoying presence of a dirty old ghost who loved to surprise mother and girls in the bathtub—a ghost whose unique charm was being headless, or at any rate, extremely blurry from the neck up.

I was invited to pass the night on the sofa and keep an eye on the stairwell where many of the disturbances were observed. Sitting up, reading, and scanning the room, it was about two in the morning when I heard a loud resonant gong. Nobody was in the room with me. I turned around and noticed a circular, amber-colored gong with a stick attached to it hanging on the wall.

"Did you ring the gong?" said Elizabeth, the lady of the house, who suddenly appeared on the stairway, looking down at me.

"You heard it?" I asked.

"That's why I'm here!"

"I didn't do it," I explained. I disengaged the stick and struck the gong. It made the sound I had just heard. Was I dreaming? I could have sworn I heard the same sound a moment ago. Obviously, I could not have been dreaming, unless Elizabeth and I were having the same dream!

"The guy without a head—he's saying hello!" she said, taking my report in stride.

Elizabeth went back upstairs and I resumed my post, delighted that the ghostly occupant had announced himself. I leaned back, feeling a little smug, and decided that the high point of my investigation with this obliging spirit was over. An anomalous event occurred in the room with me, and a second party noticed it. A few minutes passed in this triumphant mood when I noticed something quiver in the shadows by the stairwell. This flicker in my perceptual field put me on alert. All of a sudden I saw a smoky undulating quasi-human form standing several feet in front of me. It began to walk—if that's the right word—toward me. I stared open-mouthed and before I could snort, I was totally engulfed by it. An unknown field of energy seemed to lock me in its folds. I was paralyzed, and I wanted to shout, "It's here!" but couldn't open my mouth. I was thrilled and appalled at the sensation of being pinned down face-to-face with the interloper. (The face was completely blurry.) Then, just as quickly as it enfolded me, it released me, and I felt the uncanny presence beg off. I scribbled some notes, and soon fell into a restless shallow sleep until the first light of dawn woke me. The personal identity of this bully remains unknown.

Let's step back in time for an example of an identified ghostly visitor.[2] The scene now is Edinburgh, 1838. Anne Simpson anxiously calls upon a Catholic priest; for several nights she's been dreaming of a deceased woman named Maloy. Maloy, who barely knew Simpson, keeps appearing, saying she owes money to an unnamed person.

"Three and ten pence" is how much she owes, and Maloy wants a priest to pay it for her. In a letter to the English Society for Psychical Research, the priest who got involved in this case, Father McKay, wrote: "I made inquiry, and found that a woman of that name had died, who had acted as washerwoman. Following up the inquiry I found a grocer with whom she had dealt, and on asking him if a woman named Maloy owed him anything, he turned up his books, and told me that she did owe him three and ten pence." Father McKay paid the sum and Maloy stopped appearing in Anne Simpson's dreams.

And so we turn to the stuff of Jacob Marley and Hamlet's father: ghosts, wraiths, specters, fetches, revenants, phantoms, and apparitions. Words abound, each telling its own story, like the word *Ghost,* kin to the German *Geist,* or spirit, as in *Holy Ghost.* In common usage, however, a ghost may be defined (by *The New Shorter Oxford Dictionary*) as "the soul of a dead person which manifests itself to the living. . . ." Ghosts, spirits, and other visitors from the other side have been showing up since time immemorial. Much to our purpose, and inexplicably, they sometimes impart intelligence that appears to hail from out of this world.

Note the details of Maloy's conscience-stricken phantom. It appeared repeatedly showing purpose, it intruded upon a stranger, and it expressed a strong desire to pay a debt. The presence of purpose is important. Not all evidence of survival is clear about *what* actually survives. Sometimes the phantom is not so prepossessing and behaves as if it were a mere shard of memory, charged with emotion maybe but otherwise seeming pathetically aimless and vacant-minded. Other times one feels the presence of a full-blown active self, redolent with personal intention. It's not always clear that something *conscious* is present; in Maloy's dream phantom, we do find the earmarks of a conscious agent.

Simpson knew nothing of the debt or the sum involved, which was tiny. I find it hard to imagine the grocer getting worked up over it, or even remembering it; in fact, he had to look it up in his books. Assuming the story is authentic, how should we interpret it? One question one should always ask: *Whose need did the apparition serve?* (Dead or alive, we're still dealing with human psychology.) We have to assume there is some motive at work in such incidents, a motive strong enough to result in something so unusual as a truth-telling apparition. In this case, as far as I can see, the most likely source of the apparition was the deceased: a deceased washerwoman who felt motivated to ease her conscience over an unpaid debt. You can plausibly ascribe motivation to Maloy, but not to Anne Simpson or to the grocer.

However, in discussing need or motivation, we should be careful because we're limited by what we know from the reported material. Newfound facts might force us to revise our interpretation. Also, this might have been a case of deferred telepathy; in other words, Maloy may have projected her concern about the debt to Simpson *before* she died, the dying wish surfacing *later* in Simpson's dreams. In short, this might be a story of premortem, not postmortem, extrasensory perception.

Crisis Apparitions

In 1889, a Committee of psychical researchers began a five-year project of compiling what they called a Report on the Census of Hallucinations.[3] It was the first major research project of the English Society of Psychical Research, a large group effort of 410 data collectors and a critical Committee including the redoubtable Sidgwicks (Henry and Eleanor), Alice Johnson, Frank Podmore (arch skeptic), and visionary polymath, Frederic Myers.

The Committee obtained 17,000 responses. Most of the informants were educated, their stories based on responses to a questionnaire, followed by interviews from the data collectors or members of the investigating Committee. Two thousand, two hundred seventy-three people reported having hallucinations; for various reasons 26 percent of these were eliminated from the survey. To the annoyance of spiritualists, the Committee's approach was always stringent and conservative.

Most hallucinations occurred in a context of crisis, usually a death crisis. In a *crisis apparition,* you hallucinate somebody dying at a distant location. Historian Baronius recorded the story of Marsilio Ficino's experience.[4] Ficino— a forerunner of modern depth psychology—was discussing the soul with his friend Michael Mercato. They decided to make a pact that whoever died first would, if possible, appear to the other, and give a sign of his continued existence.

According to Baronius, "A short time afterwards it happened that while Michael Mercato the elder was studying philosophy early in the morning, he suddenly heard the noise of a horse galloping in the streets, which stopped at his door. The voice of his friend Ficino was heard, exclaiming: 'O Michael! O Michael! It's true, those things are true.' Astonished at this address, Mercato rose and looked out of the window where he saw his friend's back, galloping off on a white horse.

"Mercato called after him, and followed him with his eyes, till the appearance vanished. Upon inquiry he learned that Ficino had died in Florence at the very time when this vision appeared to him."

The English Census of Hallucinations reported many crisis apparitions similar to this story of Michael Mercato. (The literature also contains an interesting subset of "pact" cases.) A crisis apparition is defined as one that occurs twelve hours before or after the time of death. Eighty death coincidences were verified in the English Census study; the hallucination coincided with an external event, conveyed information, or was collectively perceived.

Here is an example from a Russian, Mr. Aksakoff, three persons having signed the report. One May day in Petrograd, Russia, Madame Telechof was in the living room of her house with her five children; a former servant had just come by for a visit.

"Suddenly," we are told, "the happy play of the children stopped, and everyone's attention was directed toward our dog Moustache, who was loudly barking and looking toward the stove. Involuntarily we all looked in the same direction, and saw by the ledge of the big stove covered with crockery a little boy, about five years old, wearing a shirt. At once we recognized the son of the milkman—Andre." Later that day the family learned that Andre the milkman's son died at the very time they saw his apparition.[5]

This is a curious story. Altogether, *eight* individuals observed the appearance of the dead boy. The first to notice Andre's ghost was a dog. Animals are widely reported to respond to the presence of ghostly specters. Thanks to Moustache, everyone stopped and noticed Andre. The dog barked furiously and followed Andre's ghost around the room. *Something* objective was clearly present. What became visible was identified as a boy known to the witnesses, and who had just died in a different part of town.

Two features of this account are striking. First, the apparition was verified; it corresponded to a boy's actual death in another part of town; second, eight individuals responded to it. It would be arbitrary to say that eight sentient beings just coincidentally hallucinated the same boy who just happened to die several miles away in town. There are connections here that need to be explained.

One more example of an animal responding to the presence of a ghost: "Miss K was caressing a kitten in her lap, when suddenly the animal got restless, rose, spit, and arched its back with every sign of terror. Then Miss K saw in an easy-chair close beside her, an old hag, with an ugly, wrinkled face, fixing an evil gaze upon her. The kitten went wild, and jumped frantically against the door. The terrified lady called for help. Her mother came, but the phantom, which was visible for five minutes, had disappeared. It was later ascertained that in the same room an old woman had hanged herself."[6]

The next story impressed the investigating Sidgwick Committee. A Senhor Ulysses Cabral of Rio de Janeiro submitted a report about a child, Deolinda, whom he had found in great poverty and taken under his care. Soon after, the girl died of consumption. Some months passed and Cabral was visiting with his friend, Barboza de Andrade. Unexpectedly, Andrade's sister took ill and was sent to her brother's house. Daily she grew worse, and Cabral offered to care for her.

"One night," he wrote in his report, "when I had taken my turn at nursing, I felt sleepy, and went to lie down. Two sisters, Anna and Feliciana Fortes took my place. After stretching myself on the bed, I was filled with a feeling of unbounded joy. I was happy, and could not imagine the cause of my happiness. I had a sensation as if someone were holding my head and placing something round it.

"Astonished at my experience, I called to the ladies who were watching in the next room, and Feliciana . . . answered me back, 'I see at your bedside a spirit child clothed in white. She places on your head a crown of roses. She says her name is Deolinda, and she comes to thank you for your kindness and charity.' I was amazed at such a declaration, for that very day was the anniversary of Deolinda's death, and neither I nor any other person in the house had recollected this. Besides, I had never spoken on the subject."

Barboza de Andrade later confirmed: "We are certain that our friend, Senhor Ulysses Cabral, told us the story of Deolinda only after the latter had been seen by Donna Feliciana Fortes." And from the sister, Anna Fortes: "I am sure that neither my sister nor I knew of the story of Deolinda before she was seen by the side of Senhor Ulysses Cabral on the night mentioned."

The cautious Sidgwick concluded that the evidence for agency of the dead in this case was "certainly strong." "If we are to exclude Deolinda's agency here, we must suppose that Senhor Cabral was sub-consciously aware that it was the anniversary of her death, and that this subconscious recollection produced by association the feeling of happiness and the tactile hallucination . . . and that the other witnesses were affected by telepathic influence from his unconscious memory. This is certainly a highly strained hypothesis."[7]

The next story is interesting because it overlaps with pact cases and deathbed visions. The experiencer chose to remain anonymous. A Mrs. B fled from her family in England to Italy. On good terms with her mother, she wanted to stay away from the rest of her relations. One warm day in Fiesole she was feeding her children macaroni. She was hurting from neuralgia, her recent baby had been stillborn, and she felt depressed and alienated. Suddenly, the wall opposite her seemed to open up.

"I saw my mother," she wrote, "lying dead on her bed in her little house at———. Some flowers were at her side and on her breast; she looked calm, but unmistakably dead, and the coffin was there.

"It was so real that I could scarcely believe that the wall was really brick and mortar, and not a transparent window."

In the slow pace of a hundred years ago, Mrs. B mailed a letter to her mother, inquiring after her health. The letter was intercepted and was returned stating that her mother had died on March 11, the date of her vision. The curious thing was this: "When I was married, my mother made me promise, as I was leaving home, to be sure to let her know in any way God permitted if I died, and she would try to find some way of communicating to me the fact of her death." The skeptical Frank Podmore interviewed Mrs. B, and also obtained supportive testimony from her husband. So here we have a death coincidence, plus the drama of a pact between mother and daughter.

Mrs. B has more to tell: "When she—(her younger sister who had been called home to attend to the dying mother's needs)—arrived at home, she entered the drawing room, but

rushed out terrified, exclaiming that she had seen godmamma, who was seated by the fire in my mother's chair.
Godmamma had been dead since 1852. She had been my
mother's governess—almost her foster-mother. . . .

"My other sister went into the drawing room to see what
had scared Kay, and saw the figure of godmamma just as
Kay had. Later in the day, the same figure stood by, then sat
on the edge of my mother's bed, and was seen by both my
sisters and the old servant, looking just as she had when
alive. . . . My mother saw her, for she turned towards her
and said 'Mary'—her name."[8]

Unfortunately, one of the witnesses to "godmamma"
soon died, and the other two wrote no testimonials. But the
case illustrates a type of deathbed apparition widely
reported; and besides the dying person, three people witnessed this ghost. So we have another case where several
people see the same ghostly entity.

Deathbed Visions

Another kind of narrative, and possible evidence for survival, concerns what dying people sometimes see. In 1878,
Edward H. Clarke, M.D., published *Visions: A Study of
False Sight*. It contains, as far as I know, one of the earliest
discussions of visions of the dying. "There is scarcely a family in the land, some one of whose members has not died
with a glorious expression on the features, or exclamation
on the lips, which, to the standers by, was a token of beatific
vision. History is full of the detailed accounts of the deathbeds of great men, warriors, statesmen, martyrs, confessors,
monarchs, enthusiasts, and others, to whom, at the moment
of death, visions of congenial spirits, or of heavenly glories
were granted."

Consider a story that a college professor told me in

September 2001: "I had never thought much about life after death until an experience I had some years ago. I was living in a two family house when my landlady took ill. It's important to emphasize that this woman was extremely unpleasant with me. She lived alone and generally gave the impression of being almost always angry and complaining. Her condition rapidly got worse. On the night of her death I was the only person present in the house with her. Toward evening, I witnessed something that to date sends shivers running up and down my spine. Suddenly, my landlady looked up at the ceiling and began to talk to what seemed like several different people.

"She continued like this for an hour or so; at one point, she turned toward me, and gently asked: 'Have we been fighting?' What shocked me, and made me tremble like a leaf, was that this woman, whom I had known only for a few months and never saw smile, suddenly looked at least twenty years younger. She literally *glowed* with health, warmth and joy. Something she saw just before she died completely transformed her. I'll never forget this till my dying day."

The first attempts to compile critical reports of deathbed visions were produced early in the twentieth century. Italian parapsychologist Ernesto Bozzano was the first to notice that dying people mainly see visions of dead folk.[9] He reasoned that if such visions were merely subjective hallucinations produced by dying brains, why not see living as well as dead people? They see people until that moment forgotten, one not especially dear, or even somebody not known to be dead, but almost invariably the dying see visions of the dead.

Deathbed visions are noted for the sudden elevations of mood they induce and the occasional *shared* vision. (See the account that follows shortly of Walt Whitman's apparition.) Nobel Prize–winning physiologist, Charles Richet, a nonbeliever in postmortem survival, said this about deathbed visions: "Among all the facts adduced to prove survival, these seem to me to be the most disquieting, that is, from a materialistic point of view."[10]

British physicist Sir William Barrett wrote a book on deathbed visions. Barrett, one of the founders of psychical research, submitted a paper in 1876 to the British Association for the Advancement of Science on his experiments in telepathy. At first rejected, the paper was later accepted, thanks to the intervention of Alfred Russel Wallace, the great naturalist and coworker of Charles Darwin. Barrett collaborated with his wife, Lady Florence Barrett, a nurse and obstetric surgeon, on his book about deathbed visions. Lady Barrett's introduction states that her husband also noticed what Bozzano had: The dying consistently see apparitions of the dead who come to take them away.

Sometimes they see people they didn't know had recently died. An anonymous vicar wrote: "On November 2nd and 3rd, I lost my two eldest boys, David Edward and Harry, from scarlet fever, they being three and four years old respectively. Harry died at Abbot's Langley on November 2nd, fourteen miles from my vicarage at Aspley, David the following day at Aspley. About an hour before the death of this latter child he sat up, and pointing to the bottom of the bed said distinctly, 'There is little Harry calling to me.' "[11] The nurse also heard the child say this. The vicar stated that he took care not to let David know of his brother's death. The puzzle here is why David saw his brother Harry, about whose death he knew nothing.

In a book called *The Peak in Darien* by Frances Cobbe, we read: "A dying lady, exhibiting the aspect of joyful surprise, spoke of seeing, one after another, three of her brothers who had been long dead, and then apparently recognized last of all a fourth brother, who was believed by the bystanders to be still living in India." A while later the family received letters from India announcing the death of the brother, which occurred before his sister's deathbed vision. Everything looks as if the fourth brother died, joined his three dead brothers, and that all together they escorted their dying sister into the next world.

The circumstances for "Peak in Darien" cases are rare, but reports continue. In a 1982 George Gallup Jr. book on death experiences we read: ". . . a woman who was in the last seconds of life looked up and in the presence of witnesses said, 'there's Bill,' and then she passed away. As it happened, Bill was her brother and he had died just the week before—but she had never been informed of his death."[12]

Doubters will dismiss deathbed visions as a form of denial or wish fulfillment. But what if more than one person perceives the vision? In the story of the English lady who fled to Fiesole, we heard of the dying mother, her daughters, and the maid *all* seeing the wraith of the deceased governess. It would be cavalier to dismiss stories like this one as mere illusion.

In reading accounts of deathbed visions, I'm struck by a difference between the twenty-first-century way of dying, which is hospital-centered, and that of the late nineteenth century, which was home- and family-centered. Narratives were then set in the home of the dying person, with family members, physicians, and ministers all present, gathered in a quiet, solemn mood. Opportunities for having, noting, and recording these phenomena surely were greater then than they are now. Our more efficient, but less human, style of dying in high-tech hospitals may be cheating us of deeply enriching experiences.

Horace Traubel was a poet, a friend and disciple of Walt Whitman. Mrs. Flora Macdonald Dension was present at Traubel's death in 1919, and reported: "All day on August

28th, Horace was very low spirited. . . . Mildred was with him a good deal and we decided not to leave him a minute. He had been brought in from the veranda and on seeing me, he called out, 'Look, look, Flora, quick, quick, he is going.'

" 'What, Horace," I said, 'what do you see?'

"Why just over the rock, Walt appeared, head and shoulders and hat on in a golden glory—brilliant and splendid. . . . I heard his voice but did not understand all he said, only 'Come on.' "

After the vision, Traubel's mood soared but soon sank again. Several days passed. "On the night of September 3rd Horace was very low. I stayed for a few hours with him. Once his eyes rolled. I thought he was dying, but he just wanted me to turn him. As I did so, he listened and seemed to hear something. Then he said: 'I hear Walt's voice; he is talking to me. . . . Walt says, 'Come on, come on.' "[13]

Especially intriguing is what Dension adds: "Colonel Cosgrave had been with Horace in the afternoon and had seen Walt on the opposite side of the bed, and felt his presence. Then Walt passed through the bed and touched the Colonel's hand, which was in his pocket. The contact was like an electric shock. Horace was also aware of Walt's presence and said so." Cosgrave gave written testimony of his remarkable experience. The vision of Whitman not only elevated the dying Traubel's mood but also made itself visible *and tangible* to another witness. Cases like this pop up in the Census of Hallucinations; a deceased person appears to different people through different senses.

In 1961, Karlis Osis of the American Society for Psychical Research undertook a scientific study of deathbed visions.[14] Osis reasoned that a more objective way to study deathbed visions would be to obtain descriptions of them from medical professionals. He sent a detailed questionnaire to 5,000 physicians and 5,000 nurses; he received in return 640. This

was followed by telephone interviews and written correspondence. Nurses, by the way, turned in three times the
observations that physicians did.

The questionnaire was designed to find out what caused
the experiences. Were there cultural (religious beliefs), psychological (expectation), or medical factors (drugs) causing
patients' visions? Or did they occur independently of such
factors, thus suggesting an *external* source? As usual, the
method is to try to infer the best explanation of the phenomenon.

Fear apparently is not the main emotion at the time of
death; indifference is more common. What was surprising
was the number of terminal patients becoming *elated* at the
hour of death. The exaltation of dying persons is often
observed to occur suddenly; the external behavior of the
dying person clearly suggests they have *seen* something. This
sudden elation is unlike drug-induced euphoria. One physician commented: "There is such a resigned, peaceful, almost
happy expression which comes over the patient—it is hard
to explain but it leaves me with the feeling that I would not
be afraid to die."[15]

The data showed a strong relationship between deathbed
elation and religious belief. There are two ways you can
interpret this. Religious belief may cause the hallucination *or*
sensitize the patient to transcendent experiences. Other puzzling observations: Some patients display "extreme strength
just before death," and two patients, a schizophrenic, the
other senile, recovered their normal mental functions just
before death. This is a classic anomaly, not easy to explain in
terms of the prevailing medical paradigm.

Osis harvested 884 cases of dying people who had
visionary experiences. What did all this data tell him? Were
there discernible trends pointing toward destruction or
toward the afterlife? First of all, this work confirmed earlier

findings. Dying people mainly hallucinate the dead. In other types of hallucination, the living, not just the dead, are "seen." The young—not just the old—hallucinate the dead. The dying hallucinate close relatives, a fact consistent with the afterlife hypothesis. Close relatives, if they survived, would be motivated to "visit" the dying. (In nondeathbed hallucinations, close relatives are *not* typically seen.)

Patients who saw deathbed figures perceived their surroundings in a normal way. Again, this differs from psychotic hallucinations where patients see their surroundings as distorted. Deathbed visions have a clear purpose: It is to take the dying person to another world. Traubel sees Walt Whitman, who keeps saying, "Come on, come on."

Osis found four cases where the apparition was collectively perceived.

Could these visions be explained by disease, toxicity, or pharmaceutical intervention? Nothing in the data supports these explanations. No correlation between deathbed visions and being medicated or delirious was found, and in fact sedatives were found to *suppress* deathbed visions. An intact consciousness is best for having a deathbed vision. "Deathbed patients see apparitions more often when fully conscious and having proper awareness and capability of responding to their environment." In other words, the patient's consciousness is not impaired at the moment of having the vision.

Could the visions reflect a superstitious lack of education? It turns out that the majority of dying visionaries was educated. Another finding was that ". . . calm and radiant peace emerge in the death situation without any apparent external cause." The immediate impression, especially when the patient suddenly gazes fixedly, rapturously, at a specific spot in the room, is that the exaltation is externally caused. According to Osis, this unexplained elation confirms the afterlife hypothesis.

In 1977, Osis and Icelandic psychologist Erlendur Haraldsson published a *cross-cultural* study of deathbed visions.[16] They compared deathbed observations of Indian and American medical professionals, and sought to determine whether the visions depended on cultural, medical, and psychological influences. For the most part, this new survey confirmed the earlier work, adding new observations to an already strange picture.

In one case, a frightened four-year-old girl was admitted to a hospital in Delhi; for three days a god was loudly telling her she was about to die. Physicians examined her and found her in perfect health. The girl stared fixedly at something invisible, shouting, "God is calling and I am going to die," so the distraught parents left her in the hospital for observation. The following day she died from circulatory collapse without apparent cause.

Could this have been caused by autosuggestion? The girl may have come to believe she was going to die, and died as a result of autosuggestion. Physiologist Walter Cannon studied cases of voodoo death, and found that some people, in perfect health, who believe they're under a spell, can indeed die by autosuggestion.[17] So it is physiologically possible; however, the Hindu child wasn't under any spell, and no one planted the idea of death in her head. Nor is there any explanation of why she might have planted the expectation in herself.

Most reported visions dispel fear and facilitate dying. But what of visions that call (Whitman's "come on!") but cause fear and exacerbate dying? These are the "no-consent" cases. No-consent cases strengthen the impression that the caller is external, not part of the dying patient's subconscious fantasy life. For example, a nineteen-year-old woman saw her father coming to take her away, but she was terrified. "Edna, hold me tight," she said to the nurse, and died in her arms.

This brings us to how Indian and American samples differ. Indians seem less inclined to go gentle into the night; the afterlife retains its frightful side; Americans seem less cowed by fantasies of hell and the devil. There is another difference. Along with the usual deceased relatives, gods and goddesses show up more frequently in Indian deathbed visions. Hindu visions include nasty Yamdoots, angels of death who terrify and rudely drag the dying person away. These invasive Yamdoot epiphanies certainly look as if they're coming from an external agent. I thought the Freudian id was supposed to shower us with soothing illusions of uterine bliss? Consider this laconic report. A young college-educated Indian is recovering from mastoiditius; he and his doctor expect prompt recovery: "He was going to be discharged that day. Suddenly, at 5 A.M., he shouted: 'Somebody is standing here, dressed in white clothes. I will not go with you!' He was dead in ten minutes." That was not a soothing illusion.

Osis and Haraldsson used a model to interpret their data. Are deathbed visions consistent with an afterlife—or with destruction of the personality? The trend of the data supports survival, according to the researchers. It showed that visions of the dying are consistent with the way ESP works, but not with the way malfunctioning brains work; the visions did not correlate with hallucinogenic or other medical factors; they were coherent, not confused or jumbled; they occurred in clear consciousness and sometimes independently of expectation; and they showed little variability. Whereas, if the data were pointing to destruction, we should see clear evidence of subjective influence. The experiencer's belief-system would stick out like a sore thumb.

This last is key to the whole model. The more variability, the more likely you have subjective and cultural differences shaping the experience. If, on the other hand, the visions show few variations, and aren't shaped by age, sex, brain malfunction, drugs, and culture, it would say something positive about their autonomous status.

I agree that it's suggestive when the "apparitions show a purpose of their own, contradicting the intentions of the patients." More telling is when they contradict the medical prognosis. "Especially dramatic were apparitions that called a patient for transition to the other world, and the patient, not willing to go, cried out for help or tried to hide. Fifty-four of these 'no-consent' cases were observed, nearly all in India. Such cases are not easily seen as wish-fulfillment, and they are even more impressive when the apparitions' prediction of death was not only correct but contradictory to the medical prognosis of recovery." No-consent cases, occurring in unimpaired consciousness, point to external causes.

Anomalous Deathbed Recoveries

Philosopher Paul Edwards thinks that diseases of aging brains like Alzheimer's and dementia testify against consciousness surviving death.[18] They seem to prove that consciousness is hopelessly wed to the brain. As the brain decays, it appears, mental function decays in tandem. Once our brains are destroyed by death, could there be anything left of us to survive?

Many of us know from experience how people, sometimes our parents or grandparents, begin to lose their memories. We can see how the personality is gradually lost, until the day comes when your own mother or father no longer recognize you.

"Mom," I used to say to my mother, "it's me, Michael, your son." She'd look straight into my eyes, and turn away without recognizing me. Isn't this a sign of irreparable loss? Unmistakable proof of the victorious onset of death?

Perhaps. On the other hand, there remains an unanswered question: Were my mother's lost memories destroyed forever by her malfunctioning brain, or have they become temporarily, not irreversibly, inaccessible? As it turns out, there is evidence of the latter, reports of brain-impaired people who recover their memories, and other mental functions, hours or sometimes moments before they expire. These reports suggest that memories aren't annihilated by brain disease, but put out of commission, temporarily out of reach. The radio on your kitchen table is broken, but radio waves still flood the atmosphere.

A pioneer study of hallucinations states: ". . . at the approach of death we observe that the senses acquire a wonderful degree of sensitivity. The patients astonish those who are around them by the elevation of their thoughts, and the intellect, which may have been obscured or extinguished during many years, is again restored to all its integrity."[19]

There are contemporary reports of this. A patient with meningitis, after a deathbed vision, recovered the use of his mind and body. Osis also mentioned two sudden recovery cases, a schizophrenic and a victim of dementia. In a personal communication, philosopher Jean Houston described her grandmother before she died. The demented grandmother no longer recognized family members; but before she died she became mentally clear and spoke coherently in Italian (her native tongue), recognized Jean Houston, and addressed her by name.

A nurse, C.X., working with dying patients in a New Jersey hospital, responded to my questions about deathbed mental recoveries. "A 92-year-old woman had been diagnosed with Alzheimer's for nine years. She no longer recognized her son, daughter-in-law or grandchildren. She believed that people were coming to her home at night, knocking over chairs and lamps. In reality, she was doing it. Twenty-four hours before she died, she recognized her family members. She also knew where she was and how old she was, which she had not known for many years."

C.X. sent me observations on other cases, in which dying patients recovered lost mental functions. "A male resident had been on the unit for five years. Had to be fed by staff. Would call out obscenities linked to his wife's name, although wife visited daily. Wife informed staff that her relationship with her husband was a loving one, and that he never swore at her. Resident never regained awareness of surroundings or family members. Apart from tactile stimuli, the patient sank deeper and deeper into unresponsiveness. On the night before he died, his wife stated: 'He was more alert and he recognized me. He smiled, squeezed my hand and when I kissed him goodnight, my husband turned his head toward me and his lips touched my face.' Resident's sister-in-law was present and verified wife's statement."

These and similar observations weaken the force of one argument against life after death. It is true that if a person has brain disease, mental abilities are lost, but whether the losses are absolute and substantial, or temporary and functional, remains an open question, along with the question of life after death.

Apparitions on the Threshold

Since few patients survive deathbed visions, we hear few accounts from them. *Near*-death experiencers, however, return from the brink and can describe to us what they have seen. Thanks to modern resuscitation technology, people are more readily revived from clinical death. Thousands have come forward with tales of the afterlife vestibule. According to a 1982 Gallup poll, about eight million Americans have had these encounters.

However, despite the powerful subjective impression of

an afterlife that these experiences produce, little research has dealt with the question. Stress has been on the dramatic aftereffects, the increased psychic sensitivity, shifts in world-view, positive effects on attempted suicides, and so forth. The experience has deep religious resonance, which materialists dismiss as brain-spawned illusion.

Certain features do combine to suggest survival. A team of researchers from the University of Virginia's Division of Personality Studies has said of this remarkable experience that mental functioning is enhanced "at a time when one would expect it to be diminishing, or entirely absent, because of diminishing physiological functioning. . . ."[20] As with the data reported by Osis and Haraldsson, the near-death experience is not consistent with the annihilation hypothesis. Being near death often leads to out-of-body experiences, which are occasionally verified.

Cardiologist Michael Sabom published a study of verified out-of-body episodes.[21] Sabom determined "to probe meticulously for details that would not ordinarily be known to nonmedical personnel." He interviewed thirty-two people who had been resuscitated from cardiac arrest. Could they have described what happened to them on the basis of an "educated guess"? Sabom interviewed twenty-five control patients with medical backgrounds similar to his near-death experiencers. The control group, who never had a near-death experience, was asked to imagine what a CPR (cardiac pulmonary resuscitation) would look like. Twenty of twenty-five made at least one major error in their descriptions; three gave correct but limited descriptions; two demonstrated no knowledge of CPR procedures at all.

In contrast to the foregoing, of the thirty-two patients who really had out-of-body experiences, twenty-six who had visual impressions of their CPR procedure made *no* errors. Six of the thirty-two had highly specific visual impressions.

In one case, a clinically dead patient described a fixed and a moving needle on a defibrillator while it was being electrically charged. According to the report, "the movement of these two needles is not something he could have observed unless he had actually seen this instrument in use." Many of the accurate visual impressions were of a technical nature beyond the patients' understanding. Some of them "were of objects and events outside the visual field of the person being resuscitated." One man correctly saw three members of his family, and what they were doing, in the hospital corridor.

An Extraordinary Case of Brain Death

Dr. Sabom recounts the story of Pamela Reynolds who underwent a daring surgical procedure called a "standstill" or "hypothermic cardiac arrest."[22] Dr. Robert Spetzler performed this at the Barrow Neurological Institute. Pamela had a large artery aneurysm, a dilated blood vessel in her brain that at any moment might have burst and killed her. To surgically enter the brain and safely clip it off, the blood had to be drained from her head, so the operating team (twenty physicians, nurses, and technicians), put Pamela's brain in a state of suspended animation.

In retrospect, the operation looks like a mind-brain experiment: put the brain of a human being into a state of biological standstill, deprive it of blood, and flatten the EEG—will the subject report any experiences? Standard medical materialism, which installs the seat of consciousness in the brain, must reply with a resounding no. But Pamela *did* report having experiences. Under meticulously observed and documented circumstances, she had a remarkable near-death experience. The documentation in Pamela's case "provides us with our most complete scientific glimpse yet into the near-death experience," according to Dr. Sabom.

Before the first incisions, Pamela's body temperature was reduced to 60 degrees. To stop her eyes from drying, they were lubricated and taped shut; this prevented her from seeing anything. Small speakers were inserted into her ears and connected to the auditory nerve in her brain stem; they repeatedly emitted 100-decibel clicks, which prevented her from hearing anything. Her heartbeat and breathing stopped and her brain waves flattened. The electroencephalogram registered no electrical activity. A test for her brain stem revealed zero activity. For the surgeon to remove the bloated vessel, the blood had to be drained from her head. In effect, Pamela's brain had to be put in a state much like physical death.

For those who think the brain is the seat of consciousness, it must be puzzling to learn that the thirty-five-year-old woman, in spite of her functionally dead brain, continued to have conscious experiences. But that's not all. "It was the most aware that I think that I have ever been," she said. (Remember Dr. Whiteman's claim that he'd never been so awake until his first out-of-body experience.) Pamela reported leaving her body, going through a tunnel, seeing the light, and meeting an apparition of her deceased grandmother. Her mind, she said, was clearer than ever.

Can we verify that she had conscious experiences? While being operated on, Pamela heard one of the surgeons say that there was a problem with the pump and her small blood vessels. In Pamela's words, "Someone said something about my veins and arteries being very small. I believe it was a female voice and I believe that it was Dr. Murray." Medical records show that Dr. Murray did indeed make the remark about the veins and arteries. "These vessels are too small. We can't use them for the pump."

The pump was necessary to reroute her blood through a femoral artery. Pamela described a Midas Rex saw, used specifically for the "standstill" operation. She told the surgeons about hearing a strange buzzing sound and observing one of them use what looked like an electric toothbrush on her head. Pamela's out-of-body perceptions were remarkable because during her operation her eyes were taped shut to stop them from drying out; it was impossible for her to see anything by normal means. Not only was Pamela conscious during her temporary brain death, but her consciousness functioned beyond the physical reach of her senses. All this is strangely anomalous. And there is more.

Near-Death Vision in the Blind

Verified out-of-body experiences suggest that conscious minds can function apart from their bodies. This seems to contradict the belief that the brain is the seat of consciousness. The same can be said of another recently reported phenomenon. For a long time rumors have flown that blind people suddenly *see* during near-death experiences. Some careful research has begun to flesh out these stories.

Kenneth Ring and Sharon Cooper found thirty-one subjects who qualified for their study.[23] Fourteen were blind from birth, ten had near-death experiences, and four had out-of-body experiences; eleven were "adventitiously" blind (meaning they lost sight after five years of age), nine had near-death experiences, and two had out-of-body experiences; six were severely visually impaired, with two near-death experiences, six out-of-body experiences. Eighty percent of the respondents said they had visual impressions; they saw the normal physical environment and an otherworldly environment. Unfortunately, it was hard to confirm their claims. Still, it's remarkable that persons born blind should claim to have *any* visual impressions.

I hope researchers pursue the problem of mindsight. It

suggests that people may have some latent "extraphysical" faculty for visual perception, which is what we would expect if they survived death. This perceptual capacity, called *mindsight* by Ring and Cooper, is like clairvoyance, an ability tested and confirmed by parapsychologists. Like mental functions recovered at the moment of death, mindsight is activated during out-of-body and near-death states.

Related to mindsight and clairvoyance are reports of so-called eyeless vision. Examples can be traced back to 1787 when the mesmerist Jacques Henri Petetin from Lyons reported that an entranced cataleptic woman could see, hear, and smell through her *stomach!*[24] If that sounds strange, more recent cases of "seeing without eyes" are stranger—for example, the well-documented case of Mollie Fancher of Brooklyn.[25]

Mollie had two accidents that left her an invalid for thirty years. Her lower limbs atrophied, she became blind, and she lost the ability to swallow, living almost without food. In the course of this terrible decline, Mollie acquired clairvoyant powers. At least four physicians, religious professionals, a judge, newspaper reporters, and others deposed detailed written testimonials. Mollie could see what was going on in distant towns, the contents of sealed letters, and she could read written text through her fingers. She exhibited four "altered" personalities, each with its own handwriting; instead of going to sleep at night she went into trances during which her alters emerged. Basic living functions—sight, movement, eating, sleeping—were suspended. You could say that Mollie became near-dead for a very long time.

I won't reproduce evidence for her living without eating,[26] or for her other paranormal talents, since the focus here is on seeing without eyes. This is a well-documented case of a woman who lost her sight and developed unexplained ways of seeing, as if to compensate for her loss. One physician, a

Dr. Speir, wrote: "We have made a careful and critical exam-ination . . . an oculist . . . and agree with him that she cannot see by the use of her eyes—at least as a person can ordinarily see."[27] Dr. Speir continues: "I recall one instance when, Dr. Ormiston and myself being present, Miss Crosby received a letter from the postman. I took the letter in my hand; it was sealed, and Miss Fancher, at the time being unable to speak, took a slate and pencil and wrote out the contents of the let-ter, which, on being opened and read, was found to corre-spond exactly with what she had written."

According to another witness, Judge Dailey, she could distinguish the colors of an object even when the experi-menter was unaware of the colors, a fact that would rule out telepathy. He adds: "That she did see, could and can see, from the top of her head and from her forehead, cannot per-mit of a reasonable doubt." Henry Parkhurst, a scientist from Harvard University, placed paper with random words and numbers in a sealed envelope, which Mollie was able to read. Again, Parkhurst didn't know the content of these let-ters, thus proving clairvoyance, not telepathy. Mollie, who "saw" unexpected visitors before they arrived, said that her gift was inconstant: "When not anxious to see, I can see most clearly."

In other cases of eyeless vision that follow the pattern of Mollie Fancher, the subject exists in a state of suspended ani-mation, living without food, and physically paralyzed. Like the near-death experiencer who suddenly acquires clairvoy-ant vision, Mollie's extraphysical "vision" miraculously seems to emerge when she is deprived of normal sense life.

Does this pattern of deprivation and compensation imply anything for the afterlife hypothesis? Mythologist Arthur Varagnac thinks that primitive humanity, surrounded by ter-rifying forces and lacking all technology, drew upon latent mental powers to cope with dangers.[28] Who knows but facing death may emancipate the clairvoyant eye? It may awaken from prehistoric slumber the deepest powers of our minds. Eyeless vision, mindsight, and clairvoyance converge toward a hypothesis: the loss of biological systems of perception, as must obviously occur in death, awakens new (or very old) systems of perception. If we really are preadapted to conscious survival of death, eyeless vision and mindsight make perfectly good sense.

Verified Apparitions Long After Death

Now on to another wrinkle in our collage of evidence. Apparitions may occur long after a person has died, as in the following three examples. Consider the well-known case of the salesman who saw the ghost of his sister, dead for nine years. That afternoon he was smoking a cigar in broad daylight and happily writing his orders; having had a good sales day, he was neither thinking of his sister nor had been in the recent past. All of a sudden, she appeared standing before him. She was looking right at him so naturally that he "sprang forward in delight," but the specter vanished. Amazed by this strange encounter, he quit work and hastened to take the next train home. He told his parents the story of what he had seen. When he said he saw a "bright red line or scratch" on the right side of his sister's face, his mother fainted, for she had accidentally scratched her daughter's face during funeral preparations. She concealed the scratch with powder, and had kept it a secret. "A few weeks later my mother died," wrote the salesman, "happy in her belief she would rejoin her favorite daughter in a better world."

As usual we ask: What was the most likely source of this apparition? The three possibilities are the salesman, the mother, and the deceased sister. The salesman is unlikely for two reasons. First, he knew nothing of the specific detail of the red scratch. Secondly, he had no pressing need to see his sister's apparition; she had been dead for nine years, and he was absorbed in the business of the day.

Perhaps the mother was the secret agent of the apparition. She was the only living person who knew of the scratch. Did she unconsciously project the apparition from her memory into her son's mind that day? Apart from there being little evidence that people can do such things, we would like to know why. Perhaps to convince herself she was going to unite with her daughter at death? For this to work we must also assume that the mother unconsciously had intimations of her own imminent death. Given these strange possibilities for self-deception, English psychical researcher Zoe Richmond offers a sobering comment: "We do not know what lengths the unconscious mind may reach, or where the limits of its power are, but generally speaking its manifestations have some purpose. . . . But so far, I do not think there is any evidence that anyone can produce, unconsciously, the ghost of another individual, and make this visible to yet another person at a distance. If this is possible, then all judgment about such experience is hopeless."[29]

If we decide against the mother, the third possibility remains that the dead girl herself was indeed the source of her own apparition. The purpose, we might guess, was to prepare her mother for death. By appearing to her brother, the daughter demonstrates her survival. The son's story of the apparition with its telltale scratch did in fact make a vivid impression on the mother, and seems to have helped her experience her death as a joyful reunion with her daughter.

The next story is weird.[30] It is important because it shows that survivors of death may retain their intentions and purposes. Evidence of purpose in ghostly appearances shows that something *personal* has survived, more than a free-floating memory fragment, a dislocated piece of somebody's mind. So, for example, a deceased man appears to his uncle and declares: "Put me in properly; the coffin is narrow, the coffin is short." A year later, the uncle meets the hospital ward who cared for his ailing nephew when he was ill. The ward took care of the nephew's burial.

"One thing was bad," she says, "no special coffin was ordered and he was put into a hospital coffin, such as are kept for emergency purposes. Well, this coffin proved to be so narrow and short, that when he was being laid into it, the bones cracked." Who would be the most likely source of such gruesome intelligence? To my mind, neither uncle nor ward seem plausible candidates. Why would the uncle or the ward subconsciously need to create such a bizarre phantasm? What motive, what *need,* could producing it have served? It's hard to imagine losing sleep over your dead nephew's cramped coffin. On the other hand, if we assume the nephew survived his death, maybe *he* was upset. Distress over one's mortal remains is common in ghostly lore, and many a tale tells of specters troubled by burial irregularities. In ancient Greece, proper burial was a sacred duty, and Sophocles' tragic masterpiece *Antigone* springs from the need to bury somebody properly.

The next story has the advantage of being inscribed in North Carolina's legal history.[31] It involves correct information, unknown to any living person, conveyed by the apparition of a dead man. James L. Chaffin died in 1921, leaving behind his wife and four sons. By the attested 1905 will, the third son, Marshall, inherited the whole of his father's estate. Unknown, however, to any living person, Mr. Chaffin had written a second will in 1919, leaving his property equally divided among his four sons with provisions for his wife. He sewed a note about this will in an old black coat and hid the

will in an old Bible. (Devious behavior, no doubt.) Soon
after, he died from a fall.

Four years passed and James Chaffin Jr. began to dream
of his dead father appearing at his bedside. He appeared
wearing his black overcoat, and said: "You will find my will
in my overcoat." This was wrong. But when Chaffin Jr. and
a witness found the coat, it did contain a note saying the will
was in an old Bible. They found the Bible and the will, and
the case was taken to court. As a result of probating the will,
the father's worldly goods were redistributed. Curiously,
after the will was found, and just before the trial, Chaffin
Senior appeared once more to his son, apparently still angry
over something.

In this case, it's fair to say that Chaffin Jr. *was* motivated
to find the second, unknown will, by which he stood to gain.
So it is possible that he clairvoyantly located it himself and
then created his father's dream apparition to reveal to himself the will's secret whereabouts. But this seems convoluted.
First, why did the whole thing happen four years after his
father's death, after the urgency to resolve the issue of the
will must have subsided? And why did Chaffin continue to
see his father's apparition *after* the will was found? Or, if
Chaffin Jr. used his psychic power to find the will, why not
clairvoyantly locate it in the Bible directly? Why go though
all the trouble of conjuring up his father? No doubt a determined skeptic could come up with answers to these questions, but in my view the best explanation still seems to be
that Chaffin Senior survived his death and continued to care
about the fate of his family.

A Remarkable Apparition Seen by Many

Several philosophers have been struck by the following
case.[32] A pamphlet titled *Immortality Proved by Testimony*

of Sense, published in 1826 by Reverend Abraham Cummings, a Baptist minister from Maine, describes the apparition of a deceased woman, Mrs. George Butler. The ghostly phantom of this lady appeared for several months on various occasions, outdoors and indoors, to groups of up to forty people. She moved about, talking at length, revealing intimate details of bystanders' lives, and correctly predicted several births and deaths. Uncannily, the phantom predicted the untimely death of George Butler's new wife. The Reverend Cummings took about thirty sworn affidavits of the hundred or so persons who witnessed the apparition. The large number of observers, the duration of the appearances, the correct information conveyed, and the affidavits make it hard to dismiss this story as a product of fraud, delusion, or malobservation.

A skeptic thought he could explain Mrs. Butler's apparitions. According to philosopher Frederick Dommeyer, some living person might have psychically produced the hallucination of the dead lady, projecting her appearance to a hundred people; this living person, moreover, could have been the paranormal source of intelligence behind the phantom's predictions, memories, and characteristic behaviors.

Is this explanation credible? It seems to me at least as fantastic as the idea that Mrs. Butler survived death. No one has any idea who the living person was who might have projected all this. But suppose the whole wild event was unconsciously engineered by some psychically disgruntled soul still breathing in a body. In that case, I would say that if human beings can perform such incredible psychic feats, what is the small additional trick of getting completely loose of the body at death?

Commenting on Dommeyer's interpretation, Robert Almeder, a philosopher from Georgia State University, argues that the psi-from-the-living explanation is less simple and less plausible than the afterlife explanation. Writes Almeder: "Never in the history of paranormal research (whether in the lab or outside) has there been any success in inducing simultaneously the same auditory and visual hallucinations in a large number of people (not always the same) on many separate occasions under differing circumstances, and then providing them with accurate information clairvoyantly obtained." Almeder points sharply to the utterly ad hoc character of Dommeyer's skeptical explanation. The skeptic should know that if his account is true, then somebody must have psychic abilities that border on omniscience. Apparently, the skeptic finds this scenario—which is an alarming one, if you think about it—more plausible than the idea of Mrs. Butler's afterlife.

Haunting Remains

They are a staple for entertaining tales, whether in Shakespeare's plays or Hollywood movies: hauntings, or localized apparitions. Is the world really haunted by ghosts and spirits walking by night? Should we at least for a moment be willing to admit with Hamlet that there are more things in heaven and earth than are dreamed of in mainstream materialist philosophy?

Stephen King once said that the reason we like being scared silly by the supernatural is that spooks imply we're not totally alone in the universe. I agree with our great storyteller that we are secretly drawn to the supernatural out of a deep fear of loneliness and a deep hope that somebody, or something, is listening out there. All that aside, let's have a look at some facts. First of all, hauntings involve assorted phenomena. The visual aspect is not all of it—hence the misleading term *apparition*. Spirits come in all colors and flavors and hauntings are multisensory: loud bangs, whispers,

moans, laughter, footsteps; smells pleasant or foul; odd luminosities; sensations of cold; hands felt but not seen, or seen
but not felt; objects apported, objects displaced. All sorts of
rapscallions turn up. Nonhumans—cats and dogs are very
popular—like to put in appearances. And now and then a
monster, hobgoblin, elf, or alien. Hauntings often give the
impression of being aimless, unconscious, stereotypical. And
most haunters suffer from what Andrew Lang called "spectral aphasia," often straining but unable to speak. Not just
old houses and ancient castles, we find contemporary
haunted fire stations, county jails, furniture factories,
libraries, churches, restaurants, theaters, airplanes, government buildings, hotels, and ballrooms.[33]

The oldest haunting story I know dates from Book VII of
the Letters of Pliny the Younger, and tells of Athenodorous,
a stoical philosopher and tutor to the emperor Augustus. A
haunted house was for sale, and therefore a bargain.
Athenodorous, not cowed by superstition, bought it, and
promptly ran into the ghost of an old man, dragging a chain.
The ghost beckoned the philosopher to follow him to a place
in the yard—and vanished. The philosopher brought this to
the attention of local judges; the yard was dug up, and a
chained skeleton was found. The remains were properly
buried and the haunting stopped.

A Boring Ghost

Now to a tale of Victorian England.[34] The case is famous
because the witnesses carefully recorded their observations.
The Morton family moved into their new house in 1882. In
the same year young Rose Morton, a medical student, first
saw the appearance of a woman in a black dress. Rose and
six other witnesses left careful accounts of what they saw.

"I had gone up to my room," Rose writes, "but was not

yet in bed, when I heard someone at the door, and went to it, thinking it might be my mother. On opening the door, I saw no one; but on going a few steps along the passage, I saw the figure of a tall lady, dressed in black, standing at the head of the stairs." This was the first of many sightings of the spectral visitor. The intrepid Rose followed it around, and attempted to speak to it, but to no avail. The figure always seemed *about* to speak. (A case of spectral aphasia.) Rose tried to touch it but it slipped away, and she tried but failed to photograph it. She tied strings to the stairway, and observed the phantom walk through them twice. Cook, gardener, charwoman, maid, relatives, and friends repeatedly saw the same rather monotonous boring phantom for seven years. What a strange picture of melancholy introversion! I suppose there might be people so wrapped up in the memories of their past lives, so full of brooding and self-paralyzing scruples about themselves, that the afterworld becomes a place they get lost in, clinging to the same place in their memory, the same obsessive thoughts.

It's hard to avoid the impression that the ghost was something somehow "out there," quite apart from the observers. Another mark of its stubborn self-centered independence: It never appeared when members of the household wanted it to, or when they watched, waited, or thought about it. On the other hand, a normally placid retriever cringed with terror at the sight of it. Could the hell of the boring introvert be so bad that it made even dogs cringe? Of a second dog, a small terrier, Rose Morton wrote: "Twice I remember seeing this dog suddenly slink away with its tail between its legs, and retreated, trembling, under a sofa."

Underscore the dog's response; it heightens the sense that we are dealing with something objective. Later it was discovered that the woman in black matched descriptions of a person known to have previously lived in the house. Adding all this up, I think we have to admit that *something* was present in the Morton house, something that resembled a known deceased person. But what that something was remains a mystery.

The Morton ghost may represent a conscious survivor of death *or* it may have been a shell, an appearance without consciousness, like images we see of our favorite movie stars in old movies. As far as I know, the behavior of some, if not most, ghostly apparitions does not give a clear impression of conscious activity. The Morton ghost, so well documented, is a case in point; it impresses one as more zombielike than actively personal. Of course, what looks boring and monotonous to us from the outside may conceal hidden dramas of heart and soul.

To Die Is Human—To Forgive Is Divine

Still, not all ghosts reveal to us only their self-absorbed exteriors. Some hauntings clearly suggest a conscious will to communicate, and show the higher centers at work, and the deeper workings of the heart. In this next story, what comes across is a strong need to forgive another human being, to salve an old wound.

Like the Rose Morton story, this one has the imprimatur of authenticity. The story of Clara Claughton is complicated, well documented, and well verified.[35] About it, Frederic Myers, one of the heroes of psychical research, wrote, "The evidence for the external facts of the narrative is absolutely conclusive." And Andrew Lang, mythologist and psychical researcher, remarked that this case was "such as we seldom meet in modern science."

One day, Clara, psychically talented but not a professional medium, visited a house known to be haunted. Curious, she settled into her room with heightened attentiveness and curiosity. In bed with one of her children, she heard footsteps in the hallway outside that stopped at the door. She lit a candle, went to the door, and opened it. There was nothing there. She went back to sleep, only to be awakened by a loud sigh. This time she saw a woman at the foot of the bed, wearing a white shawl.

"Follow me," said the phantom. Clara followed into the drawing room, where the phantom said, "Tomorrow," and disappeared.

In the morning, after recounting the night's events, two people stated that the woman Clara described was a lady who had died in the house years ago, a Mrs. Blackburn.

Clara wondered if her apparition was Mrs. Blackburn, and what she might want. Next evening, after Clara's daughter fell asleep, the lady appeared again. No sooner did her form take shape, but a dignified man also appeared in the room. He stated that his name was George Howard. "I am buried in Meresby Churchyard," he announced. Clara never heard of him or of Meresby Churchyard. These polite and rational phantoms then invited Clara to verify certain facts for herself at Meresby. "If you doubt me," said the ghost of Mrs. Blackburn, "you will find that the date of my marriage was———." The other ghost, having stated he was George Howard, gave the dates of *his* marriage and death, and invited Clara to verify them by the registers in Meresby. The phantoms then instructed Clara to go to the churchyard at Meresby and wait at the grave of Richard Hart.

So Victorian, so reasonable, they make a prediction— trivial but falsifiable. Clara's railway ticket would not be collected by the train folk. And so it happened. Later, a Dr. Ferrier, interested in the case because he owned the haunted house that Clara had her adventure in, wrote the railroad company and confirmed the prediction.

Howard's ghost also told Clara that a man named Joseph

Wright would help her carry out her mission, and that she would lodge with a woman whose drowned child was buried in the churchyard.

All this piqued Clara's curiosity, so she purchased a ticket and took the noon train to Meresby. She found a room with the parish clerk, whose name indeed was Joseph Wright—the ghost of George Howard was right. Moreover, as predicted, Joseph and Mrs. Wright did have a daughter who drowned and was buried in the churchyard.

Clara wasn't a timid lady; so just before 1:20 she found her way to the grave of Richard Hart. At the appointed time, George Howard appeared again. He instructed Clara to pick a white rose from his grave and bring it to his daughter. We are not given the details of this private matter. What we do know is that Clara picked the white rose from the grave and delivered it to Howard's daughter. She also delivered a message—unrevealed to the public—to an awed and grateful daughter. After accomplishing this, the ghosts of Meresby fell silent.

Mrs. Blackburn was fifteen years dead when she appeared to Clara Claughton; the two women never met or knew each other. There were disturbances in the house long before Clara lodged there; for years Mrs. Blackburn's daughter and son-in-law had been hearing strange noises in the house. In a letter to Clara, the son-in-law wrote: "There was a ghost before you came to stay in the house. We took the house in ignorance of its reputation." Several tenants had been alarmed by loud footsteps on the stone steps, and one person in the attic reported being sprinkled with water from nowhere.

Clara never knew Hart, Howard, or a place called Meresby, and visited Meresby only at the insistence of a phantom. A written confirmation by the clerk of Meresby stated: "The lady came to morning service, and afterwards came to vestry and asked for registers of Richard Hart and George Howard, also giving description of George Howard, which was quite correct, and dates of register also corresponded with those in the lady's journal." All the information confirmed by the clerk of Meresby Clara had obtained in advance from her ghostly visitors.

It looks like an external intelligence guided the whole chain of events and used Clara to convey information from the dead to the living. We'll never know the exact secret that Clara was entrusted to impart, except that it was about forgiveness. At any rate, this is a far cry from Rose Morton's aphasic phantom. William Blake would have liked this ghost story, for it was he who wrote: "Mutual forgiveness of each other's vice. / Such are the gates of paradise." If there is a place we might call paradise, the way there may be through the attitude we adopt toward the past. So much seems to be suggested by this intriguing ghost story.

Accounts of ghosts, apparitions, and hauntings are incredibly rich and varied. What I described above is just a handful. Scratching below the surface reveals a mass of intriguing records. I could fill a book with accounts I've collected from students and correspondents.

So the question is not whether ghosts and apparitions are "real"—they are real experiences—but what in truth are they? "In the name of truth," asks Banquo (*Macbeth*, I.iii), "are ye fantastical, or that indeed which outwardly ye show?" Shakespeare, in fact, asks the right question, whether they are "fantastical" or indeed what they "outwardly" show—conscious beings.

Some of the cases we have looked at in this chapter give the impression of being more than "fantastical." Still, there are strong prejudices today against the belief in ghosts. Today it's scientific materialism that wants to rule their existence out. I borrowed the title of this chapter, "Of Ghostes & Spirites Walking By Nyght," from a 1572 book by Lewes Lavater. Protestant Lavater wanted to prove that "Preestes and Monckes fained themselves to be Spirites." Religious sectarianism was the motive for denying there is much to ghosts and things that go bump in the night. Protestants disliked the idea of unaligned ghosts, or freethinking spirits; a ghost, they thought, had to be an Angel of God or the Devil in Disguise. The truth is that ghosts are us; they are people, or parts of people; imperfect humans stuck perhaps in the passage from one form of existence to another. It would be a step forward, if we could learn to have intelligent conversation with the spirits—the ghosts that walk in the Dark Night of the Subliminal Mind.

CHAPTER 3

The Medium
and the Message

An instrument is available to everyone for communicating with the next world now. That instrument is ourselves: our own minds and bodies, the best medium we have for tuning into the Invisible Spectrum—the Frequencies Beyond. Of course, as with any human capacity, there are ranges of excellence. There is hope for improvement with the least gifted; with some, however, the sky is the limit. Most of us can carry a tune; we also have our Mozarts and our Coltranes.

This ability to use yourself, your own organism, as an instrument of detection, a tool for communication with the Otherworld, goes under many words. A *medium* suggests a go-between; *automatist* points to the involuntary side of the phenomenon; *sensitive,* to having a well-poised receptivity. Mediums are people whose bodies—hands and vocal chords—function like transmitters; they seem to "put across" intelligence from other dimensions of being.

A medium is somebody who cultivates a certain type of

63

dissociation, a state of mind in which the routine personality is cast aside. According to psychologist Stanley Krippner's definition, dissociation refers to "reported experiences and observed behaviors that seem to exist apart from, or appear to have been disconnected from, the mainstream, or flow, of one's conscious awareness, behavioral repertoire, and/or self-identity."[1] In short, dissociation is a way of cutting loose from all our psychological moorings.

In this chapter, we look at *supernormal* types of dissociation: shamanic, psychedelic, and prophetic transports; creative inspiration, somnambulism, and mediumship. Unlike us, native societies value dissociative behaviors and use them for medical and spiritual purposes. Mediums, in the past, have distressed the bastions of power and structure, as you can see from the story of Saul's forbidden visit to the witch of Endor. The witch feared for her life, knowing she and all others of her kind could be expelled from the land (1 Sam. 28). The Catholic Inquisition wasn't fond of freelance explorers of Mind at Large either. And when mesmerism burst on the scene it was carefully contained, despite paving the way for modern dynamic psychiatry, as Henri Ellenberger has shown in *The Discovery of the Unconscious*.

A spectacular outburst of supernormal dissociation occurred in the middle of the super-scientific nineteenth century—a return of the repressed. In the 1840s, the Fox sisters from Hydesville, New York, unleashed a movement that spread through all classes of American society and eventually around the world: a pandemic of mediumistic experimentation, giving rise to an experience-based religion called spiritualism. The farmer prophets of spiritualism and the high-powered promoters like Madam Blavatsky and Arthur Conan Doyle were attacked and derided by the establishment.

Two things emerged from this wild ferment of psycho-religiosity. Spiritualism in America and Great Britain became a socially progressive movement, promoting ideas still playing themselves out, as Ann Braude's *Radical Spirits* (1989) brilliantly documents. Spiritualism did something else; it became the fuel for creating a new science. Psychical research, launched in England, eventually mutated into statistical parapsychology in America, which focused on the revolutionary task of proving extrasensory perception and psychokinesis. What began as a millenarian spiritual movement became a maverick science, which has been driven into relative obscurity.

Before we discuss mediumship and life after death, a few words about spiritualist social philosophy. This is important for us, because the next level of insight calls for broad social as well as cognitive change in our general outlook. In the nineteenth century, mediumship was a platform for women to find their public voices. (Women speaking in public was forbidden by Saint Paul.) Mediumship, like prophecy of old, became a voice of protest and reform, a voice that spoke with new authority on matters traditionally dominated by Protestant theology.

The opinions of the spirits that came through trance speakers like Cora Hatch, Emma Hardinge, and Achsa Sprague were often quite radical. Midcentury spiritualists were committed to the most progressive causes of the day. They favored the abolition of slavery. They were passionate about women's rights. They were religious reformers, claiming a new revelation and a new dispensation. They were unhappy about the medical profession, preferring the simple and natural water fast to leeching and bloodletting, and they advocated a vegetarian diet for spiritual, humane, and health reasons. They were opposed to capital punishment, and would have judged it truly barbaric to execute the mentally impaired. They were fierce about the right to free love, by which they meant the opposite of heartless promiscuity, calling for a happy voluntary sexuality, in contrast to what they perceived as the legalized sex slavery of marriage.

They were the enemies of patriarchal monogamy and insisted on the right to equal education. They stood up for the rights of women to define themselves on their own terms. They refused to see themselves as the weaker sex, naturally prone to disease, hysteria, and the vapors. They were in the vanguard against a dress code that distorted their bodies in service to male sex fantasy. Above all, they revolted against a punitive pessimistic Calvinism, which was the spiritual backbone of America's manifest destiny. To sum up, mediumship for the spiritualists was an instrument of prophetic critique of an entire way of life. To take the spirits seriously was boldly to challenge everyday life in America.

Something else emerged from spiritualism, a philosophical insistence on a more balanced epistemology. Contemporary feminist philosophers have been arguing that there are alternative ways of knowing, ways that complement sense-and-inference based approaches. The alternative epistemology of spiritualism stood by the value of intuition; the claim that important knowledge could be paranormally acquired. In short, Joan of Arc didn't have to go to West Point. Psychical research tested the powers of mediums. Could they really know things without input of sense or inference? Communicate with spirits? Most of the cases that follow are from the golden age of mental mediumship (late 1800s to the 1930s). Mediums were largely nonprofessionals, and did their thing in home circles that sprang up all over the country. On rare occasions, good mediums cooperated with scientists; controls were imposed to prevent deception and records kept for critical and comparative purposes. From the records of mediumship, then, here are some examples.

A "Proxy" Sitting

Long before the English founded psychical research in 1882, French "magnetists" and mesmerists were studying mediumship, somnambulism, and the puzzling phenomena of "secondary personality." It is a fact frequently observed: Under special circumstances, our everyday personalities may recede and make room for "secondary" personalities.

Some mesmeric experiments produced striking results. Alphonse Cahagnet, a cabinetmaker, was a pioneer experimenter in hypnotism, and worked with a young woman, Adele Maginot, a somnambulist since childhood. The entranced Adele claimed to see—and often managed to describe in detail—deceased persons she had never known. Savvy "sitters" realized that Adele might be using her talent for "thought-transference" to produce her effects, so they devised a more stringent test.

As reported in the *Celestial Telegraph* of 1848, J. J. Rostan asked his servant for the name of a dead acquaintance, a person he did not know. When Rostan mentioned the name of this deceased person to Adele, she described a woman in detail. Adele, of course, couldn't have telepathically filched her description from Rostan's mind. Still, Adele, according to Rostan, correctly described the deceased woman's "stature, age, dress, carriage, the disease and her deformed figure." This is an early example of a "proxy" sitting. The "sitter" knows nothing of the deceased; hence the medium cannot obtain information about the dead person from the sitter.

An interesting step, but not decisive. The medium could still get the information from *distant* sources, say, from the minds of people who knew the deceased or from written records about the deceased. This possibility, that the medium's mind could reach out in all directions for information, is dubbed "superpsi," a term for unlimited psychic capacity. Superpsi is one of the keys to the afterlife controversy: a key that opens the door to an immensely expanded theory of mental agency and capacity.

Why Pop Mediums Underestimate Their Own Power

Victorian times spawned the golden age of scientific mediumship. But this was an offshoot of spiritualism, an invention of three sisters in upper New York state in 1844, which swept across the world, not subsiding till 1925. In the 1960s and 1970s, again in America, the phenomenon, now named *channeling,* became widespread. "Channelers" J. Z. Knight and Jach Pursel appeared in public, on television, wrote books, and gained huge popular followings. Adept at self-entrancement, they claimed to communicate with mysterious intelligent beings. Spirit guides, interior mentors, dispensed practical advice; they were not interested in proving who they were. Perhaps they were just devices to siphon off treasure from the subliminal mind. Twentieth-century channeling was weighty with ecological preachments and the wonders of human potential. Old Greek divinities like Gaia and Chaos reappeared in modern scientific garb. Unlike Victorian and post-WWI mediumship, evidence for survival was not a concern.

In the late 1990s, however, "channeling" reverted to Victorian curiosity about the next world, perhaps because aging boomers in America were becoming more meditative about their mortality. Once again, spirit contact is claimed, and successful popular mediums appear on TV specials and talk shows (often around Halloween). People in the audience, outside callers, the host of the show—present themselves, hoping for a consoling message from a departed loved one.

The typical medium fishes, questions, guesses, flounders, gets a nibble, and sometimes scores a correct "hit." The medium may identify a name or fact relating to the person who passed. Messages are usually vague and upbeat. When the medium is on target, or seems to be, the experience can be deeply moving. As for evidence, even striking "hits" say little about life after death. At most, they prove the medium picked up information from *the mind of the bereaved person*. But telepathy with the bereaved person is not proof of life after death. In some cases, the bereaved isn't aware that it's a hit until she checks it; but a good telepath can sense what you have consciously forgotten.

Once the sensitive picks something up, he or she instinctively carries on as if they were talking to a spirit, and charisma and theatrical instinct take over. Whatever the subjective value of these performances, they're slight as evidence for life after death. Although they occur in a context primarily meant to be entertaining, they have reintroduced the idea of mediumship to the public. Let's look then at some cases that hail from the heyday of psychical research when the attempt to obtain persuasive evidence was the primary concern.

Love and Life After Death

I want to begin with a four-year-long afterlife experiment involving seven people. The case raises interesting points about the psychology of communicating with the dead, and has a powerful message about love and the afterlife. An elaborate proxy sitting, you can find the full story in a book called *The Bridge* by Nea Walker.[2]

Walker used several mediums to locate the "communicator"—the term for the alleged deceased person. (Cahagnet, by contrast, worked with one, Adele.) Walker, who served as a proxy sitter for bereaved people, was careful not to reveal the correctness or falsity of the medium's statements; the point was to prevent the medium from learning or inferring anything from the proxy, who knew neither the person bereaved nor the deceased. (Compare this to most of today's popular TV mediums, who *continuously ask for feedback* during sittings.)

Nea Walker made sure that the medium knew as little as possible about the deceased. She typically wrote down a request for contact and spoke it out loud to a group of spirits she believed were "working" from the other side. These transworld workers were known as the Group, or the Gang, and were behind the Plan. Without the sitter having any information about the deceased, and without any feedback, you'd expect the medium—unless directed by an external intelligence—to wander off in random directions. But this isn't what happened.

The story of *The Bridge* is unique; it combines passionate feeling with critical intelligence. Mary and Gwyther White were deeply and happily in love, and their life in the English countryside between the two World Wars read like a page from *A Midsummer Night's Dream,* until stomach cancer killed Gwyther at the age of 38. Mary was so dismayed by her loss that her friends feared for her life. Mary reached for solace from the church. Why did this happen to Gwyther? The cruelty of her husband's death and the terrible silence that followed shattered her faith in the "survival of human love and of personal identity." Mary, a child of the new age of Darwin, wanted proof that Gwyther and their great love had not completely perished.

This need for proof that "love and personal identity" survive prompted Mary to try the Ouija board. She discovered she had some psychic talents, and seemed to obtain some responses from the board, but her heart was full of questions and she remained unconvinced. So she wrote Sir Oliver Lodge, a famous physicist known for his research on life after death. Lodge was in America when Mary wrote, so Nea Walker replied. Walker was both scientist and helper of the bereaved, and offered to assist Mary. She would serve as a proxy sitter for her, hoping to establish a psychic link with the dead husband. "The object was to get as much evidence as possible of the personality and identity of Mr. White through mediums who had never seen or heard of either Mr. or Mrs. White, working with sitters who had also seen neither and who practically knew nothing of them and their life together." Walker aimed to rule out telepathy from the living as an explanation of experimental results.

The sittings went on and the evidence grew. The mediums kept picking up on specifics. The same personalities—the deceased husband and brothers—kept appearing through *different* mediums. What they said formed a clear pattern of cross-references. One medium would mention a moment watching a particular sunset, another revealing the same idea through slightly different associations. The evidence piled up, three mediums from Cardiff, Wales, Mrs. Dowdall, Mrs. Barnstaple, Mrs. Bewick; a Mrs. Annie Brittain, Damaris Walker (sister of Nea Walker), and finally, the strongest, Gladys Osborn Leonard. Leonard became partially possessed by Gwyther; the other mediums used clairvoyance and clairaudience. Nea Walker's job was to remain as ignorant of the Whites and their story as possible and to keep the different mediums as much in the dark as possible about the Whites and each other's responses.

The mediums kept producing statements that dovetailed and reinforced each other. For example, Damaris and the ladies from Cardiff sensed the character of the dead Gwyther, his boyish sense of humor, his touchiness if his slippers were misplaced, and so on. They described the interior of the White's house, their garden, their love of poetry, their music room with pewter pots and metal candlesticks, their favorite rugs, their love of flowers (especially roses), the umbrella stand, the hat rack, the neighboring streams and beloved towns, and so on and so forth. Trivial to us, but to Mary thrilling signals of communication from her dead lover. Also, Mary's two deceased brothers, Harold and Wellesley, came through, along with uncanny hints of Mary White's impending death.

When Nea Walker went as Mary's proxy to sit with Leonard, strong material emerged. Remember that sitter and medium knew almost nothing about Mary and Gwyther. I say "almost" because, despite her best efforts, Walker couldn't help learning something of Mary's life and her husband. She certainly didn't know that Mary's pet name for her husband was "B" or "Bee." The entranced Leonard asked: "What am I getting B for?" Leonard almost got Gwyther's pet name for his wife, which was "Biddy." Leonard said, "Lubby, Libby—that's not quite right." Later, she got it right.

In a sitting conducted by Nea Walker as proxy with Leonard, Feda, Leonard's control says, addressing Walker: "Mrs. Nea, you know the piano, you tap on his teeth, the one with the big white teeth?" Mary White comments: "Gwyther often called my piano 'the animal with the big white teeth.' " It's this kind of trivially private but highly specific impression that we find scattered fairly profusely throughout these sittings, impressions too exact to dismiss as lucky guesses.

I find it hard to avoid the feeling that these exchanges involve paranormal cognition. In some cases, the medium cannot be gaining the correct cognitions from the mind of the sitter who is ignorant of the crucial facts. In one of many possible examples, "Harold," an apparent personality calling attention to his birthday came through at a sitting with Damaris and Mrs. Leonard, neither of whom knew his name, birthday, or the fact that he was the deceased brother of Mary White.

When Mary White sat anonymously with Leonard the medium received some very striking impressions. Here, of course, the skeptic could say that Leonard obtained the correct information telepathically from Mary herself. (We discuss that possibility in detail in a coming chapter.) In the first sitting, Leonard spelled out the pet name Gwyther had for his wife that she almost identified in a previous sitting: "Biddy." "His own name for me, never used by anyone else," notes Mary. The statement, "B [Gwyther's nickname] wants you to settle your will," came through. Mary comments: "I had made a will during Gwyther's life-time, but on inquiry *after* this suggestion found that it would not be suitable." Gwyther (the self-declared spirit) warns his wife not to become attached to any puppy. Mary comments that she was in fact considering obtaining a puppy she had taken a fancy to. Gwyther laughingly refers to his wife's mania for rearranging the furniture in their home. He speaks with marked male clumsiness of a gray dress he liked—"a straight up-and-down thing." Mary confirms, describing it more exactly as "blue liberty velvet or *crepe de chine*." He addresses her with pet names such as "little woman" and "Biddy darling." He refers to "the house of sweet scents," a special phrase Mary confirms he had invented to describe potpourri.

Says the medium: "Do you know what he means about the Shrine? It is connected with that chair [a special chair they liked]. He likes to go in there at night. That is our Holy of Holies—where I meet you, so specially, so spiritually. I speak of my love to you. And there—and there, you make me feel I am going to have you again." Apparently, this is a dead husband speaking to his wife through the body of a living woman.

Mary White comments: "I do not wish to annotate this. It is full of meaning. Gwyther can give me no greater evidence of his nearness or of his intimate association with my inmost self." After this experience Mary became ill and bedridden for two years. During that time proxy sittings were continued on her behalf, adding correct and often very specific impressions about her deceased husband. She died four years later in 1924, convinced she was going to rejoin Gwyther in the next world.

What I've listed here is a fraction of the correct impressions garnered in the course of this four-year-long experiment. But these were not the whole of the evidence. The mediums also evoked the tone, mood, and special quality of the relationship between the two lovers. "The mere getting of evidential material is not, however, in the present case the whole of the evidence," Lodge said. More impressive was the atmosphere of two soulful personalities that the medium succeeded in reproducing, the feelings of intimacy and all the poetic, pictorial, and musical allusions to the two lovers when they were alive together.

Two things about this case deserve notice. A Welsh study showed that afterlife communications occur more readily between spouses who enjoy warm emotional ties.[3] To the skeptic, of course, the closer the ties, the greater the need to believe and therefore the greater the tendency to be deluded. But it is just as likely that shared memories and emotional ties create the rapport needed for afterlife communications. Independent evidence indicates that emotional ties favor extrasensory perception; lack of emotional ties would therefore impede communication, and emotionally isolated people might find it hard to imagine life after death.

The second point I want to stress is that *The Bridge* is

more than a record of a long afterlife experiment. It is also a model for facilitating the death transition. Mary died in an environment that succeeded in building a psychological bridge to her deceased husband. This suggests the possibility of improving end of life care by retaining the services of competent mediums. If our data is valid, mediums might play a role in the medicine of the future, especially in helping the dying build psychological bridges to the next world. Modern medicine is brilliant about retarding the inevitable but clueless about making the transition. In the text of *The Bridge*, there are hints on how to improve our way of death and dying.

Obsession, Afterlife, and Creativity

The search for life after death leads to surprising discoveries about the human mind. In this section, we find a story that is a strong piece of evidence for life after death. The story is also interesting for its novel conception of the creative process. Some creative people may—in light of this report—be dipping into what Emerson called the "world-soul" for inspiration. None other than Mark Twain believed this; the way he tells it, his ideas came to him from other people—using his words—by "mental telegraphy." Robert Louis Stevenson reports that his dream "brownies" gave him plots for "saleable" fictions and William Blake said his artworks were copies of the visionary worlds he had seen. The Thompson-Gifford case, which I'll now describe, has links to these famous parallels.

Frederic L. Thompson was a goldsmith by trade. One day he was suddenly seized by the impulse to draw and paint. He began to hear voices and started seeing visions of landscapes he felt he had to put on canvas. Thompson had little training in art. This unbidden impulse to make art persisted.

Thompson lost interest in his goldsmithing and began to sketch and paint. In working at his new craft, he often felt the well-known artist Robert Swain Gifford, a person he barely knew, guiding him. They had met for a few moments in the marshes near New Bedford while Gifford was painting and Thompson was hunting. Thompson visited Gifford in New York once to show him some jewelry. Gifford died six months before Thompson was seized by the impulse to paint. Gradually, Thompson became conscious of the other personality taking him over, and sometimes he'd say to his wife, "Gifford wants to sketch."[4]

In 1906 he went to an exhibition of Gifford's work. Scanning the dead artist's paintings, Thompson heard a voice: "You see what I have done. Can you not take up and finish my work?" After this auditory hallucination—of an artist he knew was dead—Thompson's urge to paint intensified. He flung himself into it, and began to produce works that not only sold, but commanded significant prices.

By 1907 the former goldsmith was questioning his sanity; there was no letup in the flow of visions. One particular scene of gnarled oaks haunted him. He made sketches from this visionary scene, and was overwhelmed by the urge to visit the original, and paint it directly. In desperation, he called on James Hyslop, a professor of philosophy at Columbia University, one of the founders of the American Society for Psychical Research, and a student of obsession and the afterlife. As Hyslop put it, he was intrigued by "the hypothesis that the dead may occasionally intrude their influence upon the living." No less intriguing is the possibility that the influence might be creative and life enhancing.

At first Hyslop thought Thompson was suffering from "disintegrating" personality, and stupidly advised him to quit painting. But Hyslop had second thoughts. He decided to bring Thompson to a medium; if the medium picked up something about Gifford, he reasoned, Thompson's story might have legs. Thompson reluctantly agreed, and Hyslop introduced him as Mr. Smith to a clairvoyante, a Mrs. Rathbun. Thompson said nothing about himself or his very peculiar situation, yet almost at once Mrs. Rathbun said she saw the figure of an artist standing behind him. She described the man, and the description, according to Thompson, fit Gifford. The medium described the dead artist's birthplace and the gnarled oak trees Thompson had been obsessing over for eighteen months. The locale was said to be a place needing a boat to reach, and turned out to be one of New England's Elizabeth Islands.

This meeting fired up Thompson's obsession; he continued to paint and sell his work to people who noticed the resemblance to Gifford's style. Heartened by this, Hyslop decided to conduct a second experiment, this time with a different medium, a Mrs. Chenoweth. This lady gave details and facts that fit Gifford's private habits, his unfinished work, his studio, misty scenes, a woman (also mentioned by the last medium), and the same gnarled oak trees. Chenoweth described the latter in careful detail, and Thompson soon set out to find the physical place itself. Before heading for New England, he left some drawings he had done two years ago with professor Hyslop. With some effort, he found Gifford's summer home, and Mrs. Gifford showed him her late husband's studio. What Thompson saw knocked the wind out of him. The easel held a painting that matched one of the drawings he left with Hyslop. Here was ocular proof of his visions. Other artworks in Gifford's studio also matched drawings Thompson had made.

Thompson learned from Mrs. Gifford that her husband was fond of the Elizabeth Islands, opposite Martha's Vineyard, so Thompson went off to explore them and encountered many scenes he knew from his visions. He photographed them to compare with his artworks. At a familiar scene, he heard a voice, like the one heard in the art gallery: "Go and look on the other side of the tree." There on the other side of the beech tree, he found the initials of Robert Swain Gifford and the date, 1902, carved in the bark.

Thompson returned home. He was still haunted by a particular storm-tossed scene with gnarled tree and broken branches. He wanted to locate the original landscape so he could paint it. Feeling consumed by forces that seemed to come to him from outside, again he enlisted the aid of Hyslop in New York. The two men returned to the islands several times until they found the locale of the haunting landscape on Nonomesset Island. At last Thompson could paint the scene and literally lay the ghost of his inspiration to rest. In recalling how it felt to make this painting, he compared it to the ecstasy of death. He named his romantic landscape *The Battle of the Elements*.

Hyslop now knew he was onto something and kept probing for more details to bolster the case. He now brought in a third medium, Mrs. Smead, who promptly identified the presence of an artist, and correctly provided his initials, R.S.G. Hyslop invited her because she resided in a backwater town in the rural South that was "almost inaccessible to information about the Thompson-Gifford story." Hyslop also obtained testimony from Thompson's wife, who confirmed many details of her husband's strange transformation. Thompson was a married man whose obsession caused him to leave his profession and go on a wild search for romantic landscapes he had seen in visions and hallucinations, and he was swept away by the desire to draw and paint them. The experience put him in doubt of his sanity. Eventually, he found his visionary landscapes were really part of the coast of New England and began to make and then sell artworks recognizably in the style of the dead artist that "spoke" to him and drove him to paint in the first place. Three different mediums confirmed his story.

The facts suggest that Robert Swain Gifford survived his death and took possession of Thompson's mind. The story prompts me to wonder about the nature of inspiration and creativity. I feel renewed respect for the ancient Greek idea that creativity is a kind of possession by the muses, except that for all we know the "muses" might be spirits who surround us and who suffer in a limbo of unrealized desires. There may be something to Yeats's idea of the "great memory" or Mark Twain's "mental telegraphy" or William Blake's "Eternal Imagination." So, in another way, as I have already pointed out, the more we follow the spoor of afterlife evidence, the more we keep meeting with surprises about human potential. It may be that in certain examples of unusual or exalted creativity, there are moments where one has already experienced contact with the next world.

The Remarkable Case of G.P.

Mediumship is a type of performance art; there is little appreciation of it today. For some it will always be a profession tainted by suspicion and skullduggery. I think, however, that an element of mediumship—of dissociation from the normal self—is found in most creative achievement. The creative "I" is often somebody else, as Rimbaud once said in a famous letter. The mediumship that interests us here is the kind that deals with communication with the dead. Let's look at an example that rises to the level of high art.

William James discovered and brought to prominence a medium who must be counted one of the geniuses of the field, a Boston lady named Leonora Piper. Piper discovered her talent when she was eight, playing in a garden one day. Something struck her right ear. She heard: "Aunt Sara, not dead, but with you still." Later it was determined that Aunt Sara died the moment Leonora heard the voice. At twenty-two Leonora married, and soon after visited a medical clairvoyant, Dr. Cocke, seeking to relieve pains from a previous accident.

On her second visit with Dr. Cocke she herself became entranced. Soon she acquired an indispensable aid to mediumship, a *control*. (We have already met Gladys Leonard's control, Feda.) Mediumistic controls go by different names in different cultures: familiars, muses, spirit guides, guardian angels, take your pick. One use of these constructs is to distract the conscious mind from impeding the subconscious flow of ideas. Controls satisfy the need to personify and therefore give the dark forms of the subconscious a recognizable face, and serve as magnetic conduits to the subliminal mind. Piper's first control was a girl, Chlorine, and then another announced itself as Sebastian Bach. Finally, a self-proclaimed French doctor, Phinuit (pronounced Finney) settled in and took over.

With Phinuit, Piper conducted séances with the curious and the bereaved, often astonishing and consoling them with appropriate and detailed communications from beloved departed ones. A Miss R said of what she took to be a deceased friend: "In a great many little ways he is quite like what my friend used to be when living, so much so that I am afraid it would take a great deal of explanation to make me believe that his identical self had not something to do with it, wholly apart from the medium's powers or from anything that may be in my own mind concerning him."

Others gave glowing testimonials of her talents. When the self-declared spirits spoke through Piper's vocal apparatus, they often reproduced the voice, tone, and manner of the dead person. But the best part was the intimate tidbits of highly personal knowledge the medium dredged up when she was at her best, though like all artists, she was not in top form all the time. She succeeded in convincing William James and his wife that she possessed specific and copious knowledge of their family life, knowledge she could not have obtained by normal means. James never wavered in his conviction of Leonora Piper's supernormal powers, and wasn't in the least shy about declaring it to his stuffier colleagues who thought such things were bunkum.

To deal with the possibility of fraud, James delegated the job of studying Piper to the skeptical Richard Hodgson. Sneakily, Hodgson hired detectives to find out whether Piper got information about her clients by normal means, but nothing she ever did roused any suspicion. Piper, modestly paid by the Society for Psychical Research, cooperated with her sedulous investigators.

Hodgson, trained in law and philosophy at Cambridge, had earned a reputation as hit man of psychic imposters. The Society sent him to India to investigate Madame Blavatsky's much-touted thaumaturgy. Hodgson returned with a damning verdict, which caused a sensation in the world press; the lady was faking her marvels. Hodgson made his reputation detailing how the credulous are taken in by their emotions, memories, and malobservations, and when he took on Piper he was skeptical about the afterlife, and ready to expose her tricks. No one, in short, could accuse Hodgson of being credulous.

Nevertheless, in the end, Leonora Piper convinced him of personal survival. One case in particular pushed him over the edge. A young acquaintance, George Pellew (known as G.P.) died from falling off a horse in New York City. Although they were not intimate friends, Hodgson more than once discussed the afterlife with G.P., a lawyer and informed skeptic. Inclined to put matters to the test, G.P. promised that in case he died first and by chance found him-

self still up and about, he'd be sure to make things as
"lively" as possible for Hodgson. Within weeks of his death,
a G.P. persona began to manifest as Mrs. Piper's "control."
When the G.P. persona became Piper's control (read "traffic
cop"), he gave copious evidence of his identity. This was very
different from the previous control, Phinuit. Although his
medical diagnoses and remedies were often on the mark,
Phinuit gave no evidence that he was a real person; he
couldn't speak French and gave no proof of medical training;
so it's safe to assume he was a dramatic personification of
Piper's subconscious. Not so, G.P.

Thus, during the time George Pellew served as Piper's
control, about 150 people came to her for sittings. Among
them were personal friends of the deceased George who presented themselves incognito. George—the apparent personality acting through Piper's voice and body—*behaved* very
much like the living George. It gave a very convincing
impression of the previous personality. G.P. recognized the
friends and family he knew when he was alive. Apparently
he did so *unerringly.* "Nor has he failed in the recognition of
personal friends," wrote Hodgson. "I may say generally that
out of a large number of sitters who went as strangers to
Mrs. Piper, the communicating G.P. has picked out the
friends of G.P. living, precisely as the G.P. living might have
been expected to do. Thirty cases of recognition out of at
least 150 who had sittings with Mrs. Piper . . . *and no case of
false recognition*"[5] (italics added).

These are impressive numbers. Moreover, George doesn't
just identify his friends by giving their names; he *relates* to
them as if he were the real George Pellew. According to
Hodgson, the G.P. persona showed the memories and emotions of the living George Pellew that were appropriate,
never making a mistake or missing a step in his reactions to
sitters. The George that comes through tries very hard to

convince the sitters—his skeptical family and the critical Hodgson—of his continued existence. Everything looks as if he is trying to keep the promise of the living George—to make things "lively." In this, says Hodgson, the G.P. persona "displayed the keenness and pertinacity which were eminently characteristic of George Pellew living." Nor were the manifestations fleeting or sporadic but steady over years and showing "the same characteristics of an independent personality whether friends of George Pellew were present at the sittings or not." In the end, the performance overcame the skepticism of friends, family, and Hodgson. All became convinced they were relating to a man whom they once knew on earth and who had survived the great sea change.

A quick example from the stenographic record. The sitting took place in the home of Mr. and Mrs. James Howard, friends of the deceased George. Piper, the Howards, a stenographer, and Hodgson were present. Since the arrival of the G.P. persona, Piper began to practice automatic writing. In the following extract, G.P. communicates through Piper's writing hand. G.P. sometimes writes using Piper's hand while *at the same time* Phinuit, or other communicators, speak through her voice, as in the following.

"Hello, Hodgson, you know me. Hello, Jim, old fellow, I am not dead yet. I still live to see you. Do you remember how we used to ask each other for books of certain kinds, about certain books, where they were, and you always knew just where to find them?"

"This was characteristic," comments James Howard. "The sitting was held in my library, where George and myself had frequently talked together and had frequent occasion to turn up references in one book or another. George, living, had remarked several times on my accurate knowledge of location of the books on my shelves."

"Hello, I know now where I am. Jim, you dear old soul,

how are you? Who is this, Louis . . . he wants to see Billie."

Then "Phinuit" (who is also present) says: "Ha! He wants to know something."

Hodgson asks: "Who is Louis?"

Phinuit replies, "He is . . . who is that gentleman, that German fellow talking to you, George, can't you tell them?"

Hodgson repeats, "He wants to see Billie, does he?"

G.P. (now writing), "Hodgson, it is I. Go out and tell him to come."

"Louis R.," Hodgson notes, "German on his father's side, was before he died a dear friend of the Howards and often sat in the library with them, and on the very chair Piper was sitting on. When Louis was mentioned the Howards did not think of him."

The remarks "He [Louis, the spirit on the other side] wants to see Billie" and "Go out and tell him to come" refer to a William Parker who lived across the street and who had previously been to a sitting with Piper and communicated with the excarnate Louis. Phinuit now spells *Foxecroft* in mirror writing, which takes some deciphering. Foxecroft was the name of a deceased friend of Louis who was anxious to communicate with William across the street.

Now, in this curious scene, it appears that Leonora Piper, in a trance state, is behaving like a human telephone, or like a switchboard, for communications between the living and the dead. At one point the voice of George says: "Get me my hair." Mrs. Howard had a packet of George's baby hair in another room, a fact she had forgotten during the sitting. The dead guy takes control of Piper's voice and says: "What can I do for you to prove it all? I am anxious, I am impatient." George—G.P.—then correctly alludes to a letter that James Howard had received about his death from someone called Orenberg.

And so it went, on and off, for about five years: the personality of a dead man coming through in intimate, detailed ways with a score and a half of former friends, one by one removing the doubts of persons disinclined to believe that he, a high-spirited New York lawyer, was still his old conscious self, an active agent, even after undergoing physical death. The brief episode I just described is a tiny fraction of the records of fifteen years of Piper's mediumistic performances. This medium of genius was closely studied, and tested, and dissected, not just by Hodgson but by William James, Walter Leaf, Sir Oliver Lodge, Frederic Myers, the redoubtable Sidgwicks, and other shrewd inquirers. What to conclude about the George Pellew case?

1. *Fraud can effectively be ruled out.* Writes Hodgson: "For several weeks, moreover, at the suggestion of one of our members, detectives were employed for the purpose of ascertaining whether there were any indications that Mrs. Piper or her husband, or other persons connected with her, tried to ascertain facts about possible sitters by the help of confederates, or other ordinary methods of inquiry; but not the smallest indication whatever of any such procedure was discovered."

   Also mitigating against fraud is the fact that in 1889 the medium visited England for several months. Myers, Lodge, and Leaf wanted to study her in a foreign milieu where the sitters and the details of their lives were completely unknown to her. Nevertheless, she performed as brilliantly as she did in America.

2. *Selectivity of the evidence.* Again, to state the most striking fact: out of the 150 people the medium met in a trance state, the Pellew *persona* recognized and interacted appropriately with just the thirty who the

living man knew. There were neither failures to recognize known friends and family nor false recognitions. This is what you would expect if a person—let's say—who had been missing, turned up in some unexpected place, and spoke on the phone with people he knew. The George acting through Piper's body recognizes the persons he knew in life and is recognized by them through his correct statements, sense of humor, gesture, voice, intonation, and so forth.

3. *The singleness and continuity of the persona.* Mediums very often fish for clues, vacillate, and beat around the bush. Before George's persona appeared on the scene, Hodgson was skeptical, especially when Dr. Phinuit was in "control." But that changed with G.P.'s arrival. According to Hodgson, his manifestations didn't have a "fitful and spasmodic nature, but exhibited the marks of a continuous living and persistent personality, manifesting itself through a course of years, and showing the same characteristics of an independent intelligence whether friends of G.P. were present at the sittings or not." If the entranced Piper were creating George's persona from the memories and needs of sitters who knew the living Pellew, the impersonation should fail, or at least flag, when there was nobody around who knew Pellew. The steadiness of the manifestations suggests an independent center of energy, and of consciousness, of the sort we associate with a human personality. Hodgson admitted his vanity was wounded in being forced to admit he was wrong about Leonora Piper: "I cannot profess to have any doubt but that the chief communicators are veritably the personalities they claim to be; that they have survived the change we call death."

The Uninvited

Ever since the days of "magnetic" mediumship, researchers have been on the lookout for more cogent evidence. For example, so-called drop-in communicators. Most people go to mediums with specific persons in mind with whom they want to communicate. Sometimes, however, the initiative appears to come from the other side. There are documented cases in which an unknown personality intrudes during a séance, an uninvited visitor who correctly names and describes himself. Cases like this are hard to explain in terms of the needs of sitters, especially if the "drop-ins" are complete strangers.

Psychologist Alan Gauld states that three things are desirable in such cases:

1. The information imparted cannot be explained by normal means.
2. The intruder must display a good reason for appearing, a reason "stronger than any which the medium might have for wishing to contact him."
3. The information from the uninvited communicator must be such that the medium had to use paranormal powers to obtain it from *several* sources.[6]

Here is a very strange case of a drowned man who lost his leg that satisfies these conditions.[7] During 1937–38 an uninvited communicator who named himself Runolfur Runolfsson appeared during a séance. The medium was Hafsteinn Bjnornsson. "Runolfur" kept saying he lost his leg. (Recall the Rumanian apparition annoyed about the mistreatment of his mortal remains.) Besides his full name, he gave his age at death, his wife's name, where he lived, that he was very tall, providing specific details of how he died. He gave the month and year of his death and the month and year his body was found; and how he had got drunk, drowned, and was swept out to sea. He named the graveyard where his remains were buried, told how his thighbone was missing, how the tide took it, where it was found, and where, after being handled by different people, it was finally dumped.

The specifics of this remarkable story were later verified. All three of Gauld's conditions were satisfied. The information conveyed by Runolfur could not be explained by normal means. No one at the séance had any reasons to reveal this information. Finally, different sources were needed for verification—different people and different written documents. Neither medium nor anyone in the "home circle" had any known motive to contact the communicator—the communicator showed all the motivation.

Given all this, the best explanation of this story seems to me that Runolfur survived the death of his body and was the source of intelligence behind the verified information. The investigators, Haraldsson and Stevenson, cautious to a fault, add by way of qualification: "On the other hand, sensitives have been known to achieve remarkable feats of deriving and integrating information without the participation of any purported discarnate personality." A certain systematic ambiguity in the evidence always ends up taunting us in the attempt to cinch the case for life after death. The case of Runolfur is compelling, but even sympathetic inquirers hold back from complete assent. We will not duck this taunt; on the contrary, we will face it, without flinching. It will open a new way of framing the whole question of life after death.

Book-Tests

Meanwhile, we need to continue our review of the varieties of afterlife narrative. Before trying to fly off to the Otherworld, we need to ground ourselves in the ABCs of the supernormal mind. So, back to Feda, Gladys Leonard's "control" who seems to have invented the book-test, another thread in the tapestry of persuasion. In a book-test, the apparent communicator, acting through the control, provides the exact location of a book, shelf and place number, and identifies a specific passage in the book. Book-tests employ books intimately related to the deceased. Words or phrases are singled out that *mean something special* to the one claiming to communicate through the automatist.

Lily Talbot wrote an account of her sitting with Leonard and sent it to Lady Troubridge on December 29, 1917 (there were two witnesses in this case). The medium knew nothing about the sitter, who introduced herself anonymously. Feda then gave "a very correct description" of Hugh Talbot's personal appearance, Lily's deceased husband, which by itself is not terribly weighty.

During the sitting, however, "Talbot" took over Leonard's body and spoke through her. An extraordinary conversation followed, and the self-declared dead Talbot tried by every means to prove to his wife that it was really he who was present and indeed had survived death. "All he said, or rather Feda said for him, was clear and lucid," reports Mrs. Talbot. "Incidents of the past, known only to him and to me were spoken of, belongings trivial in themselves but possessing for him a particular personal interest of which I was aware, were minutely and correctly described, and I was asked if I still had them."

"Feda" then began to describe a book that rang no bells in Mrs. Talbot's mind. Feda tired Mrs. Talbot with talk of this book. It was a book she would know by a diagram of languages it contained, "a table of Arabian languages, Semitic languages." Mrs. Talbot went home thinking little of the matter, but later, after dinner, prodded by her niece, decided to look for the book. After poking around for a while, she found one with the diagram mentioned by Feda, which in fact had written on it, "Table of Semitic or Syro-Arabian Languages."

Look on page twelve or thirteen, she was told. On page thirteen, she found an extract from a book called *Post Mortem* by an anonymous author describing in clear detail what today we would call a near-death experience. Lily Talbot never read or opened this book. Nor, of course, did the medium, Gladys Leonard. It was a book from Mister Talbot's library, most likely known to him only. "Feda" was right about the volume with a diagram of languages, and right about the meaningful passage. The experience convinced Lily Talbot that her husband had survived death.[8]

One more book-test. Edward Wyndham Tennant was a soldier killed in World War I. In a sitting with Leonard, December 1917, the young man, whose nickname was Bim, appeared to communicate through Feda to members of his family: "Bim now wants to send a message to his Father. This book is particularly for his Father. Underline that, he says. It is the ninth book on the third shelf counting from left to right in the bookcase on the right of the door in the drawing room as you enter; take the title, and look at page 37." The book indicated was titled *Trees*, and on page thirty-seven was a reference to a "tunneling beetle." It turns out that Bim's dad was a tree aficionado and was wild about this particular beetle, a fact so well known it was a family joke. The dead-on accuracy of the book's location, along with the beetle reference, seem beyond coincidence. The case looks like meaningful communication from one who is physically deceased.[9] Now this.

Newspaper Tests

Another test for survival emerged. The dead father of the investigator, a critical-minded Christian minister, Charles Drayton Thomas, apparently invented this one. As with the book-tests, the chief medium here was Gladys Leonard—as talented as Eleanora Piper. Gladys, by the way, began her career as an actress. Mediumship, we could say, is a specialized branch of the acting profession.

At 3 P.M., on February 13, 1920, Thomas received thirteen specific statements from the entranced Mrs. Leonard about items that would appear on the front page of the *London Times* the following day. The presumed "communicator" was Thomas's deceased father. In newspaper tests, the medium makes her remarks before the newspaper goes to press, which usually took place much later in the evening. Upon receiving predictions from the medium, Thomas recorded and promptly mailed them to the office of the Society for Psychical Research in London.

Statement given by Feda on February 13: "The first page of the paper, in column two and near the top—the name of a minister with whom your father was friendly at Leek." Needless to say, there was no normal way for Drayton Thomas or Gladys Leonard to know what would appear on the front page of the next day's *London Times*. Next day, however, Thomas found the name Perks four inches from the top on the front page, in the second column. He doesn't recognize this name, but his mother does, and his father's diaries reveal that a George Perks spent a memorable day with his father in Leek in 1873. The remaining twelve statements made specific predictions about names associated with particular people, friends, family, a former teacher, and places, schools, or previous residences.

Feda actually foretold a specific typo and its location on the front page. There were in fact numerous precise hits, including the typo! A few items were misses, but most were clearly correct and meaningful matches. Can we regard these results as coincidental? To test it, Thomas tried the predictions on randomly chosen front pages of the *Times*. He found that his communicator had seventy-three out of a possible 104 successes, but the random efforts yielded only seventeen successes out of 104. Item eleven stated: "Between that and the teacher's name is a place-name, French, looking like three words hyphenated into one." At the specified location, Thomas found the name of the Belgian town of *Braine-de-Chateau.*

Now, given that these statements emerged before the front page of the *London Times* was printed, and assuming that neither collusion nor coincidence explain the results, it looks as if someone foresaw what was to be printed on tomorrow's newspaper: names and places related to the memories and associations of a deceased person. Something insulting to logic has now entered the scene—apparent precognition. Thomas felt that the source of this had to be his deceased father. He assumed that only the dead can "see" the future. But there is experimental evidence that living people can sometimes "see" the future. So it might have been the medium herself who foresaw the front page of the *London Times.*

Perhaps this newspaper test could be explained by Leonard's paranormal powers. Let's think about what that would imply. Not only would she have to precognize the fact that the name Perks would appear in the second column on the front page of the *Times,* she would have to clairvoyantly discover that "Perks" was the name of a man whom Thomas's father spent a day with at a specific place called Leek forty years ago. Since this fact was recorded in Thomas Senior's diary, after "seeing" the name Perks in tomorrow's newspaper, Leonard would have had to scan all the written records relating to Thomas Senior to find meaningful references to Perks. Only then could she connect the two, meanwhile reproducing Thomas Senior's persona. If the test I have described is authentic, either the surviving mind of Thomas's father was the source of the newspaper "hits" *or* it was Leonard's subconscious mind. A fascinating logical disjunction.

Psychic Detectives and Life After Death

It would be wrong to imagine that good mediums vanished with Victorian times. Recently, they have been used in crime detection. Hardheaded crime fighters of the modern world are loath to admit benefits from the ministrations of mediums, but police investigators do sometimes turn to psychics for help. In a critical study of crime and psychic detectives, sociologists Arthur Lyons and Marcello Truzzi concluded that there was "a considerable body of documented cases in which psychic sleuths have scored impressive and seemingly inexplicable successes."

For a moment suppose that people do survive death and that sensitives or mediums can communicate with them; it's reasonable to suppose that if someone were murdered and survived death, she'd want to expose and catch her killers— as in Shakespeare's ghost story, *Hamlet*.

The following is a contemporary case reported by English psychical researchers, Guy Playfair and Montague Keen. On February 11, 1983, a young woman, Jacqueline Poole, was murdered in her flat in a West London suburb. Three days later a medium Christine Holohan felt a presence in her bedroom and something pulling her bedclothes; she then had a vision of a woman who called herself Jackie Hunt. She asked Holohan to help her bring justice to her killer, and the following night described the murder scene and murderer in detail. The medium conveyed this information to Tony Batters, the first detective to appear at the scene of the crime. Holohan made seventy-two statements about the crime scene and forty-two about the murderer, all of which were true or unverifiable. Jackie Hunt was Jacqueline Poole's maiden name, a fact unknown to Holohan, nor had the newspapers revealed her maiden name. The victim named her killer as "Pokie," the odd nickname of Anthony Ruark, whom the police had already suspected but could not prove was the killer. Detectives had retrieved a pullover discarded by Ruark, and kept it in storage until 2000 at which time the case was reopened and the pullover identified through new DNA technology as belonging to Jackie Hunt's killer. Pokie Ruark was convicted of murder in 2001, and is now serving a life term for his crime. Detective Batters stated in 2002 that "without Christine's information, it is unlikely that we would have procured the most conclusive evidence," the DNA-incriminating pullover.

The detectives kept detailed written records of Christine Holohan's numerous correct statements about the murder of Jackie Hunt, obtained within days of the crime. (There was one incorrect statement; the murder time was off by one day.) There was no normal way for the medium to know all the facts she revealed; she didn't know the victim or her friends and could only have learned a few facts, like the victim's marriage name, from the press. Could the medium have obtained the information paranormally, possibly by reading the mind of Detective Batters? The problem with this is that the medium revealed information unknown to the detective. Some of the information Holohan revealed took eighteen years to confirm.

The conclusion of the detectives is noteworthy. Detective Batters has "repeatedly told us [the investigators Guy Playfair and Montague Keen] that the only possible source for all the information is Jacqueline Poole." No doubt difficult for professional skeptics, Detective Tony Batters has gone on record saying: "I've accepted the fact that Jackie communicated with Christine." Batters's police colleagues have made similar declarations to Playfair and Keen. Police officials, of course, are naturally reluctant to appear credulous about the paranormal, so I am reluctant to take lightly statements like those of Tony Batters and his colleagues.

Lovers and Scholars in Paradise?

Perhaps the most extraordinary experiments to prove life after death are the so-called cross-correspondence tests. The idea seems to have come from Frederic Myers and his scholarly cohorts—*after they died*.

Myers died in 1901. He had spent his life struggling to reverse the trend of nineteenth-century psychology. Instead of a narrow dehumanizing science that modeled itself on the crude assumptions of nineteenth-century materialism, suspicious of everything mental, subjective, or spiritual, Myers created a psychology that took in the whole spectrum of human experience. His work was a synthesis of early psychical research, mesmerism and phenomena of multiple personality, and he drew deeply from the Platonic and Neoplatonic tradition.

Myers went to his grave—toward the end he looked forward to death, he said, as a boy looks forward to summer holiday—yearning to reunite with his first love, Annie Marshall, whose memory he cherished. Part of his passion to know the limits of consciousness was born of this yearning to reunite with the idol of his first love. Myers, as is plain from his poignant *Fragments of an Inner Life,* was a romantic poet, cursed in love, and driven to found a new science. If anyone was motivated to send glad tidings from the next world, it was Frederic Myers.

In 1904 an automatic script produced by Mrs. Holland, a pseudonym for the sister of Rudyard Kipling, claimed to originate from Myers. It stated: "If it were possible for the soul to die back into earth life again I should die from sheer yearning to reach you to tell you that all that we imagined is not half wonderful enough for the truth." Suppose his great love was fulfilled—one can imagine his passion to impart the prodigious good news to those of us still struggling this side of heaven.

The experiment Myers presumably devised from the other side worked as follows.[10] At a sitting with a medium, a fragmentary message, without apparent meaning, is received. Soon after, another medium, perhaps thousands of miles away, also receives a fragmentary message without apparent meaning. The automatists are unaware of what each other is receiving. Now suppose a reference comes through, a clue hinting that the scripts need to be *compared* to discern their meaning, and that an overarching meaning connects the fragments. It now looks as if two mediums, or automatists, are being used by an outside intelligence to convey a message. That is the gist of the "cross-correspondence" cases.

In one instance, for example, what seems to be a communicator writes, "Ave Roma Immortalis" and then "How could I make it any plainer without giving her the clue?" Everything appears as if the test were produced by a directing intelligence over and above the participating mediums. The allusive literary puzzles are characteristic of the mentalities of the deceased persons who appear to be making them up.

Some of the correspondences were simple enough to count as coincidental or as the product of guesswork or as unconscious paranormal nudging. However, as the scripts unfolded from the mediums—and they did so for thirty years—they became more complex, much more than coincidence could explain. Eventually, they seemed like more than telepathy from the living could explain.

The first to notice a cross-correspondence was Alice Johnson, a Research Officer of the British Society of Psychical Research. Johnson wrote: "It might be possible to obtain evidence more conclusive than any obtained hitherto from the action of a third intelligence, external to the minds of both automatists." This was a new suggestion, and had exciting possibilities. It would be as if an intelligent being from the other side had devised a jigsaw puzzle in which the pieces were parceled out to several different mediums, and left for them, or the experimenters, to put together.

This seems like a test designed to quell the fear that evidence for survival is a paranormal illusion. The cross-correspondence effect looks like something wrought by an external intelligence, the product of a group of scholars and lovers who once walked the groves of Cambridge University.

Understanding these automatic scripts is tough to do for several reasons. They are the refined products of minds highly trained in classical literature, and not too many of us today know ancient Greek or Latin. Expert knowledge and keen literary sensibility are essential.

For the test to work, the script producers need to keep the automatists and the investigators in the dark for as long as possible. In the end, what is supposed to happen is that they offer the decisive clue, the exact word, reference, or association that suddenly brings a long train of ideas into clear focus. For this to be convincing, the intelligence behind the script cannot plunk its cards down on the table all at once. Revelation must be by indirection; by evocation, metaphor, and anagram.

These experiments involved people related in a unique web of love, family, friendship, profession, educational background, and social class. They used pseudonyms. "Mrs. Willett" was a socially prominent person and first female delegate to the League of Nations. "Mrs. Holland" was the sister of the conservative Rudyard Kipling. Some scripts, because of their personal nature, have yet to be made public. Finally, the amount of material published, over fifty book-length studies, remains pathetically underanalyzed. Despite all these difficulties, the intelligence behind the scripts has seemed persuasive to many who studied them. A close friend of the deceased Dr. Verrall wrote of the medium's perfor-mance: "All this is Verrall's manner to the life in animated conversation . . . the turns of speech . . . the high-pitched emphasis." Let's look at a few examples.

The Lethe Case

On March 23, 1908, an American in Massachusetts, George B. Dorr, tried something with Eleanora Piper. Myers, who died in 1901, was supposed to be communicating through Piper, so Dorr asked "Myers" what the word *Lethe* sug-gested to him. Myers, of course, was a classical scholar, and neither Dorr nor Piper was educated in the classics. "Myers," presumably speaking through the medium, pro-duced a stream of poetic, recondite associations from the word Lethe that meant nothing to the medium or the exper-imenter. More obscure associations came tumbling out the following day. At first the classical scholars who examined the scripts could find no meaning in them. After a while, though, it became apparent they contained a web of allu-sions to several stories of Ovid that neither Dorr nor Piper had ever read or heard of.

Then, in 1910 another medium, Mrs. Willett in England, was questioned about the word *Lethe*. The investigator was the physicist Sir Oliver Lodge. "Myers" had been communi-cating through Willett who knew nothing of the Dorr-Piper experiment, so Lodge tried to elicit a characteristic response from the deceased through another medium. Writes Lodge:

"My object of course was to see whether what we may call the 'Willett-Myers' could exhibit a train of recollection similar to that of the 'Piper-Myers,' when stimulated by the one and the same question." Would the two mediums' verbal productions correspond to each other?

Lodge found that the Willett script complemented—but did not reproduce or merely echo—the content of the Piper script. If the *same* train of memories were pulled from both mediums, Lodge reasoned, it could conceivably count as a case of paranormal influence between living mediums. But the fact that the scripts were complementary argued for Myers being the source. "Myers," speaking through Willett on February 10, 1910, said: "That I have to use different scribes means that I must show different aspects of thought, underlying which unity is to be found." The statement captures the essence of the correspondence test.

The Ear of Dionysius

One literary puzzle I find intriguing is the "Ear of Dionysius" case. Willett was the automatist, Lord Gerald Balfour the investigator. On August 26, 1910, the first impression was received: "Dionysius' Ear, the lobe." The sitter, Margaret Verrall, made nothing of it. Four years later, January 10, 1914, Oliver Lodge, sitting with Willett, received this script: "Do you remember you did not know and I complained of your classical ignorance?" The script goes on: "This sort of thing is more difficult to do than it looked." These seem to have been addressed to Margaret Verrall from her deceased husband and classical scholar, Dr. Verrall. Verrall was alluding to the difficult business of producing a cross-correspondence from the "other side."

There were more sittings with more obscure associations that made no sense: The Ear of Dionysius, the stone quarries of Syracuse, the story of Polyphemus and Ulysses, the story of Acis and Galatea, jealousy, music, something to be found in Aristotle's poetics, and satire. The medium then adds: "A Literary Association of ideas pointing to the influence of two discarnate minds." Finally, in August 1915, the series ends in a sitting with clues that tie everything together. The key was an obscure poet of antiquity, Philoxenus of Cythera, of whom only a few lines remain. He offended the tyrant Dionysius of Syracuse and was imprisoned in the quarries, or echoing grottos, one of which was known as the Ear of Dionysius. After years of subtle and indirect allusions, the investigators finally tracked this information down in a scholarly book, titled *Greek Melic Poets,* by H. W. Smyth. None of this highly specialized material was known to Mrs. Willett the automatist or to anyone else involved in this experiment. *It was not until the reference to Philonexus emerged that all the pieces of the puzzle came together.*

What's so fascinating about this experiment is that the minds that produced the fragments, allusions, and associations apparently possessed *very* specialized information. And it was information characteristic of two men, Henry Butcher and Dr. Verrall: the self-declared communicators intent on proving they survived death.

If the dead Verrall and Butcher were not the authors of this prolonged experiment—this convoluted literary puzzle— who was? One possible answer seems as challenging as survival: it is conceivable that Willett, the gifted sensitive, somehow psychically extracted the information about Philonexus, Dionysius, and all the rest, and (I repeat) *subconsciously* engineered the whole performance, doling out all the sly hints, impersonating the deceased characters, and even, as Willett reports, conjuring up an apparition of Henry Butcher who announced himself to Willett as the "ghost of Henry Butcher." All in order to add color and conviction to a gigantic scam? This to me seems far-fetched but remains an abstract possibility. The American psychologist, Gardner Murphy, had this to say about cross-correspondence tests: "It is the autonomy, the purposiveness, the cogency, above all, the individuality, of the source of the messages, that cannot be by-passed . . . The case looks like communication with the deceased."[11]

A Staggering Dilemma

I've summarized a few examples from a huge database of mediumship. Reviewing the evidence with an open mind, one might reasonably suppose that some people survive death with their will, memories, intellect, and talents, still intact. On the other hand, if this is still too much of a stretch, you would at least have to say that some mediums have powers so great they can create compelling illusions of survival. However you interpret them, the facts force us to rethink our assumptions about the nature of human personality.

Author and classical scholar, E. R. Dodds, carefully monitored a series of proxy sittings, and wrote the following: "It appears to me that the hypothesis of fraud, rational inference from disclosed facts, telepathy from the actual sitter, and coincidence cannot either singly or in combination account for the results obtained. Only the barest information was supplied to sitter and medium, and that through an indirect channel." Dodds concludes: "If these hypotheses are ruled out, the experiment seems to present us with a clear-cut 'either-or': Mrs. Leonard had supernormal access on this occasion *either* (a) to some of the thoughts of a living person or persons who had never held any communication with her or with the sitter; or *else* (b) to some of the thoughts of a mind or minds other than that of a living person. I see at present no plausible means of escape from this staggering dilemma."[12]

Both horns of Dodds's dilemma imply that we need to revise our view of human potential. Certainly, the illusion that consciousness is trapped in isolated bodies and brains is wrecked, once we confront the best data of mediumship. There must be something seriously wrong with our everyday perception of the world—and of ourselves. The "I" we cling to in everyday life—the root of all anxiety—seems more like a convenient fiction than anything resembling a clear and self-contained entity. The value of the data in this chapter is to expose the fictional nature of our workaday personas, and the stories of trance induction and mental mediumship give us hints for exploring our hidden selves. As I said in the opening remarks to this chapter: We ourselves are the best instruments for exploring the next world now.

Mediumship, according to Nobel Prize–winning physiologist, Charles Richet, is a sign of the evolutionary potential of human consciousness. Once we learn to tap into that potential, a psychological reconnaissance of the next world will make more sense. What we now call paranormal will gradually come to seem normal; and Frederic Myers's *metetherial* world will be more accessible. If Richet is right, we will learn how to use our own minds and bodies to explore the next world. Now let's move on to the fourth type of afterlife evidence.

⤞ CHAPTER 4 ⤝

One Self, Many Bodies

On my first trip to Europe, I took the Orient Express from Paris to Athens, and then sailed from Piraeus to the Italian port of Brindisi. I was wide-eyed all the way, taking everything in with great gusto, but when I got off the boat—it was the first time I set foot on Italian soil—a shock of recognition passed through me. I felt like I had slipped into a kind of waking reverie.

Without thinking, I found the road to hitch a ride up the coast. Before even raising my hand, a rickety fruit truck creaked to a halt before me. A burly man with a black mustache offered a ride, handing me a bunch of green grapes. Lift after lift, it happened like that, the blue Adriatic off to my right, seeming to smile and welcome me. Somehow the landscape seemed familiar, and I felt like I was traveling through a place I had once known. I couldn't shake a feeling of unexplained familiarity. It was almost dreamlike and I felt comfortably at home as I rode up the coast on my first day in Italy, a feeling (as they say) of déjà vu, the sense of "I've been here before!"

I think we should honor such experiences—images,

moods, impressions—unexplained feelings of recognition. Whether neural-misfiring, retrocognition, or something else, no one knows for sure how to explain this common experience. One possibility is reincarnation. Suppose some of us are reborn, and turn up in the bodies of newborn babes; later in our lives, we may happen on strange places that fill us with familiar feelings, forgetting that we were there in a former life.

Belief in rebirth is almost worldwide—it is also sometimes called reincarnation, metempsychosis, palingenesis, or transmigration of souls. Reincarnation could explain at least some déjà vu experiences. If our present life is one of many, if we are one self passing through many bodies, then the haunting recognitions we sometimes feel could stem from previous lives. Once again in this chapter the data will invite us to enlarge our working concept of human personality.

A Belief Gaining a Foothold

Not at home in Western culture, or favored by most biblical faiths, belief in reincarnation has been gaining a foothold in Europe and North America. It was a tradition in ancient Greece, in Celtic and other pre-Christian cultures, and it was not until the Council of Nicaea in 325 that it was outlawed from the Christian faith. Today's resurgence of interest has several causes. The influx of Eastern religions and philosophies, most of which take reincarnation for granted, has made a difference. Many American "New Agers" have embraced reincarnation, and the view that souls undergo many embodiments has seeped into American popular culture through "past-life therapy."

People everywhere believe in reincarnation, not just Buddhists and Hindus, but Shiite Muslems in Asia, natives of East and West Africa, and many Brazilians. Northwestern

Native Americans have withstood the missionaries of their European conquerors, and still believe in rebirth. Ditto for scattered tribes in the Trobriand Islands and Central Australia and the Ainu of northern Japan. And polls in Europe, America, and Canada indicate the belief is gradually increasing from 18 percent to 26 percent. Transmigration of souls is an article of the expanding Mormon faith where it is tied to Joseph Smith's view that human beings have the power to evolve into gods. In a recent book called *Godmakers,* Mormon evangelist Orson Pratt writes of the "transmigration of the same particles of spirits from a lower to a higher organization." In the Mormon myth, reincarnation forms the basis of radical optimism with regard to human potential.

Rebirth seems less punitive than belief in life as a one-shot affair, where the wrong move can land sinners in everlasting perdition. It was a joke among Catholic kids I grew up with that one mouthful of hamburger on Good Friday, or one "dirty thought" any day of the year, could cost eternal damnation. Ours was the gallows humor of captive believers in what seemed like a harsh creed. If you believe in reincarnation, on the other hand, you can take a deep breath and relax a little, for as German writer Gotthold Lessing once said, "What need have I for haste? Is not the whole of eternity mine?"

In the eyes of many, reincarnation makes sense of life's injustices. The skeptical Somerset Maugham wrote that it "would be less difficult to bear the evils of one's own life if one could think they were but the necessary outcome of one's errors in a previous existence." And from a philosopher's angle, belief in multiple births "should cause one to take his present personality with a large grain of salt, viewing it no longer humorlessly as his absolute self . . ."[1]

Good evidence for rebirth is recent. It begins with a few

reports from travelers and explorers. In *Gleanings in Buddha Fields,* Lafcadio Hearn translated a Japanese document with affidavits documenting the rebirth of Katsugoro, a young boy who remembered his previous parents, house, and place of burial, and spoke of other matters from his former life. Eventually he found and identified his former parents. Morey Bernstein reported a well-publicized 1950 case, of an American housewife who recalled living in Ireland under the name of Bridey Murphy and seemed to possess unexplained knowledge to back her claims.[2] In 1971, Edward Ryall published an account of his memories from a seventeenth-century life spent in Somerset, England. A patient who had unexplained memories from medieval times astonished psychiatrist Arthur Guirhdom. But it wasn't until the 1960s that a new chapter in the history of reincarnation research began in America.

The Revolutionary Work of Ian Stevenson

In Dowden's *Life of Shelley,* a friend of the poet, James Hogg, shares a curious anecdote. Hogg and Shelley had been reading Plato and struggling with the idea of preexistence. They decided to take some air and sallied forth for a walk. Midway across Magdalene Bridge the two men met a woman carrying a child. Shelley stopped the woman and asked: "Will your baby tell us anything about pre-existence, madam?"

This impulse to gather evidence directly from the mouths of babes who remember past lives has driven much of the career of Ian Stevenson, a clinical psychiatrist and recently retired director of the Department of Personality Studies at the University of Virginia. Stevenson has gained worldwide recognition for his research on rebirth, having with his associates documented roughly 3,000 cases and published about seventy detailed reports. Recently, an editor from the *Washington Post* traveled to India and Lebanon with Stevenson to observe him at work and published a book describing his impressions. Tom Schroder concluded: "The only way to account normally for what people were telling us was to hypothesize some massive, multi-faceted conspiracy . . . with no obvious motive or clear means to cooperate in a deception."[3]

On September 26, 1999, an informative interview of Stevenson was published in the scientifically conservative *New York Times*. Stevenson explained that it was a feeling that mainstream theories of human personality were leaving important things out that prompted him to pursue his research. The interviewer asked how it would change the world if reincarnation were widely accepted. "It would lessen guilt on the part of parents," said Stevenson. "They wouldn't have as much of a burden that, whatever goes wrong with a child is all their fault, either through genes or through mishandling during infancy. People themselves would have to take responsibility for their destinies."

Children from all parts of the world claim to have memories from previous lives; sometimes they even behave as if they *were* that previous person. In these reports—unlike past life memories that come up via hypnotic regression—Stevenson has gathered testimony that lends credence to past life claims. Like the Cambridge founders of Psychical Research, he applies rigorous guidelines for conducting reincarnation research. You go to the scene of the reincarnation claim, conduct interviews, record reports, and gather eyewitness testimony from key informants. These are the methods of the historian and the lawyer; you try to sift authentic from dubious claims and look for the best explanation.

Stevenson traveled to India, Ceylon, Burma, Turkey,

Lebanon, West Africa, the American Northwest, South-eastern Alaska, Brazil, and elsewhere. He often had to depend on translators, and admits that occasionally distortions may occur because of mistakes in translation, but not enough to spoil the value of the evidence. He recorded the chronological order of events as accurately as possible, checked on the credibility of witnesses, tried to confirm claims, and when possible repeated interviews to ensure consistency. Often research began months, even years, after the first claims of rebirth, but occasionally Stevenson got to the case early and before the person claiming rebirth met the family whose life he remembers.

Others have taken up this extraordinary research; for example, Satwant Pasricha has done supplementary and supportive research in Southern India.[4] Virginia psychiatrist James Tucker has developed a useful "strength of case scale" and so far has entered 799 cases into a computer database.[5] Anthropologist Antonia Mills has studied cases from native populations in North America and British Columbia in which fragments of one personality seem to have been reborn in several different persons.[6] Mills has explained how the belief in reincarnation helps us understand the psychology of native North Americans. "Reincarnation," she wrote to me in an email, "helps to explain a different sort of psychology, in which what we are is not simply the result of genes and environment in *this* life, but through many lives; one is an ongoing work in progress." Personal evolution extends beyond a single lifespan. Stevenson's work on reincarnation has stirred the interest of philosophers, captious critics like Paul Edwards[7] and powerful defenders like Robert Almeder. Ian Stevenson's work may be likened to a Trojan horse inside the medical establishment, quietly laying the groundwork for revising the standard (one life) models of human personality.

The Anatomy of Reincarnation

There are five typical features of reincarnation cases. Stevenson summarized them in *Children Who Remember Previous Lives,* probably the best introduction to his work.[8]

1. The person to be reincarnated predicts he will be reborn.
2. The woman to give birth to the reincarnated person has a dream announcing the rebirth.
3. Reborn children make verifiable statements about their past lives that express imaged memories.
4. Reborn children demonstrate unusual behaviors, or behavioral memories, characteristic of their past lives.
5. A birthmark or birth defect of the reborn person is found that reflects the manner of death of the previous personality.

It is rare for a case to have all five characteristics.

Prediction of Rebirth

The first feature is often found among the Tibetans and the Tlingit of northwestern North America. The Tlingits express the desire to be reborn in more favorable circumstances. They may also predict that their new bodies will show scars or birthmarks identifying them. The lamas of Tibet speak of the locales and circumstances of their next birth; in India and Turkey elderly folk may talk about being reborn in their own family.

Can it be that our present life intentions carry over into the lives of newly born babies? We noticed, in the story of Gifford and Thompson, how the unfinished desires of a dead artist took over an unsuspecting goldsmith (which raised intriguing questions about the nature of creativity). Reincarnation reports, like some material from mediumship, force us to reflect on how subtly intertwined our lives may be. The more we examine paranormal data, especially survival-related data, the boundaries thought to separate one person from another seem less firm.

Announcing Dreams

The idea of "announcing dreams" is wonderfully biblical. A deceased person appears to a dreamer and declares his or her intention to reincarnate. The dreamer in such cases is often a married woman and potential mother, although husbands and other family members have such dreams. Announcing dreams are reported in all countries where reincarnation stories have been gathered. They come as symbolic gestures or overt requests. The candidate for rebirth enters the dreamer's bedroom and inserts himself between prospective parents, or simply says he is coming back, suitcase in hand. The dreamer may recognize the petitioner for rebirth.

It would, however, be wrong to assume that all reincarnations are intentional. If we take the Tibetan Book of the Dead as our guide, rebirth is more like falling off a boat and being sucked into a whirlpool than a trip to the shopping mall. There's probably more turbulence than smooth sailing in the afterlife, just as our dreams are more variable and surprising than ordinary waking life. In the case of rebirth, there is reason to believe that souls are forcibly drawn back to particular parents and homelands.

Imaged Memories

Children begin to make statements about previous lives between the ages of two and five. Sometimes they lack the verbal skills to communicate the images they recall and try to convey their meaning by gesture. A little girl wanted to say that her husband from a previous life owned a bicycle shop, so, to get the point across, she lay on her back and made pedaling movements with her legs. Investigators usually come on the scene after the child, who is between five and eight, begins to lose his or her memories. Children at the peak of remembering their past lives give the impression of remembering a great deal; Stevenson collected five to fifty verifiable statements from his child subjects. So have his coworkers, and those who sought to replicate his studies.

Some kids need to be reminded of their past lives, others can't stop talking about them. They often use the present tense, "I have a wife in the town of X," or the past tense, "When I was big . . ." Almost the first words spoken by a Turkish child Celal Kapan were: "What am I doing here? I was at the port." Later, this child proved he had memories of proper names and facts that corresponded to a dockworker who was instantly killed on the job—at a port. The time a child actively recalls a past life is brief. On average, memories remain fresh for three years; there are, however, exceptions. Another problem is that children, even in countries that believe in rebirth, may keep their memories secret for fear of ridicule. Understandably, parents everywhere often suppress children who say, "You are not my father" or "My mother is someone else."

Children who remember previous lives remember the way they died, most of the time, violently. This shouldn't surprise us; we know from experience that we seldom forget dramatic, sudden, and shocking experiences. Hauntings, too, often devolve on violent death. According to reincarnation data, powerful emotions can dog us across lifetimes. Children remember specific names, persons, objects, and places; they often remember the name of their murderer from a previous life. This makes verification possible. Stevenson's books, monographs, and scientific articles contain numerous detailed examples.

One wonders about the interim between death and rebirth. For the most part, few children recall what went on betwixt and between lives, although in a few cases they do. One child recalled watching the funeral of his previous self. It is strange to reflect on the possibility that as we mourn the dead at their funerals they may be calmly observing us. Little is known about what it may be like in the shadowy zone between lives. In a few cases, we hear of encounters with wise beings.

Often, at the insistence of the children who are gripped by such memories, parents take them back to the scenes of their previous lives. In good cases, they recognize places, objects, and people; they use proper names, names that had to be unknown to them. Sometimes the scene is incongruous, for example, when a small boy returns to his wife from a previous life, and acts like he still has claims on her. A skeptic might suggest that investigators could bias the response of interviewees, but Stevenson is self-consciously cautious and unsensational, and does not respond when family members ask leading questions or when they confirm the child's claims too quickly.

When a child spontaneously, unexpectedly, recognizes by name someone from a previous life, you have a first-class piece of evidence. One child noticed a cousin from his past life in the street, and cried out, "There's my Susie." Observes Stevenson: "The spontaneity with which many subjects state nicknames or make references to little, often long-forgotten episodes in the life of the previous personality seems to me one of the most impressive features of the cases."[9] Some children have their memories of past lives during a dream or when they get drowsy. The memories linger on but below the threshold of awareness, waiting perhaps for the requisite stimulus. The imaged memories may slip from the forefront of the mind and become interwined with subconscious memories and sleeping imagination.

Behavioral Memories

The images we have of the past are but one vehicle of memory. We also have "behavioral memories," which are habits built up over time. My behavioral memories—like playing a musical instrument or speaking a language—are rooted more solidly in the enduring fabric of my personality than my imaged memories. In a sense, behavioral memories are *more me* than imaged memories. Remembering *how to* do something involves me more than remembering *that* something is so. When I remember how to blow a riff on my flute I'm showing results of hours of practice; when I remember the address of a friend I visited a month ago it is more like a scratch on my personality, clear and sharp maybe, but shallow. So if a child *behaves* in a way that fits with a previous personality, I'm more tempted to think of the child *as* the previous personality.

Sometimes the child's emotions fit the previous personality: The joy, intimacy, aloofness, or repulsion is in accord with the behavior of the deceased. Children who remember past lives ending violently often have phobias relating to how they died. A child who recalled drowning in a previous life showed fear of water. A boy, Ravi Shankar Gupta, who recalled being murdered by a barber, feared *all* barbers—a serious emotional fallacy with unfortunate consequences.

Besides appropriate emotional behavior, reincarnated kids exhibit traits of their previous personalities—likes, interests, cravings, and skills. Some kids develop unexplained cravings that turn into addictions matching the personalities of their remembered lives.

It's striking when behaviors match previous personalities, but sometimes things take a mean turn. Kids with unusual tastes for food remember an upper-class life and scold their new, lower-class family for the inferior cuisine. In a related vein, Gopal Gupta refused to do his household chores because servants from a previous life did the menial work. Stevenson also studied children who act like members of the opposite sex and recall a previous life with a different gender. They may play games or prefer to dress in ways appropriate for the opposite sex. The reincarnation hypothesis may have a bearing on puzzles of sexual behavior and sexual identity.

Bodily Marks Connecting Two Lives

Now we need to look at another recurrent feature of reincarnation cases. It is a fact that many people are born with birthmarks and birth defects; it's also a fact that many of these congenital marks have no explanation. Medical science is largely content to ascribe them to genetic flukes. Stevenson thinks some of them may be explained by events from a previous life, and in 1997 published three volumes of about two and a half thousand pages of documented evidence that attempt to prove it.[10]

To pave the way for the reader to accept the idea that events from a dead person's life can influence a newborn baby's body, Stevenson illustrates how thoughts and mental images of living people can dramatically influence their own bodies. For example, some who fixate on the image of the crucifixion are known to reproduce the wounds of Christ (so-called stigmata.) Francis of Assisi and Padre Pio are two famous stigmatists. The literature of hypnosis documents the influence of mental images on bodies, for example, the enlargement of breasts and the healing of warts. A physician used hypnosis to improve by 90 percent a congenital disease known as ichthyosis, or fish skin disease; in this affliction the skin becomes black and scaly.

In some spontaneous cases mental states affect the bodies of *other* people. For example, a woman awakened from a sound sleep by a hard blow on her mouth, later learned that at that moment her husband was sailing on the lake and lost control of the tiller that struck him on the mouth. The sudden violent sensation was transferred from the husband's mouth to the mouth of his sleeping wife, miles away.

The phenomenon of maternal impressions is also intriguing. This is best seen through a horrible example: A pregnant woman saw a man in the street with mutilated feet and became anxious that her child would be born with mutilated feet. Sadly, her child was indeed born with parts of its feet missing, like the man she saw by chance. Medical journals in the nineteenth century published cases of maternal impressions like this. Eventually medical scientists realized there was no physical mechanism to explain these impressions, no neural pathway to transmit images or feelings from mother to gestating fetus. Too anomalous for mechanistic medicos, science now ignores maternal impressions. Like other anomalous phenomena they have vanished into the underground of scientific inquiry.

Now and then repressed phenomena surface. In 1997, parapsychologists Marilyn Schlitz and William Braud published a review of 150 experimental studies of what is called "distant intentionality."[11] Can some people generate positive effects on distant living organisms by means of sheer intention? Experimental studies say yes. There is evidence for distant mental influence on wounded mice and the behavior of human blood cells. In one double-blind study, subjects influenced the growth rate of bacteria. In a group of thirty experiments, subjects used images and intentions to influence electrical fluctuations in the skin of people in separate rooms. There is evidence that one person can calm another distant person by intending, imaging, or thinking calmly. So, thoughts, intentions, and images can dramatically influence our bodies (stigmata, hypnotic cure of congenital skin disease) and they can influence the bodies of other organisms (from bacteria to humans).

The next step is a leap. Here is one of numerous examples that Stevenson provides. In a high-crime district of Uttar Pradesh, India, a woman dreamed of a man who had recently been murdered, Maha Ram. In the dream, Ram spoke to the woman: "I am coming to you." Then he lay down on a cot, and the dream ended. Soon after, the woman conceived a son, Hanumant, who was born in 1955 with a large birthmark on his chest. At three he began talking about Maha Ram. He said he was Ram, and that he had been shot in the chest, which caused his birthmark. Ram was an innocent man, a victim of accidental murder while he was standing by a tea shop on September 28, 1954.

Eventually, Hanumant went back to Ram's neighborhood, and recognized people and places that fit Ram's memory. Stevenson was able to study Ram's medical records, and autopsy, which showed that the gunshot pellets had struck him in the lower chest in a pattern almost exactly matching the location of Hanumant's birthmark. The violent manner of death in the previous life apparently marked Hanumant's chest. It also left its mark on his mind in the form of past-life memories. When they correspond to wounds sustained in a previous life, physical marks provide objective evidence for reincarnation.

Few cases of reincarnation include all five features we have listed. You need to look at these cases in detail before you can appreciate the true flavor, and weight, of the evidence. So let me at least give one example in some detail. In this case from Ceylon, the behavioral memories are strongly suggestive.

A Case from Ceylon[12]

Gnana Baddewithana was born in Ceylon in 1956. At two she began to talk about a previous life in a different place with different parents, two brothers and many sisters. She gave the name of the town where her previous parents were living, specific details of the location, and names of members of her previous family. She said she wanted to visit her former parents. A family in the town of Talawakele was located that answered to her descriptions. In this family a boy named Tille had died in 1954 at the age of fourteen.

In 1960 Gnana went with her family to Talawakele, a place she had never been to before. She correctly recognized several buildings in the town. Gnana's family had never met the dead boy's family remembered from a previous life; this fact reduces the likelihood of Gnana acquiring information by normal means. She correctly identified seven members of the family of this boy whose life she remembered; and she identified two other people in the community. Her responses came in answer to the nonleading question: "Do you know this person?"

Stevenson tabulates thirty-four instances in which the girl accurately identified specific matters relating to the previous personality. They consisted of imaged or cognitive memories. For example, she recognized her uncle who taught her at Sunday school. Spontaneously, she picked an individual out of a crowd, a woman temple devotee who had a relationship with Tille. "She came to the Talawakele temple with me," she said. Spontaneous recognitions, without cues or promptings from others, are hard to ignore and support the reincarnation hypothesis.

Gnana showed a special affection for one sister over the others, Salinawathe, who was known to be the deceased boy's favorite. Showing special affection for somebody comes under the heading of behavioral memory. Warmly, too, she embraced her apparent former mother and father, who reacted to her with emotion. Notably, she requested pears from her former favorite sister; pears were not common where Gnana presently lived, but there was a pear tree near the house where Tille lived. Three times strangers were used to test if Gnana would make a false identification; she did not.

Teachers who sometimes wonder if they ever make an impact on their students should know Gnana recognized her teacher from a former life. He was a man who had gone out of his way to help her. Gnana *behaved* in the presence of this man in a way that was appropriate for Tille. "Gnana's behavior toward Mr. D. V. Sumithapala seemed impressively appropriate to the part played in the life of Tille by this much beloved schoolteacher," wrote Stevenson. "Mr. Sumithapala seems to have taken a special interest in Tille . . . The attachment between Tille and his teacher became duplicated in the fondness which Gnana and Mr. Sumithapala showed for each other."

Gnana, if she really was the reincarnated Tille, went from male to female. She told her parents: "I was a boy. Now I am a girl." According to his mother and schoolteacher, Tille behaved effeminately; he liked to sew and paint his fingernails, not the hip male thing to do in Ceylon. Moreover, the parents of Gnana found her somewhat boyish in her habits. The two children apparently shared a preference for the color blue in their clothing; and both were religious. Tille fell off a chair, sending him to the hospital where he died; Gnana showed a pronounced fear of climbing anything she might fall from. When Stevenson visited

Gnana again in 1970, she was fifteen and her memories of a previous life were fading.

Explaining the Phenomena

How do you explain Gnana's thirty-four memories and recognitions of specific things and people that Stevenson verified?[13] The two families never met until Gnana went to Talawakele. She spontaneously noticed and identified three people she claimed to know in the former life she recalled. She passed three trap questions about strangers she had never met. Besides the recognitions, there were appropriate emotional behaviors, affection for the right sister and the boy's teacher. There was the uncertainty of sexual identity. What is the best explanation of this story?

One possibility is that Gnana used extrasensory perception to make the correct recognitions. This explanation does not work very well. Children who remember past lives exhibit their presumed paranormal knowledge *only* in relationship to the people, objects, and places related to the past life they recall. Anyway, it is hard to explain skills and emotional behaviors by extrasensory perception. In cases with birthmarks and birth defects, the paranormal hypothesis seems far-fetched. For how could a child use its psychic powers to influence the appearance of its own birthmarks and defects? Deliberate or unconscious fraud is a possible explanation, but few, if any, cases provide good reasons for believing in fraud. Motive, profit, and means seem absent in virtually all cases.

So let's consider the reincarnation hypothesis. It is hard to underrate the importance of continuous, complex behaviors that specifically fit the mold of known previous lives. Moreover, if in fact you repeatedly identify with a previous person, keep wanting to leave your home and visit the home of the former personality; and if you show the characteristic social mannerisms, forms of address, emotional responses, habits, and skills peculiar to the former person, there is warrant to believe that you may *be* that person, as we say, reborn, reincarnated.

Identifying with a former person and having the right memories and behaviors may persist for years. Gnana identified with Tille for four years. She showed boyish behaviors matching the gender of the former personality. She behaved with characteristic trust and affection toward a sister and a schoolteacher known to be favorites of Tille. Such behaviors are hard to explain by fraud, errors of memory, or paranormal action; they are too closely interwoven with a unique personality that evolved over time. The only way to handle the facts and avoid reincarnation is to invoke paranormal action, but, as Stevenson points out: "We have no grounds for thinking that processes of paranormal cognition can reproduce, in effect, an entire personality transposed to another person."

An Expanded Depth Psychology

In Norman Mailer's biography, *Marilyn,* there is an interesting remark: "If we want to comprehend the insane, then we must question the fundamental notion of modern psychiatry—that we have but one life and one death . . . Yet if we are to understand Monroe, and no one has . . . why not assume that she may have been born with a desperate imperative formed out of all those previous debts and failures of her whole family of souls. . . ."

Reincarnation research gives new meaning to the notion of *depth* psychology. Norman Mailer suggests that we may not be able to understand extraordinary people like Marilyn Monroe unless we reckon on the influence of their previous lives. Stevenson's work is one of many sources that complicates and enriches our picture of the human personality. Heraclitus spoke about this *bathun,* or "depth," long ago when he declared the boundaries of the soul to be "unreachable."

Modern research into our psychic depths began in the eighteenth century when the Marquis de Puysegur "mesmerized" Victor Race and discovered his "secondary personality." Myers, with heroic insight, brought in the subliminal mind, source of our creative selves, and Janet, another neglected genius in psychology,[14] showed through hypnosis how automatisms pervade our mental life. As the poet Rimbaud once said: "There is an I in me that is somebody else." Freud probed the personal unconscious, and found the dynamics of repression. Jung explored the collective dynamics of personality. Twentieth-century split-brain experiments prove the multiple nature of personal consciousness; the unity of consciousness we seem to experience is a fragile construction that depends on many variables. If you cut the connecting tissues of two brain hemispheres, two mutually exclusive centers of awareness emerge. The surface unity of the "self" is highly volatile.

Stevenson's work enriches our working concept of self with evidence that our present selves are compounds from previous personalities. If we put stock in the reincarnation data, it would again show that behind our personas lies a many-layered being, built up across lives from different bundles of experience, more or less latent residues from previous lives, whether we are conscious of these lives or not. Most of the iceberg of our total personality remains hidden. If this is true, then, as the poet John Donne once said, "No man is an island, entire of itself," but each of us is a cross section of the history of the species. It might be liberating to remember that we need not blame ourselves too harshly for our failures and shortcomings, having in part acquired them from past lives. By parity of reasoning we need not congratulate ourselves so enthusiastically for our achievements. Similarly, we need not wholly blame ourselves for our children's shortcomings nor wholly take credit for their achievements.

The Explanatory Value of Reincarnation

Reincarnation sheds light on unexplained behaviors, and biological and medical problems. Phobias may be carryovers from previous lives, especially if death came suddenly and violently. Stevenson found that 64 percent of forty-seven cases that recalled a previous death by drowning had a fear of water. We might inherit our phobias from past lives without remembering their origins.

Other unexplained traits of childhood such as unusual interests, or preferences for games, may be seen in light of reincarnation. So might the fact that some people, without support from family or environment, seem to know their vocation at a very early age. For example, Handel's father was a butcher who sternly opposed his son's interest in music; maybe Handel was trying to finish something he started in a previous life.

The rebirth hypothesis might shed light on unexplained aptitudes, addictions, and cravings; temperament; precocious sexual fixations and confusion over sexual identity; unexplained difficulties in relations with parents; irrational hostilities, and prejudices. The case of Ravi Shankar Gupta who remembered being murdered by a barber and was ill disposed toward *all* barbers shows how traumas, carried over from another life, might turn into generalized fears or global aggressions.

Stevenson's data suggests that we should notice with respect the unexplained aspirations and yearnings that often seem to haunt so many of our lives. More than ever we have reason to alert ourselves to the possibility of influences from former lives. These may be influences pressing for a creative outlet. They may be influences that seem to have no origin in our present life but that demand that we do something about them, at the very least, recognize them as real and potent.

It would help to acknowledge—in light of the rebirth data—that our personalities contain elements we cannot explain. Just accepting the brute givens of our nature may have therapeutic value, as opposed to denying, or trying to rationalize, them all the time. We should add that research on birthmarks and birth defects suggests that emotions and traumas from former lives may be affecting our bodies. Our bodies, not just our minds and personalities, may be vehicles of unexplained forces we need to acknowledge. Moreover, it might be useful to remind ourselves that we're probably creating effects that will manifest in our future bodies.

The Appeal of Rebirth

Is the prospect of rebirth all that appealing? A few of us are said to be liberated from the endless round of death and rebirth, but for most Easterners, reincarnation is not a good but a sign of unfinished business. Reincarnation, as far as the evidence shows, is a partial, fleeting, and rapidly fading form of afterlife. Partial, because my old personality is reborn in, and identifies with, a new body; fleeting and fading because the memories last just a few years of my early life. And people who remember are often people who die violently. Gradually, the self that "I" was disappears into the new self that "I" become. "I" am increasingly diluted, and slide inexorably toward oblivion. From this perspective, reincarnation seems unattractive. At this moment, I feel and remember nothing of my past lives. The I that I was might just as well have never been.

Intimations of Past Lives?

On the other hand, suppose our surface self conceals layers of past lives, shouldn't there be hints of their existence, however fleeting and elusive? They're likely to be pretty inconspicuous, perhaps surfacing during fantasy, reverie, and dreams—exactly those states of mind when the conscious self releases its grip on everyday reality. Rarely, in fact, do we sense, or become conscious of, the occult dimensions of the self. Stevenson quotes the Bhagavad Gita: "You and I, Arjuna, have lived many lives. I (Krishna) remember them all: you do not remember." Like a person remembering his whole life at the moment of death, perhaps one day, like Krishna or the Buddha, we'll remember our past incarnations, revisit the highlights and the dark moments, and feel once more the pains and joys that now seem so distant and unreal.

We should occasionally sense, however dimly and fleetingly, the effects of our past lives. I told of my first visit to Italy, and the haunting sense of having returned to a place I knew from some former time. Memories of other lives may also spill into and tint our dreams, as we later will note in a striking case reported by Antonia Mills. Psychiatrist Stanislav Grof's psychedelic research describes people who recall flashes of past lives,[15] and there is a large literature on past-life regressions. Most of this material may not be strongly suggestive of reincarnation, but it may have therapeutic potential, and serve as a tool for exploring, even if "only" in imagination, alternate lives, viewpoints, and emotional registers. In other words, there is therapeutic value in simply becoming aware of the rich, latent, and complex possibilities that our surface personalities may conceal but harbor within.

The Door to a New Kind of Experiment

Like out-of-body flight and mediumistic data, reincarnation studies open the door to interesting possibilities for personal experiment. If the data is authentic, several practical questions may be asked. For one thing, if we have lived past lives, it would make sense to talk about exploring life *before* life. We could direct our attention to recovering, or making visible, memories, feelings, experiences from past lives. We could think of such a venture as a kind of psychoanalysis extended to prechildhood and prenatal influences.

There is another model of experimentation, though, more Eastern and introverted in spirit. Beyond my familiar surface self, and beyond *all* my past surface selves, the question arises whether there is a sovereign Self, an unknown driver, so to speak, or witness, behind the wheel? Are there ways we might learn to experience *this*? Plato called it the "spectator of all time and existence?" Is there some permanent underlying aspect of ourselves, some *atman* or eternal subject, that we can *experience now*?

In sum—based on the evidence for rebirth—we have two practical options. One is to explore the Otherworld by attempting to recollect memories from past lives, and thus seek to experience something of our life before life. However, one could also explore the Otherworld by seeking to experience the perennial core, the normally hidden but timeless center of our being. This path would coincide with the age-old quest of mysticism and spiritual life.

Reincarnation data, the physical effects and the behavioral memories, plus all the narratives we discussed in the last four chapters, suggest we can make a rational case for the afterlife. For me to arrive at this position was completely unexpected. Nevertheless, God gave us quizzical minds, and even in the best cases, problems remain and questions keep cropping up. Don your critical hat, and you may doubt these Houdini-like escapes from the last enemy. But doubt, I believe, is our friend. I find that the more I face doubt head-on, the more I feel forced to reframe and revise my whole approach to the afterlife mystery. Instead of proof, I find myself wanting certainty. Proof is indirect, based upon inference; certainty, more direct, is based upon inner conviction. In facing the extremes of life—of death—we could use the glow of inner conviction.

PART TWO

CHALLENGES

So far I've raised some problems with the evidence, but not pressed them with full force. It's time to look more closely. We need to allow the skeptic inside us a full and fair hearing. A skeptic, in the old Greek sense of the word, is an inquirer, one who hesitates and suspends judgment; skepticism in this sense is the delicate art of intellectual suspense. It is a valuable discipline. Among the ancients, the skeptical habit of intellectual hesitation was meant to calm the soul and check the dangers of thoughtless action. The skeptic, in short, is the opposite of the fanatic.

So let's probe the objections that stand in the way of the belief in a life after death. In our review, we focused on *types* of evidence. I'll follow the same procedure now with the objections to the evidence. My aim is to provide you with tools for making your own judgment, although I will let you know how *I* feel along the way.

Roughly, there are four kinds of difficulty in weighing the evidence for life after death, which I will cover in the next two chapters.

First, there may be perfectly normal explanations of our reports. We have to guard against the temptation to believe too quickly; belief can be premature when married to self-interest; and we might as well admit that self-deception is possible.

Second, we have to deal with a type of explanation that appeals to the paranormal abilities we may use to deceive ourselves. There is reason to suspect that the appearance of persuasive survival evidence could be engineered by the unconscious psychic powers of living people.

Third, there are nagging conceptual puzzles that make the very idea of life after death suspect.

Finally, even more subtle and pervasive, we have to cope with the hypnotic power of the cultural zeitgeist. The present scientific mood strongly conflicts with the belief in a life after death, and the mainline cultural paradigm has the clout to paralyze open-minded consideration of evidence.

The objections have to be faced but they needn't prove fatal. What I most value about them is that they have forced me to approach the whole afterlife question in a more direct fashion. The full solution to the afterlife problem, I will argue, lies much closer to hand than we think.

CHAPTER 5

Explanations

The first big problem is *authenticity*. Do we have true accounts of events *un*explainable by "normal" science? Do the narratives hold up? Do they bear careful scrutiny? Is something really going on here?

Most students of afterlife research agree that there are authentic cases among the reports amassed. Of course, new information or a new interpretation can put an authentic case under a cloud. For example, a recent study examines the George Pellew case that we discussed in the chapter on mediumship.[1] The author James Munves tried to undercut the strength of this case. Hodgson, he notes, had recently been accused of unfairness in his well-known attack on Madam Blavatsky. But if he was unfair, it was in the direction of disbelief.

Munves thinks that Hodgson, Sidgwick, Myers, and the other founders of psychical research were deeply troubled by the disturbing antireligious implications of Darwinism, and were too emotionally biased to be objective. This argument, of course, is a worthless *ad hominem* attack and could as easily be turned against disbelievers.

Why shouldn't *their* prejudices spoil *their* reasoning? Why trust *any* scientist to do and report any kind of research? After all, aren't they all biased by their hope for success?

Shouldn't we rather accept that people have hopes, biases, and preferences, but assume that most carry on in a mainly fair way? If we question this assumption, I don't see how we could carry on in any branch of civilized life, let alone do science or philosophy.

Munves also claims that Hodgson, like his collaborators, were ignorant of contemporary psychoanalysis and therefore couldn't see how his unconscious bias distorted his belief. Munves tells us that "the inability to attach weight to unconscious motivation probably contributed to Hodgson's spiritualist inclinations." This is worth noting but once again it is an argument that undercuts *all* pretences to objectivity—including that of Munves. If this argument is sound, why should we trust Munves's conclusions? Munves, like Hodgson and just about anybody who claims to be reasonable, must be subject to unconscious motivations. To accept the full implications of this argument is to cast doubt on all rational discussion. For how could we ever know what unconscious motivation—despite our best intentions—is biasing our thinking?

Munves suggests that "G.P." was picking up incorrect information from living sitters, not speaking the mind of a dead person. However, the point he raises about a misleading death certificate covers only a tiny part of the relevant material. He doesn't come close to dealing with those thirty witnesses to whom the medium reacted in the way the living George Pellew would have. The most we can conclude from this example is that we need to remain alert to the possibility of gaining new knowledge that might force us to reassess old cases.

Mal-observation

What we claim to know in spontaneous cases is based on testimony, and our testimony is as good as our observational skills. The truth is that we often *mal-observe*. Richard Hodgson, after exposing the conjuring tricks of the slate-writing medium Eglinton, wrote a thorough study of "The Possibilities of Mal-observation and Lapse of Memory."[2] Hodgson shows how under the special circumstances of mediumship, errors of perception and memory can easily lead to *misdescriptions* of events. What the written records say may not be what was actually observed.

Misdescriptions could be based on illusions produced by mechanical gismos, or by the medium's dexterity, or by the witness's dominant expectation. In the emotional excitement of the séance, imagination sometimes fills in where perception is fleeting or ambiguous. In reporting mal-observed events, our memories may omit or substitute one thing for another. The scene remembered is revised, transposed, interpolated; mistakes made can become so entrenched that they fuse with one's sense of reality.

For mediumship to work there must be a feeling of rapport between members, which may cause errors of observation and memory. And yet, for the group dynamics of the séance to work, too much critical awareness cannot obtrude. There seem to be inherent traps in the psychology of mediumship, for the price of rapport may be to increase the risk of error. So you have to be careful in evaluating this material, but you have to decide on a case-by-case basis.

Tricks and Errors of Memory

Afterlife evidence depends upon memory claims; but memory often plays tricks on us. One trick is called cryptomnesia, or hidden memory.[3] A delirious person may suddenly speak in a strange language he apparently never learned. At first this may seem to show a dead soul was speaking through him, until it's discovered that the person heard the language spoken in childhood. Delirium dredges up the completely forgotten experience of hearing the language, and enables one to seemingly speak in that language. Moreover, remarkable memory feats of so-called idiot-savants should alert us to the possibility that we all may, at some level, recall just about everything we experience.[4] The point is that hidden memories can explain cases suggestive of survival, so you have to be sure you have ruled out that possibility.

Entranced mediums can access deep memory sources. Eleanora Piper, whose performances we've discussed, is a case in point. William James had this to say about Piper's "control" Phinuit: "The most remarkable thing about the Phinuit personality seems to me the extraordinary tenacity and minuteness of his memory. The medium has been visited by many hundreds of sitters, half of them, perhaps, being strangers who have come but once. To each Phinuit gives an hourful of disconnected fragments of talk about persons living, dead, or imaginary, and events past, future, or unreal. What normal waking memory could keep this chaotic mass of stuff together? Yet Phinuit does so; for the chances seem to be that if a sitter goes back after years of interval, the medium, when once entranced, would recall the minutest incidents of the earlier interview, and begin the interview by recapitulating much of what had been said." The "tenacity and minuteness" of memory that James speaks of might very well be used by the medium to piece together the picture of a person and create the false impression of a surviving entity.

Another distortion of memory is called *hypermnesia*. Sometimes we remember selectively, in tune with our desires and inclinations; we focus on what suits our needs and ignore what doesn't. When memory serves belief, objective truth can get lost in the shuffle. Not the same as deliberate fraud, hypermnesia can play havoc with our ability to give accurate testimony.

Illusions of memory may also be a problem. With a little suggestion, we can be tricked into false memories. In one experiment, it was shown that the more you imagine an event the more likely you will believe it really occurred; in short, it's easy to blur the boundary between memory and imagination. Just by continually thinking about something it may eventually feel more real to our subjective memory sense.

About a quarter of adults can be tricked into believing in childhood adventures they never had. With a little coaxing, psychologist Elizabeth Loftus was able to plant false memories in children. False memory syndrome has proven helpful in child abuse cases and it could shed light on afterlife research. So we need to be aware of the tricks memory can play upon us. However, this is not a principle you can apply wholesale to demolish any claims you dislike; it can only be useful when you apply it to specific cases.

Fraud and Fabrication

Deliberate fraud explains some claims about the afterlife. There are plenty of reasons why people might fudge afterlife evidence. It could be profitable. Think of those who are desperate to believe; combine this desperation with opportunistic charlatans and tricksters and you have the perfect setup for a con. The motives for fraud and fabrication are complex and sometimes very subtle. People might deceive, or semideceive, not for pelf but for glory; for the sheer fun of it; or for the edifying pleasure of being bearers of good tidings.

Séance on a Wet Afternoon (1964), directed by Bryan Forbes, shows how money and other all-too-human motives can be a spur to fraudulent mediumship. Mediumship has been tainted by charges of fraud and chicanery since its inception in the last century, and skeptics have been good at revealing how all the flimflam works. The Fox sisters who started the spiritualist movement in nineteenth-century America confessed to duplicity. Maggie Fox stated publicly that she and her sister Kate had faked the spirit raps at their home in Hydesville. British psychical researcher Harry Price called it the most "haunted house in England," but the case of Borley Rectory now seems explainable by fraud, exaggeration, suggestion, and distorted memories. The medium Arthur Ford performed a séance on TV in 1967 that caused a sensation; he convinced Bishop Pike he had communicated with his son who had recently committed suicide. After Ford died, incriminating newspaper and obituary clippings were found among his papers, probably used to dupe sitters at séances.

Two things complicate the question. First, the records prove that some mediums mix fraudulent with authentic practice. The physical medium Eusapia Palladino cheated in puerile ways, especially when beset by hostile critics, but also produced authentic and often quite astonishing phenomena.[5] There is reason to believe, in fact, that the Fox sisters and Arthur Ford were hybrid cases; it is likely that they mixed trickery with authentic performance. Even so, charges or indications of fraud contaminate trust and should put us on guard.

Next, and of great importance, we need to distinguish deliberate fraud from unconscious fabrication. In the former, we know what we're doing; we plan to deceive other people. I think it fair to say that conscious frauds are relatively exceptional. On the other hand, most of us are, at least to some extent, unconscious fabricators. Without awareness or willful forethought, we make up stories, fill in missing parts, and are easily swayed by bias. Mediums, and other psychics, spend much of their time in dissociated states of awareness, and, as such, may be at a loss to discriminate between truth and fantasy.

In our unconscious, Freud once said, we all believe we are immortal. How could the almighty ego tolerate the idea of its annihilation? Deep down a part of us is given to fabricate on behalf of our needs and vanity. We know this from our nightly dreams; the moment the waking mind abdicates, the subconscious goes on automatic, and into the dream and make-believe mode. With this indisputable source of prevarication within us, we must beware of self-deception.

Automatism and Mythmaking

In a study of automatic writing, Anita Mühl found that stories of other worlds and supernatural beings are common with automatic writers.[6] In the "automatic zone," as she puts it, she observed a tendency to make up "spirit" messages and fairy tales. Frederic Myers was aware of this, and spoke of the mythopoetic tendency of the subliminal mind.

Besides waking graphic automatisms, there are the sensory automatisms called dreams. Our ancestors probably got the idea of an afterlife from seeing the dead in their dreams. Dreams are solid evidence of our mythmaking proclivities. In dreams the dead live on; we all produce images and narratives of dead people, and it might almost seem that we are programmed to believe in survival of death. Histrionics and a proneness to personify combine to serve the needs of the mythmaking subconscious. Add the rich store of our hidden memories, along with the ever-lurking disposition to affirm our immortality, and the keenest minds might be trapped by self-deception.

Sometimes the mythmaker blatantly reveals its devious ways. Take the often-cited case of Bessie Beals. Mediums, as we know, act like they're communicating with the dead; they have sometimes been caught "communicating" with *nonexistent* souls. Stanley Hall and Amy Tanner once asked the entranced medium Leonora Piper about a certain dead niece, Bessie Beals. In due course, a personality claiming to be the dead Bessie showed up. After talking with "her" during several sittings, Hall announced to "Hodgson"—the medium's control at the time—that Bessie Beals didn't exist. She was an invention, pure fiction. "Hodgson" stoutly insisted she was real, that there must have been some mistake, and so on. Gardner Murphy remarks: "The trance consciousness, then, is as adept in its mythmaking fantasy as it is in bringing forward those who have recently died. The purporting Hodgson, who gives on the whole a rather good evidential picture of himself, vouches for the non-existent Bessie Beals."[7]

The Super Con Artist Within

Now consider a case that shows how seductive the mythmaker within can be when it enlists the aid of psychic ability. In 1922, S. G. Soal was doing a series of sittings with the direct-voice medium, Blanche Cooper, when a strong voice began to speak in the guise of someone named Gordon Davis. Soal knew a person by that name in his boyhood, and had heard a rumor that he died in World War I. The communicator gave specific details of himself, later proven to be true, including some that were unknown to Soal at the time, for instance, that Davis had a wife and son. "Davis" also described in detail his house and its furnishings. According to Soal, Cooper gave a "lifelike reproduction of the mannerisms of speech, tone of voice and accent" of Davis. It looked like contact with the dead.[8]

Three years later Soal discovered that his friend was alive. They met and Soal was further surprised to learn that Gordon Davis did indeed live in the house described by the medium but that he hadn't moved into it until 1923, a year *after* the medium had described it. The medium therefore seems to have foreknown Davis's future abode—a remarkable performance, but damaging to the survival hypothesis. It shows that the mythmaking we found in the Bessie Beals case can prove far more misleading when the medium applies her psychic gifts. The power to make the story more convincing increases dramatically. Not only did she penetrate the past and revive memories of an old friend not seen for years but she also apparently reached into the future for more details to validate her story.

Of course, the Gordon Davis case doesn't prove that all mediumship is misleading about life after death; mediumship, in some ways like dreaming, is a psychically suggestible process, mixing true wheat with false chaff. Still, this case and that of Bessie Beals does show how capable the trance personality is of creating a false impression that somebody survived death. It's hard to assign any limits to the power of unconscious self-deception, especially in alliance with paranormal capabilities. Still, in any given case, deceptive psi cannot automatically be invoked to explain evidence away; once again, it has to be shown to fit the specific case in question. It isn't enough to show that fraud or unconscious fabrication is *possible*.

Superpsi

Researchers on life after death understand that the main obstacle to belief is not lack of evidence. Rather, it is that the evidence, often at first glance robust, may be explained by the psychic abilities of the living. This is the so-called *superpsi* explanation of afterlife data. *Super* means that the paranormal ability is beyond the known or familiar range.

Superpsi is viewed as the preferred explanatory hypothesis because it appeals strictly to abilities of living people. *Never multiply explanatory principles more than we need to* is a principle known as Occam's razor. Explain afterlife evidence by the powers of the living if you can; the simpler the explanation, the fewer the assumptions, the better. What makes an explanation better is its parsimony. Superior science explains more with less; this is what is meant by the "elegance" of a scientific theory or solution.

Take the "Peak in Darien" deathbed visions; a dying child "sees" a dead relative it didn't know was dead. Is it really stretching things too much to assume that the child acquired awareness of the unknown dead person through its own extrasensory perception? Or consider the apparition that revealed to James Chaffin Jr. the whereabouts of a hidden will unknown to any living person. Here we could say that Chaffin used his clairvoyance to locate the will, and then staged a series of dreams of his father to present the facts to himself. Once you start looking at cases through superpsi spectacles, you can talk yourself into doubting even the most compelling cases.

Superpsi combines latent paranormal ability, powers of impersonation, and psychological need and desire. Motivation is crucial. We have to ask, What is the most plausible motivation behind the impression that someone survived death? Recall the case of the apparition of a man unhappy about his ill-fitting coffin. Does it seem likely that the *uncle* needed to know about the cramped conditions of his nephew's corpse? In my opinion, the answer here is no. Chaffin Jr., in contrast, stood to gain and *could* be said to have needed to find the will hidden by his father. But if Chaffin's need to find the lost will is supposed to explain the apparitions, I would again ask, Why did the apparition appear *after* the will was found?

Of course, we can't be sure about how the psyche works in such circumstances; my point is that superpsi has to fight for its claims, and cannot be applied automatically, which is something we should guard against. The same might be said of drop-in communicators where no needs of sitters seem to be served. When an unknown personality intrudes on a séance and identifies itself, it's hard to explain the appearance in terms of the needs of those present. If the needs of no living person present come into play, the needs of the dead person remain the most likely cause.

The business of ascribing motives may itself be motivated and biased by dubious assumptions. An example is psychoanalyst Otto Rank's study of the "double" or out-of-body experience. If you work with psychoanalytic assumptions, the interpretation is bound to be slanted against survival. Rank discusses narcissism and the double: "It seems that the development of the primitive belief in the soul is analogous to . . . the pathological material."[9] Belief in the "double" or soul is automatically put into the slots of pathology, narcissism, denial of death. But this begs the question of what the "double" experience is all about. If you automatically assume that the soul idea is escapist, everything will look like evidence for escapism.

Superpsi and Experimental Evidence

Some people object that there is no experimental evidence for superpsi. But this begs the question. There is no reason to believe that experimental parapsychology gives us a complete picture of what we can do with these unexplained powers of our minds. Experiments are usually performed in emotionally tepid and existentially unchallenging environments.

Effects are mostly marginal. In spontaneous cases, where emotion comes into play, effects are more pronounced, and sometimes quite spectacular.

So I can see no reason to impose a priori limits on psychic ability. Some researchers maintain that the kind of phenomena we get is only limited by our expectations. Granting all this to be so in a general way, once again I would insist that it gives us no warrant for wholesale rejection of afterlife claims. In the end, only a case-by-case analysis allows for credible appraisals; needs, desires, and motivation have to be taken into account.

Are Special Skills Tokens of Survival?

Most researchers believe that skills needing time to build "know how" cannot be transmitted from one person to another paranormally. So if an entranced medium speaks responsively in a language she never learned—a phenomenon known as responsive xenoglossy—someone who did slowly acquire the skill must be speaking *through* her. Responsive xenoglossy should count as evidence for survival.

But can we rule out the possibility that entranced mediums acquire skills suddenly, without prolonged practice? Philosopher Stephen Braude notes that child prodigies like Mozart demonstrate unusual skills at a very early age and without much practice.[10] This is not the best example, however; Mozart was raised in a musical family and no doubt heard, observed music performed, and received musical impressions since he was an infant. In dissociated states, ordinary people may suddenly display extraordinary abilities as well as distinctly new personalities. Pearl Curran, a woman of no special education or talents, operating a Ouija board, suddenly began to pour out works of remarkable literary skill and displayed a wise and witty personality superior to her ordinary self. No strong evidence proves that Patience Worth was a real historical personality; consequently, either she was a product of Pearl Curran's subconscious mind or she came from an *unidentified* external intelligence.

The remarkable and sudden performances of Pearl Curran do give us pause about imposing limits on latent psychic potential. However, "Patience Worth," like Pearl Curran, spoke English; the difference between suddenly speaking a totally unlearned language responsively and suddenly speaking brilliantly and poetically in a language you have used all your life seems important. It is the difference between seeming to acquire a tool from nowhere and suddenly using a tool you already have but with remarkable skill. I am therefore inclined to believe that if a medium could speak suddenly and responsively in a language she never learned, it would count as evidence for survival. Well-documented reports of xenoglossy are rare, however, although Ian Stevenson has reviewed several cases.[11]

Is It Science If You Can't Falsify It?

Not to impose any limits on "superpsi" is virtually to equate our psychic subconscious with the power of Almighty God. The trouble is that you can invoke God to explain anything. Suppose somebody wins the lottery, and suppose he claims it happened because God responded to his prayers and made it happen. No one could prove this false. Now suppose our lottery winner didn't believe in God but in superpsi. He could say he won the lottery because he used precognition to guess, or psychokinesis to influence, the outcome. Like the believer in God, there is no way to falsify his claim. Because there is no way to falsify superpsi claims, according to one famous criterion, they are unscientific. Superpsi apparently bites off more than it can chew.

Retrocognition

Critical problems can assume curious shapes. Process philosopher David Griffin, who has written an important book on survival, thinks that superpsi can be framed more simply and therefore more cogently; instead of assuming the medium scans several separate sources, living minds and/or extant records, for needed information, why not say that the medium *retrocognizes* the mind of the premortem person?[12] In other words, the medium goes back in time and enters the inner world of the deceased person; from that standpoint, she succeeds in producing the illusion of that person's survival. The fact that we are forced even to consider this as an alternative explanation to survival shows how far we have come. The alternative to the survival hypothesis always seems to imply that we possess some truly remarkable psychic powers.

Braude also finds the fact that mediums can instantaneously extract needed data from multiple sources is no bar to rejecting the survival hypothesis. Evidence suggests that psychic function operates independently of the complexity of a task. "Psi," or psychic function, is goal-oriented. The medium needn't be thought of as groping among a tangle of different sources; rather, once the motivated psychic activity swings into action, the complexity of the task ceases to be a problem. The main thing is to fix on the goal; it doesn't matter whether getting to the goal is simple or complex.

The argument from retrocognition and the argument that the medium operates independently of task complexity combine to suggest that we possess almost unlimited psychic powers. When we add the example of the medium Blanche

Cooper not only conjuring up the personality of the living Gordon Davis, and passing him off as a deceased spirit, this psychic potential takes on huge proportions.

This godlike power we call superpsi, fuelled by our needs and desires, clearly has a scope and outreach unsuspected by the early researchers. For a moment, then, assume there is no cognitive or physical feat we might not achieve, and that within each of us are powers potentially unlimited. What would this imply for the afterlife hypothesis? I believe that if you are prepared to push superpsi *this* far, it can be turned *against* itself. Superpsi becomes an argument *for* survival. As psychical researcher Whately Carington once said, telepathy has "direct evidential bearing on the question of survival." According to Carington, "the ability of one mind to *communicate* with another independently of the usual sensory and motor mechanism of the body—and indeed of any physical mechanism at all—renders it distinctly more likely that a mind can *exist* independently of the body."

The more firmly you uphold superpsi and the more you admit its extravagant potential, the more you implicitly credit the hypothesis of life after death. The more you are willing to ascribe virtually unlimited powers to the human mind, the less implausible appears survival. For, if a person's mind can paranormally reach out to multiple sources, other minds, physical records, and so forth, and if it can synthesize convincing facsimiles of deceased personalities, or if it can travel backward in time and subjectively enter the mind of a now-deceased person, identify with it, and convincingly impersonate it, and if no degree of complexity need stand in the way of achieving its goal, it seems to me a short step to conceiving the capacity to *completely* escape the constraints of bodily life, which is what I take surviving death to mean. Superpsi can be used just as well to render the survival hypothesis *more* plausible, and one might think of surviving death as simply the most developed manifestation of latent psychic ability.

My conclusion is that all this leaves the afterlife hypothesis in a state of interesting uncertainty, of provocative deadlock. Stretching matters, superpsi can be invoked to explain away the best afterlife evidence; but you can just as easily stretch in the opposite direction, and see survival of death as expressing the limit of psychic capacity. Paranormal explanations cut sharply but they cut both ways. Either way, they prove that people possesses powers that surpass anything dreamed of by modern mainstream psychology.

CHAPTER 6

Imagining the Next World

Since the day I bumped into my mortality I have been traveling in odd circles. The shock drove me toward inward exploration. What I've found from my own experiences, and learned from others, has reminded me how puzzling is the nature of consciousness, and how little I know of myself. I've had a few brief glimpses of anomalous realities—the gong-ringing ghost that pounced on me in a haunted house, was one. A modest number of impossibles; more graces, I guess, than most of us normally receive. Just enough to jump-start me on a voyage of self-exploration.

I should say a few words about the philosophical funk, the paradigm paralysis I've had to work through. Even if our evidence succeeds in fighting off normal explanations, eludes our mythmaking genius, and manages to escape the demon of superpsi, the idea of an afterlife still faces daunting problems. Plenty of puzzles and conceptual irritants linger on.

So back on my head goes the skeptical hat, for I still wonder whether the very idea of personal survival makes any sense. Does the idea of a *person* surviving without a body make any sense at all? Take away the social, biological, and environmental context of what we understand to be a human person, and what's left that *could* survive? Psychic fragments, mental shards? Could our purposes, skills, and talents endure the blast of change we call death?

All sorts of practical questions come to mind. Will life after death be a lonesome drag or will our social life pick up? Will I be able to find a psychotherapist on the other side? And what about the equivalent of money and, of course, shopping? Are there jails in the other world? What about climate? Will it be humid like New York in August or temperate like April in Monterey? What will happen to our old earth life sidekick called time? Will there be clocks in paradise, calendars in hell? What about sex, good food, music, smells, colors? And if not these, what? A long embrace with the light? What will we *do* in the next world? Questions are plentiful, and it would be fun to speculate, but I don't think we should dwell too much on them. I prefer the evidence, however piecemeal, to dictate the possibilities. I also have a sneaking suspicion that if you make too many assumptions about what's possible in the next world, your experience there might be seriously constrained by those very assumptions. The French poet Arthur Rimbaud once said: "I think I am in hell; therefore I am there." Very likely, especially if you've died into a mind-dependent world.

Still, a few words about these brainteasers might be useful. After all, the idea of a person, or of a world, that lacks the solidity of matter does call for some comment. Lacking my old body, for example, how will I be identified, tagged, recognized as the person I am? What—in the next world—will be the basis of my personal identity?

People usually identify me by my bodily appearance. Does that mean that without a body I'd be nobody? Suppose I woke up one morning, looked in the mirror, and saw a totally different face and body. I would be amazed, terrified, disoriented. I would think *I* was in the wrong body.

My point: At least I could recognize myself. Even if I found myself in a disembodied world of absolute darkness, I would retain the sense of who I am through remembered feelings, longings, regrets—by the fact that they were *my* feelings, longings, and regrets. Even if I lost many specific personal memories, like my name or the color of my wife's hair, I would continue to know I was myself. Rallying around the invisible core of my remembered self, I could still think to myself: "I'm dead, but I'm still me!"

Still, there is the vexing question: minus a recognizable body, how would *others* identify me? I have to wonder about this if I want to make sense of the idea of postmortem *society*. I don't think I'd be happy carrying on as a point of solitary self-awareness. I have to try to imagine how we will recognize each other in the next world. Without that, what would be the point of surviving? How will you and your dear old granny greet each other after the great transition?

Of course, we recognize dead people in our dreams. My particular granny—a living image of her—turned up several times in my dreams after she died. We can also have perfectly lifelike hallucinations of living persons. So it's not that hard to imagine meeting each other in an afterworld society with "bodies" that are dreamlike, not unlike the ghosts we meet this side of the grave. Such afterlife mental bodies would of course behave very differently from our present physical bodies; they would most likely lack a reliably stable form. This could be a problem for some of us, depending on how attached we are to the sameness of things.

Try now to imagine an afterlife *world.* We do speak of the after *world,* the other *world,* and the next *world.* Severed from the physical universe, what could it be like? The Cambridge philosopher H. H. Price discussed the question.[1]

Price's model revolves around the familiar experience of dreams. The afterworld may be made of dreams, of mental images; Price calls such a world *imagy*—to distinguish it from *imaginary*. An imagy world would be real unto itself, governed by its own laws, psychological, though, not physical.

Religious scholar Henry Corbin calls this world *imaginal*: a place midway between abstract intellect and our sense-based world, the *mundus imaginalis* of Renaissance Neoplatonist artists and philosophers. The sense of this new hybrid dimension of being is intimated by Hamlet's question: "For in that sleep of death, who knows what dreams may come?" (Act 3, Scene 1) Price describes a multiplex theater of interweaving dreams. In this world, we would project ourselves to each other in the shape of telepathic hallucinations.

One of Price's most intriguing speculations is that in this mind-dependent afterworld, the normally repressed Freudian unconscious is likely to hemorrhage into consciousness. Our subliminal demons and angels are more likely to confront us head-on; and the more repressed we are in life, the harder it will be to cope with afterlife scenarios. And don't forget, we're as likely to run into Jungian archetypes as Freudian devils, which would complicate, if not enrich, the model of afterlife experience.

The next world promises to be mobile and volatile because the traffic laws will, as I said, be psychological not physical. To get from A to B in the next world will require "movement" more akin to mental association than bodily locomotion. Otherworld geometry will be more cubist, or surrealist, than photographic or realistic, more hyperspatial than Euclidean. If all this is correct, people of a literalist cast of mind might suffer special discomfort should they make it to the other side, and religious fundamentalists are likely to be the most disoriented.

Variety, I expect, will be the spice of the afterlife. Some writers have speculated that the afterworld will consist of many group worlds based on the laws of mutual sympathy or antipathy: Imagine a spectrum from high-speed racing through Tibetan bardos to Victorian strolls in spiritualist summerlands. It is likely that the more people identify with their everyday personas the more likely their next world adventures will seem alien. Some people may wish they never survived death.

For most of us, any attempt to imagine the next world is pure conjecture. People who have had near-death experiences, mystics and shamans used to roaming the byways of Elysium, or poets and artists with a talent for conscious dreaming, might have an advantage that most of us who are glued to the surface of life lack. Given the jolting prospects of transformation, probably the best single thing we can do to prepare for the next world is to renounce our attachment to common sense.

I received some intelligence about this once from a dream. In my dream, I was with a crowd of people playing a game near the mouth of a volcano. At first I was not amused because the point of the game was to leap headfirst into the volcano. Those who did—according to what I was told—would not fall but fly upward toward heaven itself. (In short, do the opposite to common sense.) Impulsively—after all, it was just a dream—I leaped into the volcano. Much to my surprise and delight, I really did fly up into the sky.

Paradigm Paralysis

Suppose we succeed in stretching our imaginations and getting over our conceptual cramps about the afterlife idea: There is another problem that prevents full appreciation of the evidence, sometimes alluded to as the spell of the materialist paradigm. Materialism—the popular scientific view that whatever is must be material—leaves little room for any afterlife belief. Philosophers have been wrangling over the nature of consciousness and the mind-body problem for thousands of years, so I shall not rehearse the various arguments for and against materialism.

Instead, I will go to the heart of the problem with one particular mass of data that doctrinaire materialists love to ignore; I mean the data of parapsychology and the evidence for life after death. If even one of the paranormal claims described in this book is true, materialism must be false. Nothing threatens to topple the mighty edifice of scientific materialism more than the paranormal phenomena we are describing. Psychic phenomena is the David that challenges the Goliath of scientific materialism, and on this score, the scientific establishment is in denial.

Philosopher Keith Campbell got it right when he wrote: "If some people can learn more about distant, hidden, or future fact than memory or inference from present sense perception can teach them, then their minds are not just brains. If even a single example of any of these types of paranormal phenomena is genuine, Central-State Materialism is false."[2] Campbell, however, ducks the challenge by underestimating the strength of the evidence.

Some say that even if there were good evidence for the paranormal, materialism need not be overthrown. John Godbey, contrary to Campbell, says: "Parapsychological data only demonstrate capacities of the mind which exceed any known capacities of the brain."[3] Godbey believes that some day it will be possible to explain all psychic oddities by newly discovered brain capacities. This attitude has been called "promissory materialism," the faith that in the end materialism will explain all.

Materialism today, as an efficient working program, towers over the scientific community like a colossus. You cannot see a mental event under a microscope or detect it by magnetic resonance, but this hardly proves it doesn't exist. I remember a talk I once had with a neurologist friend of mine.

"How does the mind figure in your work?"

"What part of the brain are you referring to?"

"My question was about the mind."

"Amygdala or reticular formation?"

"I mean the mind."

When he heard the word mind, all he could think of was some part of the brain. Paradigms cast spells on the brain; they make some things appear and other things disappear. In a recent very scholarly 843-page anthology titled *The Nature of Consciousness* I found in the index one trivial reference to the word *parapsychology*. The question of an afterlife is never seriously broached.

More than academic theories, paradigms are cultural straitjackets. They mold our collective minds and determine the course of our practical life. They help define the values we cherish and the scientific projects we underwrite. Above all, they dominate what we imagine is possible. The only way to break out of the straitjacket is to keep tracking the anomalies, the facts that don't square with the paradigm. Sooner or later, a critical number of scientists will converge and begin to build a new paradigm. There is, however, something about the paradigm of materialism that we're discussing that is uniquely alarming.

Afterlife Research in a Culture of Death

Paradigms determine what problems are scientifically respectable, what is researchable, and therefore what is worth funding. The belief that everything in nature is material, that people are just complex physical objects, destroys the rationale of afterlife research.

This is financially reflected in research priorities. Funds for afterlife research are pathetically small; practically speaking, they don't exist. By contrast, untold wealth is spent on defending and maintaining our power, and preparing to kill our enemies with spectacular élan. According to a recent Brookings Institute report, from 1940 to 1996 America spent $5.5 trillion dollars on weapons and weapons-related programs. Stacked up in dollar bills this would reach from the earth to the moon and back, roughly 459,000 miles. In the shadow of 9/11, the cost of the military is off the chart. America spends its public treasure to protect itself from real or imagined foes, but virtually nothing on investigating what it is we most fear. Modern science has subjugated the forces of material nature, but remains largely ignorant of the forces of inner nature.

Led by a gun lobby fanatical about the right to bear arms, America leads the world with its homicide rate. United States military power dominates the globe, and our entertainment industry is spiritually conquering the globe. Scientific materialism provides the tools to exploit and degrade the environment, and the means to destroy anyone who challenges our power. Materialism isn't just an old philosophical thesis; it has become a way of death.

Although I believe there is a surprising amount of robust data that supports the afterlife hypothesis, something is missing. For one thing, the world that we live in seems closed to exploring the implications of that data—seems, in fact, hostile to it. In my view, we're at an impasse—a crossroads—in our quest for answers. I think we've reached a stage where we need to develop an experience-based model of afterlife research. We need to get closer to the Otherworld; we need to renew our whole perspective on the problem. In Part Three, we look at some possibilities.

CONNECTIONS

Thanks to psychical research, we've never known so much about what may happen to us after death. Still, belief in the afterlife is probably at an all time low. Polls can be deceptive. For when they say that so many believe, the question is, How deeply felt are these beliefs, how dense with thought and conviction? Is it a living trust that shapes our lives? Or an insurance policy against angst and panic attack?

Now that we have looked at a variety of narratives suggesting that we survive death, I want to talk about how we can carry our search further. In spite of all the evidence for an afterlife—and the previous chapters only scratch the surface—I feel that we need a new approach. The new approach I have in mind would try to integrate this evidence, blend it into our lives in more meaningful ways. To be blunt, if we wish to enliven the afterlife idea, we have to connect it with this life; see the next world as adjacent to, and part of, the actual world we live in. Once the proximity is established, it will be possible to think about preparing for the transition; in this way the stress will shift from theory to practice, from trying to determine that there is a next world to figuring out how to experience the next world now.

A tradition from Plato to Montaigne has assumed that we can. The following chapters will spell out some connections between where we are now and where we may be going. We should connect the afterlife with evolution, the subject of the next chapter. We should connect our present psychology to that of the next. And it would help to look at cracks or openings to the next world that aren't so obvious. If there is another dimension of reality, there should be some credible indications of it, however elusive and anomalous they may be.

A new afterlife paradigm should make new experiences possible, and I will concentrate on this possibility in the last part of the book. There are steps we can take, however halting and tentative, to prove it's possible to experience the next world now. We will begin by looking at the connection between the afterlife and evolution.

CHAPTER 7

Evolution

I once let on to a serious ecologist that I was interested in life after death. He reacted as if I had set fire to the American flag or spat on the Shroud of Turin. I was fiddling while Rome burns and worrying about matters picayune and personal while Earth was reeling from corporate plunder and pollution. Wishing to survive death was the worst piece of vanity ever hatched in the brain of Homo sapiens. And I had failed to see how in the great scheme of evolution my life had no more meaning than a virus in a pig's nostril.

This chapter is for that sweet-tempered person, and for anyone who feels a need to reconcile their curiosity about an afterlife with the majestic scene of life evolving on Earth. I want to show that life after death is a perfectly natural idea, that it need not be tied to any religious ideology, and that it's consistent with caring about our much-abused terrestrial home.

Darwin and Survival Research

Darwin's *The Origin of Species* in 1859 triggered modern survival research. The theory of evolution, a naturalistic account of human origins, struck a hard blow against creationist views of life. Belief in an afterlife, central to religious faith, was also shaken. So it was that the British founders of psychical research set out to use the methods of science itself to restore the soul to something of its original status. That attempt, as we have found, produced a body of evidence suggestive of human survival of death.

One problem is that this evidence seems disjointed from mainstream science and the prevailing evolutionary outlook. I said "seems." Psychic phenomena do not conflict with science; they merely enlarge it. In fact, survival evidence fits well enough into an evolutionary outlook: the whole universe, life, human history, society, values, worldviews—all are part of a vast cosmic evolution still under way. In the four-billion-year adventure of life on Earth, is it so shocking to find evidence of another form of replication, another kind of reproduction. Is it unthinkable that reincarnation, or a next phase of mind-dependent existence, is possible? As Voltaire said, "It is not more surprising to be born twice than once; everything in nature is resurrection." The afterlife idea doesn't contradict the theory of evolution; it merely extends and makes it more interesting.

The Postmortem Environment

Frederic Myers, conscious of the evolutionary connection, theorized that supernormal ability was preadapted to postterrene existence.[1] The full scope and value of our paranormal abilities will only emerge, and be recognized by us, after death, he said. Clearly, they are not reliable, but manifest with tricksterlike spontaneity. Myers knew he was expanding the scope of evolution. He was not alone. One of the cofounders of natural selection, Alfred Russel Wallace, believed there were facts that implied a postmortem environment. So there was a growing sense, which got little play in the mainstream, that evolution was taking place in the psychological realm of humanity. Neither Wallace nor Myers favored any particular religion—except perhaps, to use Myers's words, "the religion of the ancient sage," the view that at the core of all religions are certain perennial truths of spirit. Wallace and Myers, open to all the data, strove to ground the postmortem phase of our evolution in hard matters of fact.

Myers removed the survival hypothesis from religion and put it in a naturalistic setting. He accepted the evolutionary outlook, but was driven by facts to accept a form of life ignored by most scientists—the independent life of the psyche. Psychic phenomena only pose problems for evolution when it's understood in strictly mechanistic terms. Telepathy is hard to square with what we know of terrestrial biology. Why do we have it? And if we have it, for what purpose did it evolve? Clearly, it's useless for helping us cope with ordinary life. Try driving your car clairvoyantly or conducting your business by precognition.

Psychic ability seems of no reliable adaptive use. Why then do we have it in the first place? Are these erratic capacities vestigial functions? Something we relied on before we evolved rational intelligence? There is another possibility, directly related to the question of life after death. Perhaps they are preadaptive "organs," to be used primarily in a postmortem environment. Psychic powers usually manifest so haltingly and unpredictably, you can forget that they exist. But they do exist. The question remains, Why? The answer I want to suggest is that after death, when our sensory-motor systems are defunct, they will form the basis of our whole existence. They will determine our environment as well as our ability to communicate with each other. They will, in short, make possible the mind-dependent universe we inhabit after death.

Life and Afterlife

Are there any trends in the evolution of life that point toward postmortem survival? Says Julian Huxley, a "single property of all living matter is the property of copying itself."[2] Our genes "survive" by copying themselves; if, as our evidence suggests, our minds or souls survive death, that would again be a way of copying ourselves. Life after death, one might say, is just a psychic analogue of biological reproduction; an outgrowth, a continuation, of evolution. If, as Huxley says, life is self-replication, psychic survival seems a new form of self-replication. In this sense, postmortem survival implies no drastic break with the current evolutionary outlook; it only implies a form of life mainstream biology has yet to acknowledge.

Julian Huxley believed that *progress* is discernible in living nature, and differs from adaptation and mere survival; progress means improvement that facilitates *further* improvement. Improvement, like the evolution of the wing, may be onesided, thus a bar to biological progress. The rise of the vertebrates, their increased flexibility and motor capacity, represents progress beyond the rigid arthropods. Forms of experience become available to vertebrates that are denied to the all-efficient ant or highly adaptable cockroach.

Progress is characteristic of dominant types, which exhibit greater control of, and independence from, the environment. The lung, for example, or temperature regulation, helps organisms range more freely in the environment. Mastery of the environment has been dramatic with humans whose biological progress has been spectacular. With the appearance of human language a "new method of evolution" emerged that "overrides the automatic process of natural selection," according to Huxley, thus allowing intention to rival chance as the agent of change.[3] This seems to me like a turning point, for with language new dimensions of psychosocial evolution become possible. This capacity to take evolution in hand—the recent mapping of the human genome is an example—is surely a momentous example of evolutionary progress.

Now, the idea of a soul, or mental agency, that survives organic death must count as *another* momentous turn, a dramatically *new* stage in the evolution of life's independence from environmental constraints. Mental survival of biochemical death undoubtedly represents a huge leap forward in the history of life, a new grade of liberty. The point I want to make here is this: Once we think of life after death as a stage in the ascent of biological progress, a stage of increasing autonomy from the physical substrate, it seems less remote from the mainstream view of life.

Moreover, we can connect the afterlife with evolution without subscribing to finalism, the belief that evolution is ruled by a definite, unswerving plan. Our existence, our very "immortality," may at bottom turn out to be a "glorious accident," to borrow a phrase from the late Stephen Gould. I don't necessarily subscribe to this view, but it may be correct. There is no reason to associate the afterlife with any grand design or purpose; like life, the "afterlife" may simply be a cosmic fluke. But if it were, would it be any less momentous?

Technology and Life After Death

The invention and use of human technology certainly qualifies as biological progress. Our growing mastery of nature at the dawn of the twenty-first century is quite spectacular. Space travel, radio astronomy, medicine, bioengineering, nanotechnology, virtual reality, artificial intelligence, and so on—they're all about our growing ability to control and manipulate the terrestrial environment.

The sum and drift of technology appears as a giant step, a station on the way toward life freeing itself from its physical substrate. Historian Arnold Toynbee spoke of the coming "etherization" of reality, and more recently science writer Ray Kurzweil has written about the coming age of spiritual machines.[4] As we will see in a later section, some very interesting technology may be in place (it was one of Thomas Edison's dreams) for communicating with the dead. Technology, ironically enough, may be a long spiraling path anticipating the ultimate freedom of mind from matter.

Technology is changing our relation to nature as radically as the prophets of old thought God would. The idea has been floating that we're about to experience a technological *singularity;* soon, it is said, we will reach a threshold of technological development that is going to change everything. One techno-fantasy thinks it will be possible to download human consciousness into floppy disks, or cloned babies, and achieve digital immortality, an idea that intrigued Timothy Leary before he died, but that I doubt he took too seriously.[5] A parallel but converging promise is that stem-cell technology will extend life indefinitely. Whether based on fact or fiction, there is a growing contemporary sense that technology may be the key to our immortality.

Technology in 2003 seems poised to realize the Renaissance dream of natural magic; of humans evolving into gods, and achieving forms of existence suspended between nature and supernature. The machine, it would be accurate to say, is a kind of embodiment of psychokinesis and extrasensory perception. Machines—our technological soul bodies—keep extending our perception and range of possible experience. The telephone, for example, is a technical analogue of clairaudience; television, of clairvoyance; the computer, given the ease and speed with which it performs calculations and makes predictions, of precognition.

Technology, from this standpoint, mirrors the evolutionary trend suggested by survival evidence: increased mobility, increased freedom of experience from physical constraint, and increased capacity to mold and manipulate nature. The drift of technology—from the wheel to the nanomachine—is to liberate experience from bondage to its physical substrate.

Technology foreshadows the ultimate freedom from death. That was already a vision of eighteenth-century scientists and visionaries. J. B. Priestley spoke of the "Power of Man over Matter" eventually being so great that gravity would be abolished and "our lives lengthened at pleasure." Ben Franklin agreed, and said that what the future held was "beyond what our imaginations can now conceive." Technology has served throughout history to amplify, multiply, complexify, and accelerate human experience. Psychic growth and survival—like language and reason and technology—may be thought of as extending that function to new heights and even into new worlds. It may well be the most radical and amazing instance of evolutionary progress.

Our Next World Body

The great naturalist Alfred Russel Wallace became convinced, after being "beaten by the facts," that there was a life after death.[6] (The history books studiously ignore or play this down, burying Wallace in the underground with the rest of psychical science.) But to our purpose, Wallace believed that psychic forces may explain some of the residual puzzles of evolutionary theory, and he discusses them in the tenth chapter of his *Contributions to the Theory of Natural Selection*. It's enough to quote Wallace on his point that "Natural Selection . . . is not the all-powerful, all-sufficient, and only cause of the development of organic forms."

Wallace is not alone in this refusal to believe that natural selection explains all.

More recently, English biologist Sir Alister Hardy explained how telepathy might play a role. Like Wallace, he looked at some of the unsolved problems of evolution, and suggested that nonmechanistic forces may be at work besides selection. In the seventh Gifford Lecture of *The Living Stream* (1965), Hardy asks about the role of habit in relation to bodily structure, and cautiously argues for a modified Lamarckism. The organism is capable of "active, responsive self-adaptation," he suggests. The payoff? Humans can play a role in shaping their biological destiny. Actively acquired habits could alter one's organic history, according to Lamarck. In other words, the evolution of life does not occur without some measure of self-determination. Mainstream biologists tend to reject this idea. I believe we should be skeptical about taking the established views of the nature of life as gospel truth.

Lamarck thought that *besoins*—"needs"—played a role. The mechanist will grant that human beings have needs—the need to believe in God, say, or the need to survive bodily death. But such needs only give rise to myths of supernatural beings and afterworlds, and are destined to be exposed as illusory. Scientifically educated people are determined to outgrow them, bow to sublime necessity and live without illusions. In an alternative view—Jean-Baptiste Lamarck, Alfred Russel Wallace, Alister Hardy, Henri Bergson, and more recently, Rupert Sheldrake—we read our evolutionary story differently: needs, aspirations, and internal states do play a creative role. Not just a source of delusion, our needs and desires are a powerful explanatory principle, a causal factor in the future of human nature.

Humans apparently need *more* existence, more experience, more complexity, and more consciousness. If bodies are vehicles of experience, the need for a higher body is likely to emerge, a body perhaps similar to the one described in certain wisdom traditions: the light, astral, or resurrection body. In a report titled, "Retrotransposons as Engines of Human Bodily Transformation," microbiologist Colm Kelleher thinks that enlightening experiences may induce the evolution of a more luminous physical organism.[7]

Kelleher has summarized his work for me in an email. "For about eight years," he wrote, "I have been working on the non-coding part of human DNA—the 97% of our genetic information that does not encode the physical body. There is a large body of evidence in other species that this DNA is mobile, i.e. it can jump from chromosome to chromosome, and in so doing it changes the gene structure of the locus it lands in. Mobile DNA or transposons are known to be engines of evolution.

"A long time ago," he continued, "it occurred to me if one wanted an extremely rapid and large-scale change in physical structure—for example the emergence of a new species, then a simultaneous transposition burst is the most plausible mechanism. After working closely with a Buddhist teacher for many years (who also was in close agreement with Sri Aurobindo's ideas of a physical change in the body when enlightenment is reached), I came to the idea that a transposition burst would accomplish such a rapid change that is associated with the emergence of a light body as described in some Tibetan Buddhist schools. Similar mechanisms might be involved during and after the Kundalini experience.

"In 1996," he concluded, "I cloned a stretch of human DNA from activated human T cells and I was surprised at its structure. It consisted of a tandem array of transposon sequences, arranged like beads on a string—in short the perfect structure that I had been envisioning to accomplish a large-scale speciation-type change. My paper is a summary of these findings and a testable prediction that people who have undergone near-death experiences or people who have meditated for long periods should have a higher transcriptional level of this transposon cassette."

Sir Alister Hardy believed that telepathy may advance evolution by forming a species mind, a kind of Mind-at-Large: an idea that goes by many traditional names, Brahman, cosmic consciousness, and so on. Once we posit Hardy's telepathically linked species mind, why not the next logical step? Why not a collective *psychokinetic* potential? Given this matrix of psychic power, I can imagine how our collective needs might trigger mutations toward increasingly mind-dependent organisms.

For one unfortunately neglected philosopher, Henri Bergson, real life *was* consciousness and freedom, and evolution the struggle of life to transcend matter. The more complex and evolved an organism, the greater its range of free acts, Bergson believed. If life is experience, he asked, why must it remain trapped in physical organisms? "It is not even necessary that life should be concentrated and determined in organisms properly so called, that is, in definite bodies presenting to the flow of energy ready-made though elastic canals," he wrote in 1944. Equally important, he stated that "the destiny of consciousness is not bound up on that account with the destiny of cerebral matter." Our conscious life needn't fall into "ready-made" vehicles. Life is "psychological . . . and it is of the essence of the psychical to enfold a confused plurality of interpenetrating terms." Experience is always synthetic; a rich life absorbs diversity, transforms chaos into individual form.

Language, moreover, is our "immaterial body." The pathos of our social life is stored in the immaterial body of language. Clearly, this "immaterial body" marks a new dimension in the evolution of life. But is this the last frontier of the evolution of life? Not at all; evolution needs to break the constraints of matter and to transcend death. "The animal takes its stand on the plant, man bestrides animality, and the whole of humanity, in space and in time, is one immense army galloping beside and before and behind each of us in an overwhelming charge able to beat down every resistance and clear the most formidable obstacles, perhaps even death."[8]

More recently, philosopher and cofounder of Esalen Michael Murphy has mapped with startling detail the evolutionary potential of the human body. Take, for example, the body's capacity for movement. Animal life is distinguished from plant life by motility. The human body moves with extraordinary versatility, and among yogis, shamans, and athletes we find accounts of bodily performance verging on the superhuman. Some mystics and mediums have been observed to levitate. Traveling by clairvoyance is another type of "metanormal" movement, according to Murphy.

Noticing this ascending scale of movement, we may now posit the idea of afterlife *niches,* and Murphy invites us to consider "movement into 'other worlds,' as occurring during exceptionally vivid dreaming, near-death episodes, mediumistic trance, or religious vision."[9] This latter form of movement is a case of "evolutionary *transcendence."* (Julian Huxley used the word *progress.*) Everything converges on the idea that we are presently evolving our "next world body." In fact, we find in all cultures words for this new body such as *ka, ochema, sarira.* An idea that runs deep, it seems based on a widespread family of experiences. Thus, inside our own bodies we find harbingers of the next world; and in the extraordinary moments of bodily life we begin to experience the next world now.

Do Only Humans Survive?

In the religious setting for immortality, we humans are the sole stars. In the evolutionary, we lose our privileged status. We survive, not because God loves us or made us immortal, but because nature unfolded it. As to why or how, we remain pretty much in the dark. Immortality, naturally acquired and intrinsically possessed, it seems, is a property of consciousness, not a consequence of divine fiat.

And so we might ask: If humans survive, why not apes, monkeys, elephants, cats, dogs, ants, worms, or crabs? The way creatures survive probably depends on their cerebral development. A dog is likely to survive in a more interesting way than a gnat because a dog's mental life is richer. Rupert Sheldrake's study of psychic animals[10] reports that creatures like lizards and snakes that are not sociable, and form no bonds with other creatures, are devoid of psychic sensitivity; they probably lack the psychic equipment to survive death. Dogs, cats, horses, and birds do bond and do give evidence of psychic sensitivity, and therefore might survive. Also, as we know from parapsychological studies, humans with emotional ties have more psychic experiences. The difference between us and other animals seems less than we think.

In *The Descent of Man* (1871), Darwin wrote a chapter titled "Comparison of the mental powers of man and the lower animals." "My object in this chapter," he wrote, "is to show that there is no fundamental difference between man and the higher mammals in their mental faculties." In this and the next chapter on moral sense, Darwin tried to show that, as people differ in their physical constitution from other animals only in terms of "numberless gradations," so do they differ in their mental powers and moral sense only in degree. If Darwin is correct, survival among species must differ only in degree. I can see no reason to deny that some animals other than humans might survive death.

The idea that untold numbers of living creatures—besides humans—survive death must seem odd or absurd. But this is due to our speciesism and impoverished imagination. Darwin argued that animals other than humans exhibit memory, wonder, curiosity, happiness, suspicion, fear, humor, loyalty, attention, deliberation, resolve, reasoning, jealousy, emulation, and imagination. Parapsychological data shows that nonhuman animals have psychic abilities, and ghost hunters have collected accounts of animal apparitions. We also know that cats and dogs are very sensitive to human apparitions.

In my opinion, survival ceases to be a privilege of one species. Survival depends not on thinking skills, but on the ability to sense and feel and have experiences. In the evolutionary model, we prefer to minimize the suffering of animals and to learn to respect their inner life.

Are We Evolving Our Ability to Survive?

Another adjustment in our thinking is called for. We have to ask whether we are still *evolving* our psychic "organs" for postmortem survival. Most of us assume that either we all survive or we all do not. But this assumes too much. Complete human survival may not be a fait accompli, but a potential of nature still struggling to emerge; it may still be in the early stages of emergence. We humans may be passing through an unresolved phase of evolutionary "progress" or "transcendence." It would be a mistake to assume the process is complete, and that we all automatically survive death, and with the same inner equipment.

To give what must be a crude analogy, in the evolution of flight, not every random experiment could have been successful. Who knows how many efforts floundered in the long struggle to master flight? Perhaps not all humans survive death, nor for an equal time, nor in the same way. Some might survive as passive, solitary fragments of selfhood, with only occasional flare-ups of well-rounded self-awareness. Others might make it to a more socially interactive environment. Still others might move on to advanced modes of being beyond what most of us can presently imagine. I have a feeling that our mixed evidence reflects the mixed forms of survival actually achieved. Some ghosts behave like zombies; others are active, intelligent, and show heart.

Some people, mystics, mediums, shamans, and near-death experiencers, are convinced of next-world realities, while others are riddled with doubts. Some have experiences that convince them there is another world; others never have so much as a hint of things to come. It is also conceivable that our different attitudes toward survival will determine how, or whether in fact, we survive. The next world might be filled with people who have yet to fully realize they have passed into a new mode of existence.

So how—or even if—we survive depends on our psychological preparation and spiritual level of development. The Catholic idea of purgatory is consistent with this evolutionary perspective; it claims that different things happen to us after death, and that change (symbolized by "purgatory") is possible. The afterlife, like life itself, seems to be a place where challenge and change continue. The English philosopher of religion John Hick, in his remarkable book, *Death and Eternal Life*, has discussed this view of the next world, which he views as a scene of unending growth and development.

Homer's Hades differs from Calvin's hell and both contrast with Sufi paradises. The form and duration of our afterlife are likely to reflect cultural conditionings, inner evolution, and psychological self-awareness. As in this world, so in the next, we can expect the challenge to adapt, with a variable potential for learning and making progress. To sum up: I find no problem putting the afterlife in an evolutionary setting. In fact, I believe we may still be in the process of evolving our ability to survive death. And we are still evolving the tools we need to cope with the next world. Life is a school and death begins our postgraduate education.

CHAPTER 8

Mental Bridges

My life *after* death must connect with my life *before* death. For without such connections, without bridges of meaning between the "before" and the "after," talk of an "afterlife" would float in a lost zone, a derelict from nature. But there are such connections; in fact, they lie before us in plain view. Of course, they cannot be our familiar bodies, social status, personal possessions, financial resources; what else could they be but our mental possessions, our inner resources? These are the bridges to the next world.

If there is an afterlife, what will it consist of? An intensification, it seems likely, an unfolding of our inner selves, our memories and desires; whatever lies buried, tangled, and latent within. One might in fact define death as a radical confrontation with oneself: having all the masks removed, an apocalypse, an unveiling, of the psyche.

Like traveling to a strange country for the first time, we can expect some rough spots and anxious moments—or worse. So it makes sense to talk about preparing, boning up, so to speak, on one's traveling skills. We should therefore look at the mental bridges between the two worlds, the parts of ourselves that define who we are, the parts with legs that stretch from here to the hereafter. These familiar aspects of our mental life are bridges connecting this world to the next.

Remembering the Future

Memory, for example, is one of our mainline bridges to the next world. Our memories form the basis of personal identity, the continuous thread we fall back on that defines us in our passage through time. But there's a problem; if memory depends utterly on the brain, the adventure will be curtailed by bodily death. If, on the other hand, memory could be described as *using* the brain, the way we use our clothing or cars, survival would make more sense.

Memory, as it turns out, is difficult to localize in the brain. In the 1950s, the Canadian surgeon Wilder Penfield observed that electrostimulation of specific areas of exposed cortex evoked memories of specific experiences.[1] This at first seemed to show that memories and specific places in the brain were closely tied in a one-to-one relationship. But Penfield found that when he stimulated the same parts of the brain again, *different* experiences were evoked. This loosens the relationship between brain and memory, and argues against strict *identity* of memory and any specific part of the brain.

I remember that I rode the Wonder Wheel in Coney Island when I was a boy. Is there a one-to-one relationship between that memory and a specific location in my brain? It is very hard to prove there is, but one could still say that my memory of Coney Island is distributed across multiple and shifting patterns of neural activity. In that case when my brain dies, it would be the end of my memories. On the other hand, there is evidence suggestive of the nonlocality of memory. When, for example, a medium telepathically pulls a memory from my unconscious, that suggests that memories may not be locked into physical substrates. Reincarnation cases—in fact, all cases suggestive of survival—point to the independence of memories from brains.

Other anomalies suggest that memory can operate free from brain process. A fascinating example may be found in a book called *An Adventure,* written by two English women who tell how in the summer of 1901 they were walking in the gardens of Versailles when they mysteriously slipped into a time warp, and found themselves in the Petit Trianon circa 1793, the year that Marie Antoinette lost her head to the guillotine. The two English ladies noticed specific scenes, people, and objects that they did not know and could not have directly observed in 1901. The two women took pains to confirm the historical reality of their observations during their experience. No plausible brain story could account for this strange memory adventure, a story that suggests the possibility of *retrocognition,* clairvoyant or telepathic awareness of past events.

There are puzzling features of memory. Some people have an almost limitless potential for remembering what they experience. Others, on the threshold of death, remember in vivid detail all the highlights of their lives. Your whole past seems to file by you; and you relive all your experiences, not just from your point of view but from the inside of all those you touched in life. Mythology speaks of the "akashic" records and poets like William Butler Yeats of the "great memory."

So-called idiot-savants have prodigious memories. Medical investigator Darold Treffert describes a savant who could remember what the weather was like every day of his life.[2] A good savant can listen to a complex musical composition once and repeat it, note for note, nuance for nuance. Most people can retain seven digits in short-term memory;

savants vastly exceed the normal powers of recall. Seemingly unlimited powers of memory may be evoked in normal people by hypnosis. One researcher reviewed the memory-enhancing effects of hypnosis and said: "There do not seem to be any theories that explain all these effects of hypnosis on memory."[3]

Physicians have known for decades of a new memory anomaly. Organ transplant patients sometimes claim they have memories belonging to their dead donors. Claire Sylvia received a new lung and heart from an eighteen-year-old youth who died in a motorbike accident. She began to exhibit his tastes, habits, and thoughts. She craved foods she formerly disliked, was attracted to new colors and, unlike her usual self, became impetuous and aggressive. She dreamed of a man called "Tim L.," who (she later found) fit the name and appearance of her heart donor. She never met or knew Tim whose identity was concealed from her as a matter of medical policy.[4]

Memories are supposed to be stored in the brain, but Claire received a new heart and lung, not a new brain. It is well known that some psychics who touch objects may receive correct impressions about the owners of the objects. Sorcerers operate on this principle, using people's hair or nail parings to cast spells on them. So, Tim's lung or heart, now a part of Claire, might have enabled Claire to receive impressions of the dead Tim. Such documented transplant cases—they need to be carefully studied—make it hard to confidently equate the seat of memory with the brain. And to mention once more, in cases of severe brain disease, memories apparently destroyed for years are sometimes retrieved. Memory, then, despite its often wobbly performance, is a highly elastic thread of the self as it ricochets through time.

In the ancient world, in medieval times, and during the

Renaissance the art of self-recollection was a revered spiritual practice. In our age of print and electronic prosthetics, we tend to rely much less on our memories. We don't feel the need of traditional cultures to learn things "by heart." This may have unhappy repercussions on our inner life. It is enough to say in conclusion, that inside memory we find intimations of a wider life. Memory is one of the bridges we're always walking across, the mental cable connecting our present and our future life.

The Will as Bridge to the Next World

According to the Chandogya Upanishad, "Man is a creature of will. According to what his will is in this world, so will he be when he has departed from this life."[5] This ancient Hindu text is clear: The will, the common capacity to choose and act and focus our attention, forms a mental bridge between where we are now and where we might end up on the other side. The road to the next world is paved with our intentions—whatever they may consist of.

Once again I want to suggest that something we all take for granted and associate with a common word—*will*—constitutes a critical mental bridge to the Otherworld. I said there was something funny and mysterious about memory; ditto for what we call will. For example, in a well-known theoretical paper, two English psychical researchers argue that ESP and psychokinesis are "merely unusual forms of processes which are themselves usual and commonplace."[6] ESP, they say, is just an unusual expression of normal perception and psychokinesis an externalized expression of our common motor, or muscular, activity. To put it another way, ordinary acts of the will (I move a spoon to stir my coffee) are "psychokinetic," and are part of one and the same process. When I raise my hand and the appropriate motor neurons fire, I'm doing *endosomatic* psychokinesis—"in-the-body psychokinesis."

Everyday acts of the will are psychokinetic; they work *like magic*—you think, and your arm moves. Volition and psychokinesis operate "teleologically": based on mental focus, they are *goal-directed*. I will to move my arm and the neuromuscular events needed to bring about the movement are *automatically and unconsciously* set into motion. (I have no idea what's going on in my nervous system, just as I might not know what's going on in my car when I turn the ignition key.) Willing to raise your arm and willing to control the fall of the dice in a psychokinesis experiment—*both operate in a goal-oriented way.* Native people call this magic.

If the Upanishads are right, the way to experience the next world now is to train our wills—and become masters of our "magic." (I will say something about this again in the last chapter of this book.) Let's put it this way: If and when we find ourselves transported into the next world, our voluntary skills will skyrocket in practical value. The will is spiritual power, the part of us that affirms or denies, persists in spite of obstacles or wanders off course at the first sign of a dark cloud.

In the day when all our outer trappings fall away from us, we will have nothing to rely on except our inner resources. Without a keenly responsible sense of our voluntary selves we are apt to be at the mercy of every thought and impulse bubbling up from the inferno of our subconscious minds. Our inner life is no less unstable now, but here we have solid landmarks to pacify the inner turbulence. (Turn on the TV, raid the fridge, call a friend.) Then, when the glass is shattered, we'll have no choice but to confront the turbulence. As in Edgar Allan Poe's story *The Black Cat,* the thing we tried to kill will be staring at us with black penetrating eyes.

I think we will need to keep our wits about us in the

next world, as much as if we were visiting a foreign country whose climate, people, laws, and customs were new,
unfamiliar, and probably dangerous. Dante made provisions for this. If you take his guidebook for afterlife travelers seriously, each of us had better sign up for a Virgil guide
and a Beatrice guide, in other words, each of us will need
our volitional and our emotional skills honed to the highest
pitch.

What Dreams May Come

Why did Hamlet hesitate to commit suicide? He wondered
about "what dreams may come"—after death. Are dreams
portals to the world beyond? Professor H. H. Price thought
so, and again according to the Upanishad, "the Spirit of man
has two dwelling-places: both this world and the other
world. The borderland between them is the third, the world
of dreams." Nightly, we leave the bodily world through the
door of dreams. Dreams? Again, what could be more common? But they are endlessly surprising and very puzzling.

Most people are fascinated by dreams, and a lagging conversation is apt to perk up when the talk turns to a dream
somebody had. Dreams are a common feature of our mental
life and contain intimations of the next world. We spend a
third of every day in an altered state called sleep, and during
sleep we dream. In the average lifespan, one spends about
five years dreaming. The dream is an element with threads
that run through history, religion, myth, magic, and inspiration. In the last century, science tackled this enigmatic form
of human experience, and a vast literature was produced.
But in spite of piles of data, basic questions still nag
researchers.

There is little agreement among experts on *why* we
dream, as Virginia psychologist Robert Van de Castle's com-

prehensive 1994 review shows.[7] Some think dreams can be our wisest teachers, if we could learn to listen to them; others see dreams as "reverse learning," devoid of higher or symbolic meaning, a way of flushing junk from the nervous system, a kind of neural enema. Interpretation and theoretical bias range widely.

We might recall Lord Byron's poem called *The Dream*. Sleep and dream, wrote a bipolar Byron, have their own world, "A boundary between things misnamed/Death and existence." Dreams become

> A portion of ourselves as of our time,
> And look like heralds of eternity.
> . . . The mind can make
> Substances, and people planets of its own
> With beings brighter than have been, and give
> A breath to forms which can outlive all flesh.

The first step in linking dreams to the world beyond is to understand their affinity with the paranormal; the most likely occasion for most of us having a paranormal experience is during a dream, say the experts. Dreams have long been seen as paranormal bridges to higher worlds. Homer's *Odyssey* speaks of true and prophetic dreams that come through the gate of ivory and of ordinary dreams that come through the gate of horn, and we have seen how some ivory dreams point to the survival of consciousness after death.

Precognitive and clairvoyant dreams have been reported throughout history. Abraham Lincoln dreamed of his funeral before he was assassinated. Mark Twain dreamed of his brother Henry lying in a metal coffin with a bouquet of white flowers and a red rose on his chest. A few days later, Henry was killed in a boat accident; Mark Twain went to his brother's funeral and found him just as he appeared in the dream: metal coffin, white flowers, red rose. Death is the theme of over half of all paranormal dreams.

In 1973, researchers in New York City proved that waking subjects could deliberately influence the dreams of sleeping persons.[8] Agents concentrated on randomly selected images, paintings or photographs, and significantly influenced the dreams of people sound asleep in different rooms. Dreams, it would seem, are a common mental vehicle for breaking free from the physical envelope of our existence. The question we are asking is, How far might this vehicle take us? Could it take us as far as Shakespeare's "undiscovered country"?

On dreams there are two schools of thought: Locke thought they were by-products of sensations; Leibniz thought they expressed independent intelligence. In accord with Leibniz, Carl Jung once wrote: "The images and ideas that dreams contain cannot possibly be explained solely in terms of memory. They express new thoughts that have never yet reached the threshold of consciousness."[9] If so, we may be able to learn something about the mystery of death from dreams. Jung has shown how dreams anticipate death. In a dream my father had before he died, he climbed to the top of a mountain and entered into a light he later described as heavenly. At the top of the hill he found men digging a grave. My father was not a literate man, but he sensed the dream foreshadowed his death, and became depressed; but he was also struck by the light, and more than once spoke of his dream with awe and wonder.

Wrote Jung: "The unconscious mind is capable at times of assuming an intelligence and purposiveness which are superior to actual conscious insight." This seems to have been the case with my father, who was both puzzled and amazed by the dream he had not long before he died. Dreams sometimes reveal the onset of death; they may, as they did with my father's, also point to a world of light. Light, of course, is a symbol of consciousness. The "new thought" for my father was to couple the images of death and light. Common sense associates death with darkness.

Science today understands a great deal about the physiology of sleep and dreams. American psychologists Nathaniel Kleitman and Eugene Aserinsky discovered the relationship between rapid eye movement (REM sleep) and dreaming, REM cycles, brain wave and respiratory patterns, and so forth. But advances in descriptive physiology have not led to insight into *why* we dream. Dreaming itself is not a physiological fact. As David Foulkes, one of the pioneers in the physiology of sleep, said: "Whatever brain events accompany dreaming, the dream *is* a mental fact." Another important dream researcher, William Dennet, said: "Never before in the history of biological research has so much been known about something from a descriptive point of view, with so little known at the same time about its function."

Dreams have spatial properties of their own; they occur in their own space, at right angles, so to speak, to the three-dimensional brain. Dream space differs from the physical space that brains occupy. Suppose by a scanning device some Peeping Tom probed my brain while I was dreaming. It would be of no use to him; my dream would remain in a suitably private world, inaccessible in its own mental space.

At the same time, my private dream images have spatial properties. In a dream, I might see somebody with red hair *walking to the left* of a tall tree. There are directions of movement, and sensations of rising or falling, although exact measurement is impossible. The qualitative reigns over the quantitative. Everywhere on the planet billions of people constantly and periodically are entering dream spaces that jut out, invisibly, in all directions from their brains. Every dream is a kind of quantum leap into another world. This leads to my next point.

Dreams have another remarkable feature: They are *creative*, and in a rather strong sense of the word. They possess the singular property of being *world-making*. Moreover, this world-making, or "creative," power of dreams is virtually infinite. Writes Gordon Globus, a professor of psychiatry and philosophy at the University of California, Irvine: "The dreaming life-world is created *de novo*. Thus our dreams are first-hand creations, rather than put together from residues of waking life. We have the power of infinite creativity; at least while dreaming, we partake of the power of immanent Spirit, the infinite Godhead that creates the cosmos."[10]

Globus boldly identifies the creative power of dreams with the infinite Godhead. This is very different from those who see in dreams a garbage disposal system. I have my own reasons for betting on Globus. I do not see how this infinite, novel, and autonomous world-making power of dreams could be explained by any set of brain mechanisms. I am perplexed by this strange ability to fashion virtual people, landscapes, dramas, all from what? Eyelids grow heavy, muscles relax, and suddenly we find ourselves *elsewhere*—wandering through rapidly shifting theaters of experience. Every dream is a kind of out-of-body experience, a vestibule into the "next" world.

Fragmented, but often more vivid and intense than waking life, dreams are ruled by psychological, not physical, laws. This has implications for "transportation" in the next world. "Movement" in dream, or Otherworld, space is by mental association, not by Newtonian mechanics. Although we haven't the foggiest idea of how dreams come about, they furnish a credible model of the next world. The dream may be thought of as a halfway house to the afterlife, so we could say that our dream life equips us with a handy mental bridge for linking the mainland of familiar consciousness to islands of the afterlife.

Case histories collected by Jungian therapist Marie-Louise von Franz show that dreams sometimes monitor the approach of death; judging by many of these dreams, the subconscious mind views death as a portal to a new phase of existence.[11] Dreams relate to the afterlife hypothesis in another way. According to anthropologist Antonia Mills, nightmares and night terrors may sometimes be related to traumatic memories from a previous life. Mills reviews three cases of children who were troubled by recurrent nightmares that seemed unrelated to any experiences they had. For instance, a girl from British Columbia kept dreaming that bricks had fallen on her head. She'd wake up screaming, insisting she was bleeding, and reported headaches after the dream. The child was phobic about being touched and disturbed when she saw bricks, believing a house had fallen on her when she was "big" like her mother. Unable to trace the source of this pattern of nightmare and headache, Mills reminds us to keep an open mind.[12] Ian Stevenson also reports cases of children who have nightmares related to their reincarnation memories.

The dream may be a halfway house to the next world, but why is the typical dream so jumpy and incoherent? Are all dreams really so lacking in stability and solid reliability? I believe there are exceptions; there may be hidden structures to the dream world. For example, there are recurrent dreams, and not just nightmares or throwbacks from traumatic stress syndrome. For years I've been returning to dreams of the Bronx Botanical Gardens, a place I loved to visit when I was a college student in the Bronx, and which leaves me with unexplained feelings of lightness and happiness.

A wonderful example of returning to a dream comes from an autobiographical story by Mark Twain called "My

Platonic Sweetheart." For over forty years Mark Twain had a recurring dream. He always dreamed of the same fifteen-year-old girl; he would meet her in India, in England, in Hawaii, in Athens, and in America. Her name would change, her face and voice would change, but he always knew her to be the same girl whom he loved with a chaste and reverent heart. One night he dreamed of her in Hawaii, and she died. He was stricken beyond any grief of his waking hours.

Later he dreamed of a temple in Athens in which she appeared to him again, and he realized she had never really died. "It may be that she had often died before, and knew that there was nothing lasting about it," he wrote. Mark Twain was faithful to his platonic sweetheart. "In our dreams—I know it!—we do make the journeys we seem to make; we do see the things we seem to see; the people, the horses, the cats . . . are real, not chimeras; they are living spirits, not shadows; and they are immortal and indestructible. My Dreamland sweetheart is a real person, not a fiction."

And what's more, the dream is *more* real than the everyday world: "more deep and strong and sharp." Mark Twain holds this up against our waking "artificial selves" and the "dull-tinted artificial world" and finds the waking world wanting. To the author of Huck Finn, this dream world is what we step into when we die. "When we die we shall slough off this cheap intellect, and go abroad into Dreamland clothed in our real selves." The dream is one of the most dramatic bridges we periodically cross to catch glimpses of the Otherworld.

Artistic Imagination

In the beginning I looked for answers to the enigma of death in the teachings of the mystics and shamans. I soon realized that science had to be consulted, and I found much useful knowledge in the underground of psychical research. Yet all along I've suspected that precious intuitions were available through art and inspiration.

Artistic imagination combines the spontaneity of dreams, the depth and complexity of memory, and the goal-directedness of the will. It is yet another bridge to the next world that we can cross, another way of trying to connect our present lives to the ether of otherness that may await us beyond. Laura Dale was for many years the editor of the *Journal of the American Society for Psychical Research,* and a long-time student of the afterlife problem. I remember one day discussing with her the best evidence for survival. Suddenly she stopped, looked up at me sharply, and said: "You know what really convinces me that there's another world?—listening to Beethoven's *Missa Solemnis.*"

This came as a surprise from someone so immersed in the scientific afterlife literature. Still, some of us get our best sense of other realities from sublime scenes of nature or beautiful works of art. Moments of such inspiration may be rare; not every movie we watch, or novel we read, can have such an impact on us. But it does happen. There are moments in our lives—inspired by art or nature—that raise us above our normal selves to states of mind thick with transcendent feeling.

Like the mystics and shamans we have discussed, many artists tell how inspiration comes to them from something larger than themselves. William Blake spoke of his poetry being dictated from Eternity. The letters of Vincent van Gogh reveal in touching detail how raw spiritual need evolved into a great painter's passion. Wassily Kandinsky created nonobjective painting based on certain theosophical ideas that inspired him. Whether practicing artist, or devoted seeker of beauty, the spiritual overtones of art and creativity are familiar themes.

Frederic Myers defined creative genius as an unusual ability to channel the vast resources of the subliminal mind. Because we are so busy with the practical business of everyday survival, most of us stay opaque to the creative influx of our subconscious selves. The exceptions are seers, mediums, and creative folk of all stripes. Mark Twain liked to say he got his best ideas from some great elsewhere via "mental telegraphy" and Robert Louis Stevenson obtained plots for "saleable stories" from the brownies and incubators of his dream life. André Breton, who knew the work of Frederic Myers and read the French psychical researchers, was intensely interested in forming bridges between dream and reality, a special place he called *surreal*. It is a place where "the contradiction between life and death" disappears, according to this medical doctor turned surrealistic dream fabricator. Like the mystic's eternity, or the shaman's ecstasy, the surrealist roams the twilight zone between waking and subliminal mind, a place he calls *ethernity*.

Are the arts avenues for tracking possible afterdeath worlds? William Blake said that true religion is art, and that "imagination is eternity." To the ancient Egyptian, art was a technique of "retooling for eternity," part of a tradition that lasted for thousands of years. Egyptian artists believed they could call into being objects material and immaterial that "might bridge the gulf of death" and pave the way to the next world in recognizable shapes and forms.[13] The aim of art was to create an "incorruptible body," a "subtle body" for navigating the next world. In his poem, *Sailing to Byzantium*, Yeats writes:

Once out of nature I shall never take
My bodily form from any natural thing,
But such a form as Grecian goldsmiths make
Of hammered gold and gold enameling . . .

Works of art, acts of creative imagination, reshape the material world as well as our inner life. We may think of them as doodlings of eternity, as practice runs not only for an expanded life here and now but also for an expanded life in the next phase of our existence. Egyptian tradition offers an intriguing gloss on the now-rusty idea of the avant-garde; from Fra Angelico to Kandinsky, artists have deployed their craft as spiritual practice, a way of channeling sacred power. In Plato's *Phaedrus,* godsent madness inspires people of genius, an idea that spoke to Shelley and Michelangelo. The notion of art as a technique for reconnoitering the next world lies deep in experience.

For Blake the true religion was art; Jesus and the Apostles, he blithely insisted, were artists. "This world of Imagination is the World of Eternity," he wrote, "it is the divine bosom into which we shall go after the death of the Vegetated body." So what we imagine today will define our reality tomorrow, and our true business here on Earth is preparing to build the mansions of eternity, through what we call "creative imagination."

After my father died I saw him once quite vividly in a dream; he looked younger, radiantly alive. "What on earth are you doing here?" I thought, when he appeared before me. With the "vegetated" time-anchored façade cast off, I now saw my father under the guise of his eternal poetic nature. Imagination, at its creative best, is another bridge to the next world, another medium for exploring the next consciousness. "Imagination," as Blake said, "is eternity."

Every moment of existence is a possible bridge to the next world. Painting, sculpture, music, dance, poetry—all forms of imaginative life—are ways of freeing us from the grip of mechanized perception. The "eternity" that Blake spoke of—Yeats's "great memory"—is not given; we have to wrest it from raw experience. Art heightens our perception of the world; it offers, as Wordsworth said, "intimations of immortality."

According to Columbia University psychical researcher, James Hyslop, creative imagination is the key to understanding what actually survives death. In the postmortem universe, we enter a world without sensory input, a world of pure experience. "It is the creative functions of the mind that survive," Hyslop said. "If this be true, the mind could create its own world after death just as it does in dreams, in deliria, and hallucinations. . . . Daydreaming and poetry in our normal lives are the best analogies of what these might be."[14]

The word *poetry* in Greek means "making," and poetry is a kind of searchlight into our postmortem future, a reconnoitering of possible afterdeath worlds. This may seem strange, even ludicrous, but art critic Suzi Gablik has written a book calling for the "reenchantment" of art, arguing that art today has lost its soul, its magical potency. In *Living the Magical Life,* Gablik tells how art became for her a new form of existence, a spiritual practice. Making art transcends esthetics, for "the choice to live magically and symbolically in a culture based on rationalism and materialism is a challenge that puts one's whole being at risk."[15]

What we blandly dub "creative imagination" is more powerful than commonly supposed. Alexandra David-Neel, the famous explorer of Tibet, tells a story that proves this in a startling way. She knew a Tibetan artist who specialized in painting wrathful deities. One afternoon she bumped into him, and noticed he was being followed by a half-shaped, shambling form that resembled a wrathful deity. The artist was unaware of his materialized sidekick, but David-Neel touched its cool gelatinous substance, and watched it melt away. She tells of her own adventures with a *tulpa,* an entity in Tibetan lore said to be made by intense visualization. After months of trying, she managed to materialize a pudgy monk who developed an independent (and nasty) will of his own. It took her months to get rid of it.

Art today has fallen from its once-high station, lost its metaphysical power, and too often turned into shallow entertainment in a commodity-crazed culture. I have discussed some of the old magical ways of making art, of building bridges from here to eternity; art as it was used by Paleolithic cave painters, Egyptian sculptors, and medieval icon makers: a ritual of seeing heaven in a wildflower; of building bridges to the life beyond. The chasm between the two worlds is not that forbidding. Our ordinary mental life contains intimations of transcendence. The everyday mind, says the Zen adept, is the Buddha Mind.

Our memories form the bedrock of the world to come, our wills the effective force to shape its course and quality. When we dream, even when we daydream, we're casually designing, building the mansions of William Blake's eternity. And in following the torch of creative imagination, we ride the vanguard of future life. Conscious of it or not, day by day, we're all crossing mental bridges to the next world.

CHAPTER 9

The Otherworld Nearby

Eventually it dawned on me that if there is another world, it must in some sense be nearby—the equivalent, so to speak, of a mental stone's throw. Suppose it is nearby, shouldn't there be all sorts of cracks or doors leading inside, like the light that scientists say leaks out from a black hole? And if we can't just open one of these doors any time we please, there must at least be more than a few keyholes we can peek through.

This chapter is a short catalogue of such keyholes. (I might use other metaphors such as gates, portholes, windows, openings, and so forth.) As it turns out, the more I looked and thought about what was in front of me, I found all sorts of hints, sometimes very dramatic, suggesting that we really are interpenetrated by Something Else. We know, of course, that we're awash in electromagnetic radiations carrying signals via radio, satellite television, and the Internet. On the physical plane, the right receptor can, with a flick of the finger, make invisible seas of information available. If there is an Otherworld—a parallel psychic universe—where are the receptors picking up the psychic signals?

What follows is a sketch of places in human experience that suggest passages to the Otherworld. So far we've examined several patterns of direct evidence that consciousness survives death. In this chapter, we try to fill in the picture with several patterns of indirect evidence. English parapsychologist Whately Carington once said that some evidence may "be of *indirect* value in disclosing previously unsuspected properties of the Universe," properties that support the idea that consciousness survives bodily death.

History, in fact, is filled with narratives that suggest the presence of "other worlds." They may tell us nothing about any particular person, but they do suggest "properties of the Universe" that bolster the next-world hypothesis. They indicate a richer ontology, a wider range of human capacity. Above all, they point to a universe with more girth than official science recognizes.

Traditional Openings to the Next World

The first category of opening is traditional. By this I mean those experiences that form the bedrock of beliefs in alternate realities—higher, greater, other worlds. At all times we find claims that some exceptional individual has special knowledge, or gnosis, of these other worlds or influences. Broadly, the claims emanate from the shamanic, prophetic, and mystical life of humanity.

The point I want to make here is limited. In looking at descriptions of these experiences, there is always the presumption of another world as well as of the human power to transcend this world. People claim to see, hear, experience worlds, powers, symbols, dimensions, and beings beyond the limits of their routine selves. These traditional openings, taken en masse, testify to the fact that people have always believed that transcendence is possible. These experiences represent a massive influence on human history. Humankind's spiritual evolution is steeped in assumptions about the Otherworld.

Prophet, Mystic, Shaman

Prophecy is pretty much at the core of the religious claims of humankind. The prophet, from Zoroaster to Muhammad, sometimes a founder of a world religion, is one of the central figures of human history. The prophetic experience interests us because it gives the appearance of individuals being seized from the outside by supernatural agents. Prophecy is a type of possession, and a prophet is a medium, channel, or mouthpiece of God, a living conduit who conveys revelations and instructions from a source alleged to be divine.

Distinct from divination or soothsaying, prophecy is not based on technique but on inspiration. Here is how Ezekial describes his seizures: "There the hand of Yahweh came on him" (Ez. 1:3). Something outside takes hold of him. The Hebrew word for *prophet* (Greek for "forthtelling" and "foretelling") is *nabi*. *Nabi* has two senses: a verb form, "to be beside oneself" and the noun "he who is called" or "he who proclaims." Says the prophet Jeremiah to Yahweh: "You have overpowered me; you were the stronger. I am a laughing-stock all day long; they all make fun of me. For whenever I speak I have to howl and proclaim. . . . I would say to myself, 'I will not think about him, I will not speak in his name any more,' but there seemed to be a fire burning in my heart, imprisoned in my bones. The effort to restrain it wearied me" (Jeremiah 20:7–10). The prophetic experience suggests an invasion from an external source.

Of course, it's also true that the prophet may prepare himself by prayer and fasting. So, Habakkuk (2:1) is trying to make himself receptive with conscious intention, when he says, "I shall station myself on my watch-tower, watching to see what he will say to me." Prophecy is of course associated with foretelling, but that isn't the main job of the prophet, which is primarily to warn, guide, and encourage. Most of all, the prophetic function was to establish a direct relationship between God and the people. This channeling of God was facilitated by psychic powers. Elisha was reputed to have paranormal knowledge of distant events (2 Kings 6:12) and Ezekial to enjoy detailed knowledge of events in Jerusalem while residing in Babylon (Ezk. 8–11). Sometimes dreams were vehicles of inspiration among the prophets, as in the case of Jeremiah (31:26), who heard the word of God in a dream. It is impossible to take prophecy seriously without assuming a transcendent source behind the scenes.

Appearing in preliterate, indigenous societies, the shaman is another representative type proficient in transcendent experience. If the prophet is disposed toward possession by the god, the shamanic maneuver is to become ecstatic, to vacate oneself from the body. Mircea Eliade calls the shaman an expert in "archaic techniques of ecstasy." As we said, ecstasy is the core datum of survival research. The shamanic experience is based on the assumption of a working model for conducting next-world psychic excursions.

Shaman making involves ritual death and dismemberment. Australian anthropologist A. P. Elkin describes making "aboriginal men of high degree" in Australia, a rite of transition that follows a traditional pattern. Being "pointed" with the "death-bone" ritually kills the candidate. Followed by a period of mourning, the ritual corpse and bones are cleansed and purified. Entering Dreamtime, communing with spirits of the dead, the candidate is restored to life, having forged a link to the Otherworld and presumably gained his special powers. Making people of high degree is a harrowing ritual designed to awaken the candidate's psychic powers. In Australia, initiation is symbolic of "being killed," and the initiate is duly mourned. He may be killed by a "death bone" or swallowed and spewed up by a water snake that sails down from heaven on a rainbow. An abdominal incision is made on the ritual corpse and magical substances such as quartz crystals are inserted, thus creating a new body and restoring life.[1]

Everywhere early people discovered techniques designed to dismantle ordinary behavior and perception and exhibit the cracks in the shell of our mundane existence. Today the near-death experience parallels the shamanic initiation. The story of Dannion Brinkley, first published in 1994, is a case in point.[2] Dannion, like certain shamans, was struck by lightning, recovered from the brink of death, and acquired healing, clairvoyant, and prophetic powers. According to research, near-death experiencers sometimes acquire psychic powers, reminiscent of aboriginal "men of high degree" said to walk on fire, levitate on a magic cord, disappear and reappear, project telepathic hallucinations, and run with paranormal speed. Psychic powers, the acquisition of a psychic body, and the ability to navigate the cosmic axis, are the fruits of experimental ritual "death." In this context, "death" refers to an altered state of consciousness, to entering Dreamtime and the Otherworld. It's assumed there are "gates" leading there that the living can step through—if one is willing to prepare. This shamanic model for exploring the next world seems well suited to a hopefully more tolerant twenty-first century psychology. Much the same might be said about the spiritual methods of yoga and mysticism.

Yogis and mystics the world over have claimed to go behind the scenes of ordinary reality. As the shaman undergoes a ritual physical death, mystical trances have their distinctive physiology. In structure, they mimic death; respiration is minimized, cold sensations and catalepsy mimic rigor mortis. Augustín-François, an expert on Christian mysticism, states that "the ecstatics sometimes no longer seem to have either pulse or heart-beat. And more than this, one can just barely remark a last vestige of the body's natural, vital warmth."[3]

Mystical practitioners attempt to suspend, even to invert, the current of the life force. Catholic mystics speak of *ligature,* the suspension of all the faculties, and mental absorption in the Supreme Idea. Danish religious psychologist Ernst Arbman claims that *inhibition* describes the essence of mystical practice. Patanjali, who compiled the Yoga Sutras, uses the word, *nirodha,* or "restriction." Yoga is defined as restricting the fluctuations of our mental life, the aim being to achieve *kaivalya* or "release." Mystical experience, like survival of death, implies release of conscious existence from bodily constraints, and both veer in the same transcendent direction. One of the key terms of Sufism brings out the idea of ritual death, *fana,* which means "annihilation." Arbman comments on this term, speaking of the "extinguishing of the waking or normal mental life and the total ecstatic absorption in the object of belief." All these experiences seem to nest in metaphors of ontological breakthrough: new planes of being, the "other side," the "other shore."

Now these breakthrough experiences often give rise to tangible powers and evidence for Otherworld contact. So, for example, Patanjali's Yoga Sutras describe the *siddhis,* or supernormal attainments, said to result from yogic practice. *Siddhis* point to other worlds and to powers of the spiritual body: levitation, teleportation, the ability to enter and possess *other* bodies, acquiring the strength of wild animals, invisibility, immunity to hunger, knowledge of the time of one's death, and so forth.

For anyone concerned with practice, Patanjali offers a simple key to the acquisition of these powers: *samyama,* the integration of three psychic skills: *dharana, dhyana,* and *samadhi;* concentration, meditation, and the capacity for total absorption. We are told that by performing *samyama* upon an elephant, one acquires the strength of an elephant. Indian spirituality is rife with magic and miracle, and testimony from Catholic saints and Victorian mediums confirm the reality of many of these wild claims.

The aim of yoga, according to Eliade, is to immobilize the flow of thought, breath, and sexual secretions.[4] *Asana, pranayama, ekagrata* are the holy trinity—motionless posture, breath restraint, one-pointed thought. The Catholic mystics called it "ligature"—suspension of the senses. Ligature means complete dissociation from the world; curiously, it's a picture, functionally, of "death." The extraverted life current is put into reverse and effort made to funnel it inwardly. Yoga is a system that gives guidelines for a kind of experimental induction of near-deathlike states. It is one of the many ways human beings try to experience transcendence.

To summarize: There are traditional forms of human experience, forms that reveal Otherworld realities for most of humanity. Traditional belief-systems are rooted in original experiences. They represent pathways to direct experience of alternate realities.

Certain common psychophysical procedures are involved; they occur spontaneously or may be coaxed into manifestation by specific techniques. The prophet is invaded, the shaman is ecstatic, the mystic is emptied. These all seem to me variations on a theme: The ordinary threshold of awareness is drastically displaced. The displacement is so fundamental, it can be likened to death itself. A massive tradition, largely forgotten by everyday believers, testifies to this intuition of Something More.

"Miracles" and the Otherworld

The siddhis and charisms, or special powers, associated with yoga and mysticism qualify as cracks, or openings, to a possible Otherworld. These are phenomena quite out of place in the closed universe of scientific materialism. The premise of this book is that we must draw on the underground banks of repressed data, if we want a more complete and accurate picture of reality. So I am eager to ferret out the exceptional experience.

Let me start with two examples that might shake up anybody's complacent sense of what is possible. If they are real, afterlife phenomena seem unremarkable by comparison. Moreover, on the face of it, materialization and dematerialization imply the existence of another world, a hidden dimension, something decidedly *extra* or *super*. For materialization refers to objects erupting into public space from elsewhere. Dematerialization is the reverse trick; something tangibly ensconced in familiar space is sponged out, vanishing without a trace. Together, they suggest some kind of traffic between worlds, one thing popping in from elsewhere, the other unceremoniously exiting our space-time bubble. As usual, folklore and myth is cognizant of such ideas; for example, in the elfshot Scottish Highlands, one hears tales of secret places, holes, or passageways that lead to the Otherworld.

Take a contemporary case, alleged by many witnesses to be authentic. The famous Hindu avatar, Sathya Sai Baba, is either a supremely gifted con artist or Christlike in his miraculous prowess. Materializer extraordinaire, here is a man who seems able to whip hot food, jewelry, exotic out-ofseason fruit, and enormous quantities of sacred ash from nowhere. Icelandic researcher Erlendur Haraldsson has collected eyewitness reports that Baba produces specific objects *on demand,* not the sort of thing illusionists can do.[5] The ash, moreover, reportedly materializes from his photographs around the world. He's been doing, or seeming to do, all this, day in and day out, for roughly fifty years. If he's a scam, he must have coconspirators, and well-stocked factories to draw on for all the stuff he's been doling out. Jesuit researcher Herbert Thurston, moreover, has garnered eyewitness accounts of Catholic saints materializing food. So maybe the Catholic saints are conning their flocks, too—or maybe there is something to these accounts. Let's just say, if the reports are authentic, they enrich the prospects of the afterlife idea. They are the sorts of things consistent with the effective reality of an Otherworld.

The example of dematerialization I want to focus on dates from September 21, 1995—a story that made headlines around the world. On that day just before dawn, a man from New Delhi dreamed that Lord Ganesha, the elephant-headed god of wisdom, wanted some milk. The man dashed out to the first temple to make an offering, which he placed under a statue of Ganesha. Much to his amazement, he watched the milk disappear before his eyes. By day's end, reports of "milk-drinking" statues were coming from all parts of India and from Hindu communities from Bombay to Jersey City. The entire phenomenon, witnessed by millions, fizzled out roughly after twenty-four hours.

Hinduism Today reported: "The 'milk-miracle' may go down in history as the most important event shared by Hindus of this century, if not in the last millennium." Ordinary life in New Delhi came to a standstill while liter upon liter of milk vanished into thin air. The stock market in Bombay came to a halt as people rushed to temples and talked about the miracle. Skeptics' sneered and called it "mass hysteria."

Arpana Chattopa of New Delhi published a letter in the *Hindustan Times:* "I am a senior scientist of the Indian Agriculture Institute of New Delhi. I found my offerings of milk in a temple being mysteriously drunk by the deities. How can the scientists explain the copper snake absorbing the milk I offered with a spoon kept at a good distance from it?"

People from all walks of life were dumbfounded as they watched milk slowly disappear into empty space before their eyes. Worldwide press coverage was spectacular. I myself watched milk dematerialize on CNN, as demonstrated by a startled BBC reporter. By chance a young Hindu student of mine, Deepak Bhagchandani, was in India on the day of the "milk-miracle." I quote from his written report: "I have personally witnessed and experienced the opportunity to feed the Lord with my own hands in a temple, in New Delhi. I stood and waited in a queue at the Ganesha temple. It was astonishing and unbelievable when my turn came to offer milk to the Lord. I took a spoonful of milk in my hands and placed it near the sculpture. The milk disappeared slowly and gradually. It was not flowing down or being wasted. As a matter of fact, I could see no traces of milk anywhere."

Deepak adds that he went back on the queue several times for a repeat performance. He was also kind enough to write an account of his witnessing "bhabutti" (sacred ash) materializing from a Sai Baba photo. This latter phenomenon, as I said, seems very hard to account for by invoking Baba's talented sleeve.

Materialization and dematerialization stories aren't, of course, proof that anyone survived death. So why insist on calling attention to them? They are of value for at least two reasons. First, they rudely challenge the mainline view of the way things are supposed to be. They seem, for example, to contradict the law of conservation of matter and energy and suggest that our understanding of space is deeply flawed. We have no theories, as far as I know, that explain how empty space can "drink" (cause to dematerialize) a macrocosmic substance like milk.

My second point is this: At first glance, it looks as if the milk disappeared *into* another world or reality; Sai Baba's ash, conversely, seems to emerge *from* another world, *through* another dimension. The complementary effects give an impression of invisible structures and processes that point to a more comprehensive reality.

Evidence for holes in our picture of physical reality is found in other traditions. Thanks to the legalistic obsessiveness of the Catholic Church, much of the best evidence for extraordinary physical phenomena has been collected and critically sifted. Reaching into what may seem a grab bag of assorted wonders, I piece together a composite image of a "vehicle" for the navigational needs of our postmortem consciousness.

Looking, for example, at the types of phenomena that Thurston discusses in great detail, some groupings begin to form. The unifying idea for me is the *expressive* nature of Catholic mystical phenomena.[6] For example, there are hundreds of accounts, more or less well documented, of levitation. Levitation is complete or partial lifting of the body, or other physical objects, in apparent defiance of the law of gravity. Observations of the famous flights of Saint Joseph of Copertino and Saint Teresa of Avila's self-reports show that levitation is a by-product of a special state of mind—ecstasy. In Angelo Pastrovicchi's biography of Joseph, written when the saint was beatified, we find a chapter on ecstasy and levitation. The author notes that "whenever he [Joseph] heard songs or music in church, or a conversation about God, or the names of Jesus and Mary, he would be enraptured and cry out, 'O love, O love!' "

It was during these enraptured states, triggered by thoughts of divine love, that Joseph's aerial jaunts took place. In some reported cases, he imparted immunity to gravity to people around him. According to an account based on sworn testimony: "Great was the surprise and terror of Father Custos on one occasion, when solemn Vespers had been sung in honor of the Immaculate Conception in the chapel of the novitiate. Joseph entreated the father to repeat with him the words, 'Beautiful Mary.' He then seized the father and, pressing him close and exclaiming with louder voice, 'Beautiful Mary, Beautiful Mary!' rose with him into the air."

In expressiveness, stigmata and bodily elongation seem related to levitation. Stigmata are wounds resembling Christ's that appear on the bodies of saintly and some mentally unstable people. Evidence indicates that stigmatists, in effect, mimic the statue or painting of the crucified Christ they happen to be fixating upon. Typically, wounds appear on the palms of the hand, as represented in traditional art; but Roman crucifiers impaled their victims through the wrist bone. So it seems that some people, by intense concentration on an image, can literally transform their bodies. As Patanjali understood it, whatever you perform *samyama* upon, you become.

Bodily elongation seems straight out of *Alice in Wonderland,* yet testimony deposed under oath states that the bodies of ecstatics become elongated, shrink, and are morphed in ways we normally deem physically impossible. So-called tokens of espousal are very curious; related to the stigmata, they consist of anomalous formations on the skin, or of oddly persistent and contagious hallucinations. Tokens of espousal are strange icons of religious romanticism.

Certain saintly women were convinced they saw marriage rings on their fingers where in fact ring-shaped prominences and discolorations appeared.

Many mystical phenomena rotate around themes of light and heat. Credible witnesses recount the luminous phenomena of the mystics, heat-related effects such as immunity to fire, or the supernormal fire of love. Immunity to fire and anomalous heat seem two sides of the same coin. These heat prodigies express the ardors of mystic love. Such anomalies point back to a Dantean universe where love moves the stars and Newton's gravity ceases to hold sway. The same can be said for mastery of fire in other traditions, the Tibetan practice of tummo yoga, and the Hindu preoccupation with "kundalini" energy.

The expressive function of miracles is clear in the odor of sanctity and in bodily incorruption. Persons noted for heroic sanctity often produce unexplained fragrances. Padre Pio made himself known at a distance by the smell of roses and oriental tobacco, and there are reports of fragrant incorrupt bodies of saintly servants of God. Herbert Thurston in 1952, and more recently, Joan Carroll Cruz in 1977, reviewed eye-witness testimony on the mysterious effects of bodily incorruption.[7] It is a fact that the dead bodies of certain holy people resist the common ravages of corruption. Contrary to nature, they stay soft, flexible, lifelike in color, and occasionally seem to move, bleed, and exude fragrant oils.

Something is making these pious cadavers behave very oddly. All I wish to say here is that an expressive force seems at work, an agency that wants to exhibit meaning, retarding and even reversing the physical effects of death, thus eroding our complacent view of the way nature is supposed to behave. Whatever the elusive agency behind these effects, I consider it part of the indirect evidence that adds general credence to our picture of an afterlife-friendly universe.

Two last examples of saintly marvel will round off the picture. Thurston discusses what he calls mystic hunger strikers, as well as the disconcerting ability to see without eyes. (We talked about the latter in connection with people born blind who suddenly "see" during near-death.) Inedia and eyeless vision contradict the powerfully held belief that we need nutrition to sustain life and eyes to have visual impressions.

Suppose it's true that certain people can live without physical nutrition and see without their eyes. The idea that I could live without my normal body seems inconceivable unless I *define* "living" in terms of normal bodily mechanisms. These reports of physical phenomena add to the composite image of a hypothetical spiritual body—a "body" that could live without physical nutrition, see without eyes, assume a luminous shape, manifest anywhere in space, and so on. In our attempt to think credibly about life after death, we need to keep all these exotic facts in mind, and try to integrate them into a coherent picture.

Aliens and Flying Saucers

Among shamans, prophets, and mystics, we find reports of effects that imply influx from ultraphysical dimensions. Documented accounts of "miracles" and other supernormal wonders at the very least serve to enlarge our perspective on what may be. I want to look at another pattern of experiences with otherworldly overtones. Aliens and flying saucers are not often linked to parapsychology and may seem remote from matters of life after death. Nevertheless, there are suggestive overlaps.

To begin with, UFOs and alien abductions show many earmarks of psychic phenomena. Various writers have commented on this, beginning with C. G. Jung who thought that the shape of the flying saucer represented a mandala or symbol of wholeness.[8] For Jung the fact that people were seeing UFOs in the sky was a sign that changes in the collective psyche were imminent. Whatever their physical status, UFOs were part of a collective death and rebirth experience.

Researchers like John Keel and Jacques Vallee have detailed the connections between UFOs, fairy tales, the demonic, and the psychic realms, and parapsychologist D. Scott Rogo theorized that UFOs were collective poltergeists. Mysterious lights, a staple of ghostly and visionary lore, recur in UFO sightings. UFOs sometimes assume the shape of structured disklike craft, but behave unlike familiar physical things; they divide and unite, appear and disappear, make right angle turns at incredible velocities, and behave in a manner more thoughtlike than physical.

The occupants of these strange "craft" indicate a profusion of types. Patrick Huyghe's *The Field Guide to Extraterrestrials* raises questions about the ontological status of alien visitors. Huyghe shows that behind the popular media-focused image of the small humanoid "gray" with huge almond-shaped eyes lie reports of a bewildering variety of forms, ranging from tall blond humans to lizardlike monsters and little aggressive blobs. Could so many different kinds of aliens really be visiting us from distant planets and galaxies? The variability suggests the psychic, the mind-dependent, and the mythical.

UFO craft and occupants behave like mind-matter hybrids and remain maddeningly elusive and surreal, more like the antics of ghosts than machines from outer space. We hear of levitation, telepathy, apports, teleportation, strange light and heat phenomena, and materialization effects. UFO effects and survival effects both challenge the dominant worldview on what there is. UFOs and aliens, like ghosts and apparitions, behave as if they were not subject to normal physical constraints.

Social psychologist Ken Ring compared psychological profiles of near-death experiencers and abduction narrators.[9] The subjects in his study shared an "encounter prone" profile; they tended toward states of dissociation. Not necessarily pathological, this could as well predispose one to be more psychically receptive. Ring asks: "Could it be that the world of the NDE and that of the UFO abduction, for all their differences, are not, after all, universes apart, but a part of the *same* universe?"

Harvard psychiatrist John Mack has studied the alien abduction phenomenon and is convinced that his clients have encountered something so extraordinary and so powerful that it has traumatized them.[10] At the same time, they show no known pattern of psychiatric disturbance. The abduction experience is a psychiatric anomaly, and Mack has concluded that an unknown agency is impinging upon significant numbers of human beings in ways that defy Western understanding.

In a conversation with John Mack, I asked if he would comment on the possible links between afterlife and alien abduction data: "UFO abduction investigators are sometimes reluctant to admit that there's a whole range of phenomena encountered," he said, "from simply the sense of energy, light, or presence to something resembling nonmaterial light or astral bodies. There is also what abductees often call the collapse of space-time; they experience themselves as not operating within the ordinary space-time universe and can travel throughout space, throughout history, throughout the dimensions. Then you have more specific kinds of experiential evidence for the separation of the self from one's physical body, namely, past-life experiences.

"Some of these experiences are very powerful and seem

to show the patient has made contact with something larger than the ordinary self. Somehow the energy from the encounter dislodges memories of past lives. I haven't traced any of the specific memories described in my cases, but this could be done. I think that the main point to be made is that this phenomenon, like so many of the transformational types of experience, manages to rip open the connection between the self and the body. It has the power to make people travelers in consciousness. That seems to me the first step toward proving life after death."

I find it significant that Mack was prepared to state that alien abductions are only one type of encounter experience pointing to other dimensions of reality. Given the psychic nature of so much in the UFO world, it's plausible to insist on a possible tie-in with the Otherworld we are exploring. UFO-maven Jacques Vallee speculates that UFOs may be coming from another dimension, noting that physicists today talk about hyperspace and multidimensional space. Early psychical researchers discussed the fourth dimension as possibly related to the mechanics of the afterlife.

In a possible scenario, the abduction mystery would be about real otherworldly visitations, beings of a kind perhaps related to apparitions of the Virgin Mary, or fairies, or demons, or other creatures of an elemental, discarnate or excarnate nature. These beings would in one sense originate from "outside" our personal world but also from "inside" our collective mental life. They would be creatures of a third zone of being that fuses objective and subjective realms but that is neither, entirely or exclusively. Some scholars have called this third fused mode of being the *Mundus Imaginalis*.

In this light, we can begin to understand the telepathic style of communication, the levitational capers and transmaterial skills, and the surreal variety of ways these beings appear to us. Clearly, in this scenario there is room for discarnate minds. The imaginal hyperspace or parallel world that might lodge aliens, angels, demons, Marian goddesses, fairies, and elves, appears vast and rich enough to accommodate dead souls. If I am right in stressing this continuum of visitation, the Otherworld has many ports of entry. Anybody curious to know about the afterlife fate of human consciousness should keep an ear cocked to the strange unfolding of the UFO story.

Poltergeists

The phenomena I describe in this chapter are not usually understood as directly bearing on the afterlife question. My point is that if we look more closely at them, they may indeed provide us with signs from a nearby Otherworld. At best, they provide supportive background or indirect evidence.

The term *poltergeist* is German for "noisy spirit." Poltergeists, those puzzling outbreaks of physical effects, in the past were indeed seen as mischief-making delinquent spirits. Modern parapsychologists are more inclined to believe that *living* persons are the unconscious agents of these disturbances, but no one quite knows for sure. There are, however, poltergeist cases that do not appear to involve any credible living persons as probable cause. In these cases, the ruckus may be caused by a provocateur from the Otherworld.

For example, in 1982 Karlis Osis and Donna McCormick reported a case of poltergeist activity that lasted about ten years in a gift shop in New Jersey owned successively by three different people.[11] Along with unexplained noises and apparitions, objects moved without apparent cause and equipment broke down for no apparent reason. At least twenty-four people observed the phenomena. No one ever identified a living agent. There were disturbances when no one at all was in the gift shop. In this poltergeist case, according to the authors of the report, a discarnate agent might well explain the phenomena.

In 1992 David Fontana of the English Society for Psychical Research reported another fascinating poltergeist case with afterlife implications.[12] The title of the report, "A Responsive Poltergeist," suggests one of its unusual features. The poltergeist agent, which was personified as "Pete," had all the earmarks of a conscious agent that responded intelligently to witnesses. The scene of the phenomena was an engineering workshop and retail facility in a shopping district of South Wales. The investigator observed many, though not all, the phenomena.

Consider a partial list of some of these effects, which persisted about two years, itself unusual for cases of this type. Stones, coins, and bolts inexplicably moved and impacted on floors and walls. Witnesses were sometimes struck but not hurt by missiles. Objects, like paint scrapers, disappeared and reappeared, sometimes hot to the touch. Objects on the premises were teleported from one place to another, often in response to a need or a request (like pens and coins). Old pennies of unknown origin and dating from 1912 dropped to the floor from nowhere. There were unexplained sounds of large stones crashing and clattering on the roof. Fluorescent light tubes exploded and carburetor floats were found stuck in the ceiling. There were unexplained smells of burning. Witnesses were barraged with phone calls at their homes, the lines going dead when the phones were picked up; British Telecomm engineers found no explanation for these calls. Heavy wooden planks, apparently from the yard outside, were mysteriously thrown into the shop. Stones were thrown in the retail shop while customers were present. Keys of unknown origin appeared from nowhere. Unknown cutlery appeared in the kitchen, sometimes arranged in meaningful patterns.

Many phenomena seemed intentional and occurred in response to witnesses. Dust was thrown down the necks of witnesses and some were hit with stones or pricked with needles of carburetor floats. When witnesses (as well as the investigator Fontana) threw rocks back in the direction that seemed the source of the invisible agent, the rocks were hurled back. (The flight of these returns was usually invisible; they would appear suddenly.) Phenomena were reported that presumably occurred overnight when the workshop was empty and locked. Large amounts of grass seed and fertilizer were scattered around the premises, plates were smashed but the pieces were found perfectly arranged, a mowing machine was found to be running in the workshop in the morning when the owners opened up, cutlery was found arranged on the floor and tables, as if in preparation for a meal. In response to a request for money made to "Pete," five-pound notes appeared, and, finally, on three occasions apparitions were observed by at least one witness.

As David Fontana observed, the only possible *normal* explanation of the phenomena is fraud. Four adults (two married couples) were the chief witnesses and proprietors of the workshop. No plausible motives or even opportunities for perpetrating a deliberate fraud were found. The apparent agent was intelligent and responsive. Unlike many poltergeist cases, no emotionally disturbed children were involved. The witnesses were mature adults whose emotional stability and personal probity seem unquestioned. Even when there was no one on the premises, effects were produced. Finally there were sightings of an unidentified apparition.

In view of the intelligent nature of some poltergeist outbreaks, especially in cases where there is no living person who is the likely cause of them, an Otherworld cause remains possible. But even when disturbed adolescents are involved in poltergeist cases, Otherworld causality may still come into play. The reason is that we do not know if emotionally disturbed children cause poltergeists themselves, or whether they provide the psychic energy for possible discarnate agents to make their tangible mischief. The whole poltergeist phenomenon, in my opinion, may well be another sign of the proximity of Otherworld agency and intelligence.

The "Old Hag"—A Nasty Visitor

"Old Hag" is an expression used by medical folklorist David Hufford to describe a familiar experience.[13] It's called "nightmare," "incubus," "night terrors," or "sleep paralysis." Hufford found that over 15 percent of the general population had the experience at least once.

You wake up suddenly during the night and find yourself paralyzed. You sense a presence nearby, footsteps, voices, laughter. A powerful weight presses on your chest; fear and terror grip you. I've had the experience several times, and can testify to its uncanniness. My own informal surveys of students over the years show that perhaps more than 15 percent of us have this experience. In 1996 I interviewed a distraught man who said he was being badly "hagged." Waking from sleep, he often sensed footsteps behind him and heard a voice laughing maniacally. This happened to him several times a week. No, he passed all the psychiatric tests, and was perfectly sane.

According to Hufford, hagging, or night terrors, are not pathological, and the experience, moreover, is cross-cultural. The man whose "Old Hag" laughed maniacally wasn't crazy or hallucinating. The Old Hag experience has its own stable, complex structure, and is probably the phenomenon behind many traditions of supernatural assault. The experience is the cause of the traditions, says Hufford, not the other way around, although different traditions favor different *interpretations* of the experience. Something similar seems to happen in reports of near-death and alien encounter. The common feature of these experiences is having contact with something seemingly from *elsewhere*.

What is the value of the Old Hag experience for afterlife research? Hagging isn't usually related to afterlife research because these shadowy gripping presences give no hint of their personal identity, but Hufford offers some hints in a chapter called "The Old Hag and Culture" where he shows how the psychic basics of hagging turn up in hauntings, witchcraft, and reports of demonic and other supernatural encounter. In the story I told in Chapter 3, I was attacked and paralyzed by a blurry humanoid entity—an assault reminiscent of the Old Hag.

If there are excarnate souls conscious and active, some of them may, as we might expect, be more aggressive, violent, and unruly than others. Who knows what spectral terrorists, what psychopathic revenants—careless of social niceties—might be out there, and what they might be up to? In my view, if there is an Otherworld, we should *expect* to see more breaches in the partition separating it from our sense-ensnared world. And there is no reason to suppose all these breaches must reveal sweetness and light. Poltergeists and hagging would seem to reflect the rowdy side of the Otherworld.

Physical Mediumship

Physical mediumship differs from mental mediumship; the effects are more tangible and sensational. In Victorian times, there were so many allegations of fraud and trickery that researchers refused to bother with physical mediums. The phenomena of physical mediumship rarely suggest that particular persons survive death, but they do, taken en masse, add to our reasons for believing survival is a credible possibility.[14] Icelandic medium Indridi Indridason; D. D. Home, that spectacular Victorian; and the Neapolitan Eusapia Palladino—all display roughly the same kinds of ability. The physical effects include inexplicable knocks, blows, movements, and levitations of objects. Mediums, like saints, reportedly levitate. Indridason, like Padre Pio, was thrown or dragged along the floor by invisible forces. The force inflicted painful blows upon both men. I agree with writer Colin Wilson when he remarked on destructive poltergeists that it seemed difficult to view such effects as coming from the medium's unconscious mind. Still, I would say that we should never underestimate how self-destructive people can be.

In this menagerie of strangeness, we observe the opposite of movements: the bodies of mediums, and objects associated with them, are immobilized. Objects become heavy or light on request. Strange lights are reported, immunity to the effects of fire, inexplicable moans, sounds of laughter, footsteps, ringings, whistlings, chirrings, chirpings, and assorted buzzings.

Near some physical mediums, whole environments extrude into local space. Besides mechanical and electromagnetic oddities, physiological oddities push the envelope: bodily shrinkage, bodily elongation, silhouettes, and by far the most spectacular, breathing materialized human beings. In a Palladino, Indridason, or Home séance, hands sprout from nowhere and pull, push, squeeze, and poke participants. And, I am happy to report, invisible detached lips reportedly kiss participants; the Victorian séance was often an erotically toned, sexually charged, event.

How does this relate to the afterlife and connect with the

possibility of experiencing the next world now? That hands or heads or whole bodies, alive to the sense of touch, have, under special group conditions, been observed to emerge for a short time from "nowhere" should be of interest to anyone curious about life after death and about how it might be possible to slip through one of the cracks to the next consciousness dimension.

Consider a striking example. In 1871, Sir William Crookes, president of the Royal Society and physicist who discovered thallium and invented the radiometer and the Crookes tube, described his research with D. D. Home, one of the great physical mediums: "The phenomena I am prepared to attest are so extraordinary, and so directly oppose the most firmly rooted articles of scientific belief . . . that . . . there is an antagonism in my mind between reason, which pronounces it to be scientifically impossible, and the consciousness that my senses, both of touch and sight, are not lying witnesses."[15]

Although Crookes moved on from psychical research to experimental physical research, he held firmly, without retraction, to his findings in psychical research. He goes on to state: "In the light, I have seen a luminous cloud hover over a heliotrope on a side table, break a sprig off, and carry a sprig to a lady. On some occasions I have seen a similar luminous cloud visibly condense to the form of a hand and carry small objects about.

"A beautifully formed hand rose up from an opening in a dining-table and gave me a flower; it appeared and then disappeared three times at intervals. . . . This occurred in the light of my own room, whilst I was holding the medium's hands and feet. To the touch, the hand sometimes appears icy cold and dead, at other times warm and lifelike, grasping my own with the firm pressure of an old friend."

Crookes tells us how he put things to a test: "I have

retained one of these hands in my own, firmly resolved not to let it escape. There was no struggle or effort, but it gradually seemed to resolve itself into vapor, and faded in that manner from my grasp."[16] Materialized hands have been reported of Indridason, Palladino, Kluski, and others. Notably, some of these extruded hands resembled the hands of known deceased people.

The Master of Lindsay, later Earl of Crawford, one day missed a train and had to sleep the night in the same room with D. D. Home. "I was just going to sleep when I was roused by feeling my pillow slipping from under my head, and I could also feel what seemed to be a hand under it. . . . Then I saw at the foot of my sofa a female figure standing in profile to me, and asked Home if he saw anything.

"It is my wife; she often comes to me," said Home.

In the morning, Lindsay was able to identify the dead Sacha Home in a photograph. On another occasion, Lord Adare and Captain Smith claimed they observed Home's dead wife materialized. It must have been fascinating—and unnerving—to be in the presence of Home.

Teofil Modrzejewski, known as Franek Kluski, was a physical medium, poet, and Warsaw banker. Kluski, who was studied by Gustave Geley, Charles Richet, Camille Flammarion, Thaddeus Urbanski, and throughout Europe, never accepted money for his services and was known for his honesty. Kluski, a mysterious fellow indeed, was famous for producing full figure materializations. Recognizable deceased human beings appeared in his presence, moved about, interacted with the home circle.

Cesare Battisti, a well-known Italian military figure, materialized for a full count of eighty-eight times. In 1984, Urbanski published a statement in the Polish Academy of Science attesting his observation of Battisti's phantom in the 1920s.[17] Adam Zoltowski, a professor of philosophy of the

University of Poznan, also witnessed Kluski's materializations, and wrote: "None of the manifestations were known
to me, except that of Cesare Battisti, the Italian hero, whose
appearance to me was familiar through photographs."
Roman Bugaj quotes other statements from competent witnesses who saw phantoms of known deceased people at
Kluski séances.

In a famous study conducted in Naples, the English con-
jurer W. W. Baggally testified to the phenomena of Eusapia
Palladino, and stated that he sensed about her the "action of
an independent energy." Coinvestigator, Everard Feilding,
felt that the phenomena he observed, in themselves worthless
and futile, were "symptomatic of something which, put at its
lowest must . . . profoundly modify the whole of our philosophy of human faculty." This is very close to the aim of this
book, which is to offer the reader an enlarged philosophy of
human faculty or potential. Feilding continues to comment
on mediumistic materialization phenomena. In the end, he
says, we "*may* ultimately be judged to require an interpretation involving . . . relations between mankind and an intelligent sphere external to it."

By means of a special group dynamic, it may be possible
to contact this "intelligent sphere external" to us. So it
seems rash to dismiss cases of materialization. They are relevant to afterlife *theory*. As Feilding said, they widen our
view of "human faculty." They give examples of the "vehicle" we might use to navigate the next world. At *most*, the
physical phenomena prove an "intelligent sphere" that is
"external" to us. The séance, moreover, furnishes a proto-
type of the group dynamic for producing paranormal phenomena, as described by English parapsychologist Kenneth
Batcheldor.[18] In light of this sprawling pattern of anomalous data, it seems a little less daunting to entertain the
afterlife belief.

The Machine as Porthole to the Next World

If people survive death, they might try to communicate with us through technology. We know from experimental studies that living people can influence machines paranormally. We've seen the effects produced by physical mediums. Why shouldn't the dead, assuming they survive, communicate with us through machines?

There is a phenomenon called "direct voice" mediumship. The presumed voice of a dead person seems to emanate from nowhere. Trumpets are usually handy and are taken to amplify the spirit's "voice." Also, no doubt in some cases, they were handy to expedite a scam. Even so, might there be something to the idea of using mechanical devices to register signals communicated from the other side? With classic Yankee temerity, Thomas Edison toyed with the idea of inventing a machine for communicating with the dead. In a 1920 interview for *Scientific American,* Edison spoke of his plans to build a machine that would "facilitate human communication with the dead."

In 1959, filmmaker Friedrich Juergenson claimed he obtained voices of dead people on an audiotape he was using to record the sounds of birds. Psychology professor Konstantin Raudive began to experiment with audio devices and produced voices claiming they were spirits. Machine mediumship of this kind flourished in Europe, Asia, and North and South America, and people today say they are picking up audio and video signals from the dead on a variety of electronic devices, including the telephone and the computer. There is, in fact, a well-known book by D. Scott Rogo and Raymond Bayless entitled *Phone Calls from the Dead.*

At first skeptical, independent investigator, Peter Bander, translated, published, and introduced Raudive's audiotape work. Unknown to Bander, colleague Colin Smythe performed an experiment with recording tape, following the instructions of Raudive's book. He turned on the tape recorder and asked if anybody was there. The tape recorded the voice of someone unknown to Smythe. Bander listened to the tape; he was shocked to hear his mother speak to him in German.

"Why don't you open the door?" she said. Although the voice spoke rapidly in a strange rhythm, he recognized it at once. He had corresponded with his mother by tape recorder for eleven years before her death. In other experiments Bander conducted, voices spoke in languages unknown to anyone present.

More recently, investigator Mark Macy has been reporting developments in ITC—"instrumental transcommunication"—mediumship and divination by machine. Macy describes one group receiving intelligence from an entity known as the "Technician," whose job it is to start "interdimensional communication." Macy claims that the "Technician" and cohorts are causing copy to appear on computer screens as well as images of deceased persons on television screens. Macy once called me up and cheerfully announced he had just spoken with Konstantin Raudive, a dead man, over the telephone. I asked him how he knew for sure that he was talking to Raudive. Was he familiar with the dead man's voice? Had he considered the possibility that someone was playing a joke on him? Unfortunately, the response to all my questions was negative.

We're on more solid ground with communications psychologist John Klimo, who has been investigating EVP/ITC (electronic voice phenomena/instrumental transcommunication).[19] Klimo, who wrote a comprehensive study of "channeling," has been experimenting with devices for recording signals from excarnate minds. Klimo wants to design machines sensitive enough to amplify elusive discarnate communications. Examples of these futuristic "transcommunication" devices include "radionic" cameras for photographing spirits, "flame-speaker microphones," "plasma receptors," "bio-mirrors," and something for using the "zero point energy vacuum."

Klimo is aware of the outstanding problem of survival research. How can we make sure that we're communicating with the dead and not with paranormal projections of the living? Klimo will disappoint anyone hoping for a mechanistic solution to the supreme mystery. Despite his hope that technology may help us break the Otherworld barrier, he says that "the psychological/spiritual state of the hardware operator is crucial to the success of the communication process." Klimo has therefore taken up the practice of prayer and meditation to make *himself* more receptive to possible otherworldly transcommunication.

Video, audio, and computer technologies are now available for those who wish to try to "transcommunicate" with the dead. In 1986, parapsychologist Robert Morris reviewed the evidence that people can paranormally influence the output of random event generators and electronic oscillators. In addition, there is a great deal of anecdotal evidence that computers, and other machines, go haywire in the presence of people who are stressed out. If living people can paranormally influence the behavior of machines, why not the dead?

Photographing the Spirits

Sparks, swirls, balls, and clouds of supernormal light often appear in afterlife narratives. Ghosts appear haloed in light, Mary apparitions are resplendent, and UFOs tweak reality under bright disguises.

As it turns out, ever since the invention of photography,

there have been claims of "extras," images of dead people turning up on photographs.[20] The specter of fraud haunts this scene, but there are things worth pondering.

In 1861 William H. Mumler produced a photograph on which a ghostly extra of his dead cousin appeared. "This photograph was taken by myself of myself and there was not a living soul in the room beside myself," he stated. Mumler's fame and success as a spirit photographer spread, but he was arrested in New York for producing fraudulent spirit photographs. A U.S. Court of Appeals Judge, John Edmonds, began by trying to entrap Mumler, but became convinced that he was genuine, and, in the end, testified on his behalf. The case against Mumler was dismissed. He was famous for photographing Lincoln's wife, on which an unexplained image of Abe at her side appeared on film.

More recently, psychiatrist Jule Eisenbud investigated Ted Serios, a man said to be able to mentally project images directly on Polaroid film.[21] For years Eisenbud and his parapsychological associates took every precaution against Serios producing fraudulent effects, and were driven to conclude that the former bellhop was indeed able to project specific thoughts that materialized on film. How does this *thoughtography*—to use Eisenbud's term—tie in with the survival hypothesis?

For one, the more we understand that such exotic human abilities exist, the better to decide what we're dealing with: simulations or excarnate minds? Eisenbud relates Serios's psychokinetic imagination to apparitions. Apparitions could be psychokinetic projections of our own subconscious minds—or projections of somebody who survived death. What Ted Serios could do with film is evidence of the mind's creative power. Could this creative power to materialize images—also found in dreams—be evidence for the power of mind to survive death? Could we, by consciously exploring this power, find a way into the next world? Eisenbud wonders about the reality we see before us: "It is not a long step from matter as an electronic ghost to thinking of it as the objectified image of thought."

Perhaps the next world is made of materialized images, a place where our thoughts, memories, and desires find their "objective correlative." Psychic photography—the objectifying power of thought and imagination—proves we have this potential. If it can be done on Polaroid film, why not in a mind-dependent Otherworld?

The Otherworld nearby? A mental stone's throw? We're handicapped here by the limitations of language. If there is a separate mind-dependent world, it could *only* be "nearby." Various circumstances are liable to shatter the partition, or cause some crack or fissure in it, making us receptive to messages—or messengers—from the other side. A mind-altering drug, fatigue, hunger, a fainting fit, an illness, trauma, daydreaming, falling asleep, dissociation, any one of these might lower the threshold of resistance and force us to turn inward—deathward, as it were.

Traditional spiritual experience always presupposes an Otherworld. In the experiences reported in prophecy, shamanism, yoga, and mysticism we find the bedrock of faith. We live on the spiritual adventures of those who came before us. The miracles, which we discussed, have played a major role. They are sometimes very potent indications of next world powers. What could be more basic than materialization and dematerialization?

Many people experience the next world as victims of an overwhelming power, as something invasive and shattering: for example, in alien abductions, or with the more playful but quite unruly poltergeist, or the uncanny Old Hag or the nightmares that sometime assault us in our bedrooms. Very strange, of course, are those stunning accounts of mediums who materialize hands, breezes, perfumes, whole recognizable human forms—warm and moist to the touch. I wish I had time to pursue further the link between psychic photography, especially the extraordinary work of Jule Eisenbud with Ted Serios, the creative power of dreams, the artistic genius of a Blake or Michelangelo, and, more extreme in a different way, Alexandra David-Neel's success in materializing a phantom with a will of its own. All these patterns of experience point to unexplained, albeit latent, powers. So indeed there are more things in heaven and earth than are implied by scientific materialism. From time to time they overflow into our world from some Unknown Dimension X.

PART FOUR

PRACTICE

Coping with the idea of my mortality has been a profound stimulus to my mental life. When I was a boy, the Catholic Church taught me to believe I had an immortal soul, that my true home was heaven in God's loving presence. But growing up I had to face modern science—Copernicus, Darwin, Freud, and all the rest. In my need to carve out a living truth for myself, there were questions I had to ask: What really are the boundaries of my existence? What exactly is this thing I call my consciousness?

What I found was that the boundaries of mental life are far more fuzzy and uncertain than I had instinctively guessed. The question that now intrigues me, How far can I really go? What are the limits of experience? There is, as I believe, a strong measure of human testimony that bears on the idea of an Otherworld—a greater existence. Is it possible to initiate an encounter with this other existence? Many people claim to have done so. Ecstatics leave their bodies, people see ghosts, mediums produce messages from spirits, children have memories of past lives, and so on. Well-documented reports of shamans, mystics, and yogis, and their astonishing powers, challenge our customary conception of human capacity. Some people seem to know things most of us accept or deny on faith or willful prejudice.

My ignorance irritated me into this exploration. I wanted to find out what was really going on behind these reports of the marvelous and the impossible. So, bit by bit, I have decided to approach the mystery—or maybe I should say the mysteries—with the resolve of being more frontal in my attack. Gradually, the question reshaped itself in my mind. What can I do to increase the likelihood of having experiences that will satisfy my metaphysical curiosity? Is it possible for me to move beyond the pallid prescriptions of religious belief and the dull dogmas of mainline science?

The task, I came to see, involves shifting my attention from looking for evidence of something *after* life to certain kinds of immediate evidence, or experience, *in* life. In other words, shift from trying to prove the afterlife to trying to enter fully into the depths of this life. In Chapter 8, we talked about psychological "bridges" to the next world; the new step is for us to start crossing those bridges.

What exactly do we mean when we speak of experiencing the next world now? The question is paradoxical, but the paradox is reduced once we think of *dying as a change of consciousness*. Suppose that after we shed our bodies we do enter another existence. What could we bring with us but our consciousness? Of course, without the customary physical body to filter it, our consciousness will necessarily change—probably very profoundly. If we could tease out *that* consciousness now, it might be possible to gain a foothold in the next world.

The Buddha is supposed to have said:

One could live a hundred years,
And never see the Region of the Deathless—

It is better to live a single day,
And see the Region of the Deathless.

Better one powerful personal experience that gives conviction of "the deathless" than bare hope or shaky speculation. So we're at a turning point: We are led back to ourselves. And there is a question we are forced to face: What lies below the threshold of *our* familiar consciousness? We've heard and read about the experience of others—what about us? Isn't it time to stick our own heads through the crack in the cosmic egg?

CHAPTER 10

Flatliner Models

In Joel Schumacher's 1990 movie *Flatliners,* some adventurous medical students attempt a dangerous experiment. They decide to induce temporary death in themselves in order to steal a peek of what may lie beyond. "Religion and philosophy have failed us," says Nelson, one of the characters—"our last hope is science."

So in this chapter I'm going to describe a "flatliner" model of afterlife research: research that encourages direct experience—personal experimentation. By *research,* I mean "searching back" into yourself, looking to pass beyond conjecture, living your own truth, breathing your own mythology.

Of course, I'm not suggesting that we literally flatline ourselves. Still, if we hope for some light on this topic, we may have to push matters a little. Nowadays, to study physics, scientists use powerful technologies to produce collisions of high-energy particles. To test a theory, you intervene in nature, rough things up a little, devise a way to force nature to answer your questions. If this method is valid for physics, it is also valid for psychology.

As it turns out, we already have models at hand for a modern flatliner "practice of death." For example, the near-death experience is said to offer direct knowledge about the next world; people who have the experience say they've *been* there and *seen* things. One knows by intuition—the experience speaks for itself. Like modern near-death voyagers in Schumaker's movie, shamans and mystics are said to visit the underworld and celestial realms, and come back from their hero's journey with the boon of knowledge.

Meeting the Spirits

It may happen spontaneously, without preparation, or it may be induced. From early times people have known ways to trigger meeting the spirits. The mystic retires to a mountain hut; the prophet retreats to the desert. Native North Americans go on vision quests, fast in solitude, exhaust themselves, pray for signs, open themselves to omens and visions. Techniques vary, but every indigenous culture has its kit of tools.

Anthropologist Peter Freuchen lived among the Eskimos for years and observed the *angakok* or local medicine man go into trances.[1] Freuchen watched Eskimo children who played games choking each other until they lost consciousness. Kids who were good chokers became *angakoks* when they grew up. Eskimos had simple but effective methods for inducing trance. "One way is to starve and thirst until the feverish mind starts the proper hallucinations. Another way is to obtain concentration and paralysis of the conscious mind by going to a lonely place and rubbing a stone in a circle on a rock for days and hours on end." Any everyday action, if it is repeated, can be used to distract the conscious mind, and pull the lid off the subliminal.

John Lame Deer, a Sioux medicine man, described his

first *hanblechia* or vision-seeking experience.[2] He lay crouch-
ed in his "vision pit," a body-size trench on top of a hill,
wrapped naked in a blanket, alone, no food or water for
four days and nights. Light-headed and dizzy after a session
at the sweat lodge, he was told: "You'll know it, if you get
the power." Sweat lodge, solitude, and fasting prepare one
for a power vision.

In Lame Deer's world the spirits of the dead are always
nearby, and his forefathers rise from the earth and crowd his
visionary eye. In the earthen pit Lame Deer feels a great bird
near his body and hears strange voices saying, time is brief,
so use your life to work, to heal, to teach. "All at once I was
way up there with the birds," he writes. From shapeless fog
a vision of his great-grandfather took form, his chest bloody
from wounds inflicted by a white man. There on the hill
Lame Deer knew and saw for the first time the *nagi* or soul
essence that he was, and awesome power surged through
him, just as the spirits foretold. Lame Deer entered full man-
hood when he shared his vision with the elders and gained
their approval. *Hanblechia* is ritual burial, an experience of
regeneration. The general idea is somehow to break down
one's normal resistance to a radical change of perspective.
The native way of doing this is by cutting off the flow of
everyday sensation and action. As the examples below suggest, there are many ways of doing this, and we are free to
adapt the main idea to our mentality and circumstances.

Modeling ourselves after the native vision quest, we
would cultivate the experience of solitude. Traditionally,
becoming spiritually mature meant going on solitary
retreats. Jesus began his public ministry with a forty-day fast
and a solitary retreat. Buddha began his search for enlightenment by wandering alone in the forest. Unfortunately, everything about our machine-ridden culture seems designed to
make solitude very difficult. Current mantras are about get-

ting wired, networking, connecting. Solitude, isolation, dissociation are tarred as antisocial, pathological.

Periods of deliberate isolation and conscious dissociation, however, are tools for breaking the everyday trance. No need to retreat for a forty-day fast in the desert, but set aside time each day for silencing the inner chatter, time for the gesture of making oneself porous to the unknown. Perhaps the most powerful step we can take is into periodic silence and solitude. If you have to, snatch some on the run; the choice to be choiceless; the will not to will.

Otherworld Telescopes

The first humans who looked at their reflections in still ponds, or saw mirages on the horizon, must have been amazed. Ambiguous perceptual spaces were the first Otherworld telescopes, the first natural technologies for inducing visionary experiences. It is a fact of perception that when the mind is uncertain it fills in the empty spaces and fashions form from the formless. Spontaneously we project our thoughts and feelings on ambiguous spaces, like Rorschach blots, clouds, wrinkles, transparent substances.

That is the basis of the art of scrying or crystal gazing, a technique for inducing visions of distant persons, lost objects, or deceased spirits. Scrying is mental concentration on transparent or reflective substances like water, crystal, or mirrors. It is, says Theodore Bestermann in *Crystal-Gazing,* "a method of bringing into the consciousness of the scryer . . . the content of his subconsciousness . . . and of bringing into operation a latent faculty of perception."[3] Scrying, please note, could mislead a person into thinking she made contact with a spirit. English psychical researcher Ada Goodrich-Freer saw a newspaper announcement of a friend's death in her crystal, whom she didn't know had died.[4] Later she discovered the previous day's newspaper contained almost the exact announcement, which she had glanced at but had forgotten. Scrying recouped the forgotten memory.

During the Middle Ages, Thomas Aquinas believed scrying worked best with the help of a devil. During the Renaissance, the technique was deployed for espionage, and it was believed that "innocent children" were good scryers. Today researchers are using mirror gazing to induce apparitions of dead people for therapeutic purposes.[5] Scrying is an ancient technique for stimulating the visionary faculty. The habit of gazing into shiny, polished surfaces sometimes induces visions; images of the "next" world may flash on the inner eye.

Experimental psychiatrist Raymond Moody calls his vision-inducing mirror-contraption a *psychomanteum*.[6] Dr. Moody gives an intriguing account of one of his own early experiments with the psychomanteum; while immersed in its dark, perceptually ambiguous environment, suddenly (as if on cue) his deceased grandma appeared before him. What flummoxed Moody even more than his grandma manifesting in front of him was her stepping right out of the mirror, and scolding and chasing him around the room.

The *ganzfeld* is a modern laboratory procedure that works a little like scrying.[7] Instead of using transparent substances to create perceptual ambiguities, you cover your eyes with halved Ping-Pong balls, expose them to a uniform light source, and listen through earphones to monotonous sounds. Before long you tune out the external world, which enables you to tune in to your inner world. The "ganzfeld" is a psychic magnifying glass, and parapsychologists have succeeded in using it to facilitate extrasensory perception.

Something like this technique could also be used to induce otherworldly experiences. "Ganzfeld" situations occur in nature: listening to the drone of waves, staring at a field of grass, feeling a steady wind blow on your face. The monotony and uniformity of perception heightens receptivity. Doing something simple and monotonous, like washing dishes or raking leaves, could put you in a ganzfeld state. Using low-tech, natural procedures, one might induce aspects of the visionary near-death experience. Everything depends on lowering the threshold of resistance. To the open, receptive mind, Otherworld "telescopes" may be found everywhere.

Being Beside Yourself

As we saw in Chapter 1, the out-of-body experience can sometimes be veridical. It's the core afterlife phenomenon, and can show us what it feels like to exist without a body. The first yogis, mystics, ecstatics probably became convinced of an Otherworld precisely because they had such experiences. Like people who have this experience today, they would have become convinced of the world beyond.

We know there is evidence for life after death; the next step in our search is getting acquainted firsthand with the afterlife terrain. One way is by learning to be beside ourselves, inducing the feeling of conscious departure from the body. This is the sort of thing that promises insight into the spiritual dimension of death. There are ancient methods of releasing consciousness from attachment to the body and methods may be learned from talented out-of-body travelers like Oliver Fox, Sylvan Muldoon, or the South African philosopher-mathematician, J. Whiteman.

One method that worked for me was "dynamic concentration."[8] On three occasions, I just concentrated on projecting myself out of my body, and succeeded—to my own satisfaction. During a visit to the tiny Greek island of Aegina, for example, I thought intensely about leaving my body before going to sleep. I thought about it during the day, reminding myself as often as possible. Not long after drifting off one night, I seemed to break loose from an ordinary dream I was having, and shot out of my body, like popcorn out of a gun. Gliding like a balloon over the deserted moonlit streets, I peered down on the beachfront. I felt absolutely clear, light, and free; during this brief but powerful experience, I recall repeating to myself: "This is the way to be! This is the way to be!" Anyone can try this before going to sleep.

Progressive relaxation is a useful technique. Physician Edmund Jacobson recommends systemically tensing and relaxing all muscle groups, insisting that without muscular tension, anxiety is impossible. Anxiety impedes the Platonic "departure" of the soul, although extreme terror may also facilitate it. Relaxation or life-threatening stress can trigger out-of-body flights. (Sorry, nothing is fixed or certain in the psychic world.) The aim of progressive relaxation is to experience yourself as effort-free. Complete relaxation eliminates distracting neural "noise," which enables one to be absorbed in mental imagery. In practice, these are states of consciousness resembling mind-dependent afterdeath states.

An American computer engineer, Robert Peterson, taught himself to become a seasoned out-of-body traveler, and his book explains how to induce the experience.[9] His first two trips happened while he was dreaming. He makes a good point about needing to feel safe. After all, trying to leave your body is not like driving to the shopping mall or taking a plane to Disneyland. Peterson was raised Catholic, and had to deal with his fear of demons. To ensure a sense of his safety, Peterson provisionally reclaimed his old Catholic belief in guardian angels. He called upon his guardian angel and boldly proceeded to experiment.

Fear is nothing to trifle with in the flatliner vestibule. If leaving the body is a kind of reconnoitering of death, it could get frightening. Fear caused Peterson to apply the brakes on his first flights. Fear prevented me from going all the way on my maiden out-of-body voyage. My first thought was "Great!" until I thought: "What if I get lost?" I immediately snapped back in my body, like a jack-in-the-box.

Peterson observes: "I reasoned that some day, when I die, I will be forced out of my body, and I'll have to deal with the issue then. It seems better to learn the rules before I die, so I can handle it better when my time is up. If I explore the out-of-body state while still alive, perhaps my transition to the waiting world will be smoother. When I die, I will be cast into a strange new world, just as an infant is cast into our world."

I have used the term "technique" in this section, but the challenge is philosophical, not technical. It's not just about having a special experience. More important is to form an attitude in the face of existence, living in radical openness, without fear of impermanence. It's about a way of looking at things, a way that keeps us poised for departure, and helps us to think *transitionally*.

Lucid Dreams

A model for a mind-dependent afterdeath state is the lucid dream.[10] Another way to experience the next world now, then, is to learn to control your dreams by becoming "lucid" or conscious that you are dreaming. Combining dreams with self-awareness and volition was not something scientists believed was possible, until psychologists Keith Hearne in England and Stephen LaBerge[11] in America proved it could be done. In experiments conducted by Hearne in 1975, subjects were able to signal by prearranged eye movements to experimenters that they had become lucid in the course of dreaming, while physiological tests confirmed that they were actually dreaming. Dreaming has been called the Third State of Existence; lucid dreaming might count as a Fourth, combining the fantastic properties of dream consciousness with the abilities of the waking voluntary mind.

There is clearly a sense in which lucid dreams resemble out-of-body experiences. In a lucid dream, you have full-blown experiences in realistic dream environments. Lucid dreams reportedly serve as launching pads into out-of-body excursions. There are reports of lucid dreamers meeting up with deceased friends and relatives, whether phantoms of the dreamer's imagination, or appearances of excarnate minds, is difficult to verify.

Most people have a lucid dream at least once in their lifetime. Still others experience lucidity more frequently. It is possible to learn how to become lucid. The first, and simplest, method is simply to consciously intend to, repeating to yourself your intention to wake up in your dream. Carlos Castaneda, in *The Journey to Ixtlan,* explains how his teacher Don Juan recommended looking at one's hands in a dream, as a way of recognizing one is dreaming. This is more likely to work if you look at your hands in the course of the waking day, and prime yourself to remember to look at them when you dream.

LaBerge designed a simple computerized device called the Dreamlight, a mask to wear during sleep. This registers rapid eye movements during dreaming, which cause a red light to flash on the closed eyes, signaling one to wake up—*while still dreaming.* LaBerge recommends that when you wake up from a dream, you should visualize yourself back in that dream; this can help you become lucid next time you do dream. Another technique for entering this Fourth State of existence, which resembles what André Breton meant by "surreality" and Frederic Myers by "genius," is to program yourself to notice incongruities in a dream. This, too, might remind you that you're dreaming. The main thing about these techniques is trying to be more reflective and activating the voluntary intelligence.

Anticipating perhaps the research of the present and the potential progress of the future, Tibetan scholar Evans-Wentz wrote, "By applying the yoga of the dream state, of the Bardo and of Transference, mankind would become masters of all states of consciousness, and be able to pass at will from the waking-state to the dream-state, and from the state called life to the state called death, and vice versa."[12] The Tibetan *bardo* refers to mental transitions. Learning to experience the next world now is about learning to navigate the transitions of mental life: from waking to dreaming, from being in to being out of the body, and from life to death. The guiding principle is to cultivate introspection, self-observation, to become aware of the fluctuations of one's inner life as much as possible. Psychic amphibians we are, like frogs straddling land and water, continually jumping back and forth between worlds.

Awakening the Mystic Light

Late one night I was drinking black coffee in the Twin Brother's Diner of Greenwich Village. A guy in a dark shabby suit, sitting beside me at the counter, and looking seraphic or sepulchral (I couldn't quite tell which), turned and twanged in my ear: "Have ya seen the light?"

The idea of the inner light is as old as the hills; reports are found everywhere in the literature of higher consciousness. The light is at the heart of the near-death phenomenon. Pediatrician Melvin Morse, known for his work with children's near-death experiences, studied hundreds in his Transformations project. Morse found that what really changed people was experiencing the light. "Those changes are the most profound in the near-death experiencers who have experiences of light. This was true whether they had a vivid and powerful memory of a flower-filled heaven bursting with light, or just a brief and fleeting memory of seeing the light."[13]

Experiencing the light reduces the fear of death. "Decreased death anxiety does not come from nearly dying or from believing that near-death experiences are the gateway to an afterlife. It comes from actually seeing that light at the end of the tunnel." The light experience enlarges perception and palliates the fear of death.

Morse brings out something else: "We also found that people who have a mystical experience of light—whether in a lucid dream or simply tripping into an altered state, *without being near death*—are just as transformed as those who have a near-death experience." In other words, the experience is possible for anybody, not just during cardiac arrest. "Most of these people experience the mystical light as the result of a life-threatening situation, but some have 'seen the light' while driving cars, jogging, watching television, or taking walks in the forest. These are ordinary people. Yet they have had the same experiences as great mystics and religious leaders." Dr. Morse's testimony to the power of the light experience is of great value for practical research. If the light is the core variable, can we induce it experimentally?

Spontaneous Illuminations

A person in normal health may suddenly experience the light. After a presentation I once gave, a soft-spoken stranger approached me, and told me how once at a party in South Beach, Florida, he stepped outside for a minute. The noise and the smoke, he said, were getting to him. Suddenly, for no apparent reason, a powerful light seemed to engulf and render him speechless, sent feelings of incredible bliss streaming through his body, and filled him with sacred emotion. His routine sense of self evaporated on the spot. Years of automatically held beliefs were erased. His lifestyle suddenly appeared ludicrous. Things he craved, emotions that disturbed him, now seemed unimportant. The light jolted him from his normal life orbit and all he wanted was to go back—and fill himself with the light. When I met him he'd been on the road for a dozen years. He was gaining, he said, on what he called his "sublime prey."

Canadian physician Richard Bucke had been reading Walt Whitman with friends. Driving home in a hansom cab, he slipped into a meditative mood. Writing about it in the third person, he said: "All at once without warning of any kind, he found himself wrapped around, as it were, by a flame-colored cloud. For an instant he thought of fire—some sudden conflagration in the great city. The next instant he knew that the light was within himself. Directly after there came upon him a sense of exultation, of immense joyousness, accompanied or immediately followed by an intellectual illumination quite impossible to describe. Into his brain streamed one momentary lightning flash of the Brahmic Splendor which ever since lightened his life. Upon his heart fell one drop of the Brahmic Bliss, leaving thenceforward for always an aftertaste of Heaven."[14]

Bucke named his experience "cosmic consciousness," a state of mind he felt foreshadowed the evolution of humanity. Total conviction of immortality would mark the new consciousness: "Each soul will feel and know itself to be immortal." Bucke saw this vision vibrantly alive in his friend, Walt Whitman, the poet of *Leaves of Grass,* who wrote, "Death is different from what anyone knows, and luckier."

Today we have thousands of stories of Whitman's cosmic light, and Bucke's prophecy gains some edge. A woman described her light experience to psychologist Kenneth Ring: "The mist started being infiltrated with enormous light and the light just got brighter and brighter and, it is so bright but it doesn't hurt your eyes, but it's brighter than anything you've encountered in your whole life . . . And this enormously bright light seemed to cradle me. I just seemed to exist in it and be part of it and be nurtured by it and the feeling just became more and more ecstatic and glorious and perfect."[15]

I soon found people who had light experiences who weren't near death. They saw the light in dreams. I myself once had a dream that left me with an "aftertaste of heaven." In the dream, I was lugging a coffin-shaped boat up a hill. The sun rose over the hill, and a ray of light poured into my heart, pervading me with bliss. I now knew from experience what the light was like. I have never forgotten the ineffable quality of that illuminating dream, and whenever I find myself slipping into the doldrums, I do my best to recollect it.[16] As Morse says, it can happen to anybody and under various and unpredictable circumstances.

Eskimos know the light as an experience called *qaumaneq*.[17] According to anthropologist Knud Rasmussen, a "mysterious light which the shaman suddenly feels in his body, inside his head . . . an inexplicable searchlight" enables him to read minds and perceive the future. *Qaumaneq* is associated with "feelings of ascension and the ability to see spirits." The light confers speed, agility, and the power to converse with the dead. Contemporary research has found links between experiencing the light and increased psychic powers in near-death incidents. In fact, we keep finding converging strands of evidence that link the approach of death with the symbol of light, an association clearly contrary to expectations of the ordinary waking mind. The ordinary waking mind associates death with darkness and the extinction of consciousness.

The Answer to Death

A sacred Hindu text tells of a young seeker of truth, Nachiketa, who did something I'd love to do: interview Yama, the Lord of Death. "When a man dies, there is this doubt: Some say, he is; others say, he is not," muses Nachiketa, begging the Lord of Death for the boon of knowledge.[18]

The problem is not like any other, says Yama; if you want to know the answer, a new way of knowing is needed, a shift from reason to gnosis. "The ancient, effulgent being, the indwelling Spirit, subtle, deep-hidden in the lotus of the heart, is hard to know." The reply, a little off-putting, veils a certain optimism. For the way, though like balancing on a razor's edge, is not impossible. It demands more than intellectual prowess but inner discipline. "The wise person, following the path of meditation, knows the light and is freed alike from pleasure and from pain." If Yama is correct, our search has led us to a crucial turn. We can know "the indwelling Spirit"—the answer the Lord of Death gives—but only by changing certain deeply ingrained psychological habits.

Yama's view has support from modern research: Meditation stimulates paranormal experiences. Of course, the experience the Lord of Death is talking about is unique; it's not just about acquiring some bit of information. It is about transformation, reversing the outward flow of consciousness, and turning inward. "Rare is he who, longing for immortality, shuts his eyes to what is without and beholds the Self."

According to Yama, the riddle of survival research can only be solved by insight into our hidden Self, by experiencing the "birthless, the light of whose consciousness forever shines." The answer to death is a type of intuitive knowledge defined by a quality of transcendent joy. It is a joy we have to long for deeply. Enlightenment, in short, is a cooperative venture. As in any relationship, you have to take a chance, expose yourself to the risk of failure and disappointment. The good news is that Nachiketa's boon—the answer to death—lies coiled inside us, ready to spring forth when conditions are right. Everything said so far has been leading us toward this shift in perspective.

Flashpoints from Beyond

The Lord of Death is not the only one to tell us that light is the hallmark of the *numinous*—the enchanting radiance of the Transcendent. Tales of transcendent lights, fires, halos, and scintillas are well documented. There are, for example, photos of the "Lady of Light," who appeared three years running at Zeitun, Egypt (1968 to 1971) that show living beings made of pure light. In a spectacular demonstration of the power of the light, thousands witnessed these Egyptian luminosities take the form of birds, stars, and the Virgin Mary.

Silently she appeared, the *theotokos*—as she was called—the "god-bearer." She never spoke a word but stretched out her arms and bowed gracefully before the multitudes. She floated on the dome of Saint Mary's, nodding to the crowd, and giving signs of peace: Christians and Arabs prayed together, forgetting the usual hostilities. She blazed away like some celestial Mae West, night after night, like a twentieth-century Isis or Persephone, sending a mute message of love from another dimension. And she was kind enough to leave traces of herself on photographic film for waffling skeptics.

In Southern Italy she was venerated for generations as the Bona Dea, and for two thousand years the ancient Greeks wooed her at the Mysteries of Eleusis. They came from all parts of the Mediterranean world, fasted and drank the sacred brew, and beheld amazing light in the shape of a beautiful maiden. People have sought and found these flash-points of transcendence, and though the forms change from epoch to epoch, the core light experience seems ingrained in nature. Persephone, Isis, Mary, and now the Being of Light of the near-death experience. According to Gregory of Palamas, an Orthodox Archbishop: "He who shares the divine energy . . . becomes himself in some sort light."[19] Religious ecstatics light up the cells they pray in, according to reports. Saint Seraphim of Sarov was famous for the mys-tic fireworks he displayed. A disciple wrote: "I looked and was seized with pious fear. Imagine the face of a man speak-ing to you from the center of the sun, from the brightness of their dazzling midday beams."[20]

Accounts of light and fire phenomena suggest something so intense it is beyond language and metaphor. I quote from the biography of a Carmelite nun, the Venerable Serafina di Dio. Under oath, sister nuns swore she became incandescent during prayer or Communion, and observed her "face glow-ing like a flame and her eyes sparkling. It scorched them if they touched her, even in wintertime and even when she was quite old. They heard her repeatedly say that she was con-sumed with a living fire and that her blood was boiling."[21] The spiritual passion raging behind these physical symptoms is clearly powerful stuff.

Strange heat effects are reported in Tantric circles. Tibetan Tantric Buddhists practice tummo yoga, a method to induce body heat coupled with sensations of bliss. They use erotic visualization to generate heat-and-bliss experiences, a practice with counterparts in Plato's erotic mysticism and

Hindu kundalini yoga. All this may seem strange, even blasphemous to the puritanical, but in much of the world coupling sex with spirituality is not only acceptable but a common option.

The light can be coaxed into manifestation—that is the telling point. An effective way is to simulate death: slow breathing, minimal movement, and a shift from sensory input to internal attention states. In effect, do what shamans the world over and the old Greek philosophers did: Practice ritual death. Socrates bluntly called philosophy a "practice of death and dying." Cicero and Montaigne agreed, recommending a certain laissez-faire attitude toward life as the best practice for death. Eastern seekers have been bolder, and developed specific methods. The Tibetans, the Chinese, and the Sufis, for example, evolved very specific light-inducing (consciousness-expanding) practices. Here are a few suggestions and possibilities. I include them as aids to jog your inventive imagination, not as formulas to follow mechanically.

The Tibetan Way

Tibetan spirituality challenges many assumptions of Western psychology and theology. Psyche and deity, for example, are understood as inseparable just as theory is inseparable from practice. The light experience is central, and there are several techniques designed to induce it. The essence of these techniques is to let go of the fear, anger, desire, concepts, and psychological conflicts that merge to obscure the inherent light-nature of our minds.

According to the Tibetan Book of the Dead, we all see our light-nature at the moment of death. "As soon as your breath stops, what is called the basic luminosity of the first bardo . . . will appear to you . . . open and empty like space, luminous void, pure naked mind without center or circumference. Recognize it then, and rest in that state." The most important thing is to recognize and understand that you are the source of the light. It is not outside of you; nothing can save you but your own efforts. The Tibetan belief that you see the light at the moment of death is supported by modern research; nowadays reports of light encounters on the brink of death are commonplace.

However, our practical assumption is that we can experience the light now—not just on the brink of death. The essential technique is that "all the life processes are reversed, turned topsy-turvy: Breathing is stopped as far as possible, thinking stopped, hearing stopped, seeing stopped." We set up psychological conditions for experiencing mind in a state at once aroused but clear of inner distractions.

The habit of introspection is essential: "Again and again look within your own mind." Watching at the point just before a thought becomes manifest, you may meet "the self-originated Clear Light." The light, says the text, may not literally be visible; rather, you experience your mind as void of quality, as "transparent." Ramana Maharishi told how he was enlightened through deep introspection. One day as a young man, in perfect health, he panicked for no apparent reason at the idea of his death. He looked into his mind, and asked, Who is feeling this terror? Who is thinking this thought of death? All at once he experienced his pure mind, saw the light, and was forever changed.

Soon after death, say the Tibetan texts, we experience all kinds of lights, seductive and frightening. The challenge is always to recognize these lights as projections of our own minds. In daily life, we also project "lights" and shadows onto people and things. In this respect, daily life is a daily death. In life, too, we have to recognize our projections—our blinding prejudices, presumptions, and assumptions.

Tummo yoga, the yoga of psychic heat, is a practice most Westerners would likely find strange. You coordinate breathing and visualizing exercises and aim to create sensations of warmth, bliss, and light. Visualize the Buddha, or any divine image you like, depending on your belief system. In Tantric heat yoga, one arouses the energies by visualizing having sex with various deities.[22] Reports of intense heat phenomena are also in the annals of Catholic sainthood, and Christian mystics speak of the *incendium amoris,* the "fire of love." The difference is that the Catholic tradition of exploiting sexual tensions and energies for spiritual purposes is unconscious.

One might try the Tibetan "yoga of the illusory body." This practice is designed to free you from fixation on your habitual body image, a strategy for separating consciousness from the body. Visualize your body expanding and shrinking, old and young, as god or goddess—whatever helps you detach your mind from your normal body image. None of this, it must be said, implies ascetic abuse of the body. Tibetan methods are gentle and follow the Buddha's middle way; the aim is to convert habits conducive to anxiety to habits conducive to well-being.

Tibetan Tantric methods use natural forces for spiritual purposes: breathing, sexual impulses, imagery, dark and troublesome emotions. One natural force shrewdly employed is dream life. In Tibetan dream yoga, you play the trickster who blends waking and dreaming forms of consciousness. "To think continuously in the daytime that all one sees, hears, touches . . . is in a dream, will greatly increase one's chances of recognizing dreams at night." Seeing the world as a dream while awake is practice for becoming lucid, a way of creating a bridge between the two worlds, spanning the divide between waking and subliminal mind. This attempt to mingle the two modes of consciousness is a way to open the door to the inner light.

We are told to pay heed to the "interval between the waking-state and the sleeping-state," the twilight states of mind psychology calls *hypnogogic* and *hypnopompic*. In that space-in-between, on the islands of uncertainty that Tibetans call *bardos*, the great light is poised and waiting to dawn upon us. It is most likely to happen during the "interval between the cessation of one thought formation and the birth of the next."[23] This is a practice that calls for careful self-observation, for how are we supposed to locate such intervals? What we find when we look closely is that the surface of the mind is agitated. Sight of the depths is occluded. When the turbulence subsides, the surface becomes smoother, more translucent, and one can glimpse the depths. By meditating we create intervals of relative calm; the acquatic marvels below are then more likely to manifest. We don't have to *do* anything to make the light appear; we have to *stop* doing.

As a useful exercise, try the Tibetan practice known as *phowa*. Here you practice transferring your conscious viewpoint from one place, perspective, or body to another. *Phowa*, or projecting awareness into different beings, can be an incentive to compassion and understanding, a method for tweaking, eclipsing, and expanding one's everyday self-identity. There are practical ramifications; think of the value of learning to see and feel the world from centers of consciousness *other than your own*.

Phowa is a method for enhancing the quality of relationships with others. It also offers to open us to the light, to our consciousness in its "naked" and "primordial" form, that is, the form in which it is *conscious of itself*. Anything, let us recall, that tricks us out of our routine perceptions, anything reversing the habits of ordinary life, could crack open the cosmic egg, and give us a glimpse of the light beyond.

All these methods—recognizing projections, manipulating one's body image, dissolving boundaries between dream and reality, stirring up psychic heat and erotic bliss, and entering the viewpoint of other beings—all are centered on the idea of experiencing the light *before* dying. That is the goal we hope to achieve. Every tactic is designed to help us realize what we never noticed before, that we ourselves, our essential consciousness, *are* the "fundamental clear light."

Enlightenment Now

It's important to underscore the shift of emphasis in this chapter. Experiencing the light is not only part of the near-death scenario; it has deep roots in the history of mysticism, yoga, and other spiritual traditions. Enlightenment itself is often described as an event, an experience of a powerful light. Experiencing this light is what convinces people that death is like stepping into another room, a transition into a new dimension. The light experience does infinitely more than convince the mind; I know from my own brief encounter that it also convinces the heart. And people experience the light—our best "proof" of immortality—spontaneously, in various circumstances, not just during near-death episodes.

The evidence for life after death is very suggestive, and in some cases I would say it borders on being compelling, but, as we discussed earlier, thanks to ESP and the dramatic powers of the subconscious, there's a chance that even the strongest afterlife evidence may be brilliantly delusional. There is, I believe, an elegant way out. Our evidence shows that the light experience changes one's consciousness; as the Canadian physician Richard Bucke predicted a hundred years ago, cosmic consciousness would produce absolute conviction of one's immortal nature. Experience the light (or some equivalent) and the problem of life after death is dissolved. The next step, I submit, is intensely personal; it is about trying to induce the light experience. This light, or related experience, is what we need to more fully confirm. The proposal is that we reframe life *after* death into a question of enlightenment *now.*

Taoist Methods

Given that the light experience is so powerful, and has such interesting aftereffects, it is not surprising to find spiritual traditions that discuss techniques for inducing it. Consider, for example, *The Secret of the Golden Flower,* which was first published in eighteenth-century China. Based on a tradition of automatic writing, séances, and the "flying spirit pencil" or planchette, the Golden Flower sect inspired fear of sedition and was persecuted—not unlike the Falun Gong sect in China today, which is severely repressed by the Communist party.

The Chinese text claims to transmit a "secret." The secret is rather subversive, and in tune with our speculations on the evolutionary connection to the afterlife. It is that we have to form our spiritual bodies in this life if we hope to survive death in a conscious form. Chinese spiritual psychologists think that the trauma of death tends to shatter our psyches, especially if they are poorly integrated. The "Golden Flower" is the spiritual embryo, the imaginal body of "light" that each of us creates through meditative practice. The more we nourish this embryonic light-body *before* we die, the better will we fare in our afterlife journey.

A simple but fruitful idea is behind all this: Harmonize consciousness with life. The "light-body" is a symbol for a fully conscious life. We live but sometimes we live without being conscious that we are living. The Taoist gospel tells us to pay attention to whatever happens; embrace life in all its colors, shades, moods; be present to the details, to the moment-to-moment specifics. Above all, unite opposing forces, try to strike a dynamic balance, play up the contrasts and discords, and look for new harmonies. According to the Chinese text, the more our oppositions are resolved, the "brighter" our light-bodies.

If we take these old masters seriously, confronting our own death offers the greatest chance to expand our consciousness. Jung's friend, Richard Wilhelm, wrote that cultivating the "golden flower" meant preparing "for life after death, not merely as a shadow-being doomed to dissolution but as a conscious spirit." It's hard, however, to die consciously if one starts out in denial of death. According to this Chinese tradition, we should prepare for death by living consciously. Living consciously is the best preparation for death, the way to be a "conscious spirit" after death.

It is important to breathe consciously. The first step is *pranayama,* controlled breathing. We could call it lucid breathing because it's like lucid dreaming: It fuses different realities into a new form of existence, the automatic (breathing or dreaming) and the voluntary (the waking self). Soul, psyche are words that *mean* breath. Breathe gently, slowly, rhythmically; feel, long for, visualize the inner light. Right breathing is essential to experience the "golden flower."

The circle is a symbol of the "secret"—a visual aid signifying consciousness centering on life. Centering on life is the best way to practice for death. "When the light is made to move in a circle, all the energies of heaven and earth, of the light and the dark, are crystallized. That is what is termed seed-like thinking. . . ." The recommended style of thinking is "seed-like," seminal, throwing out filaments, uniting opposites, androgynous: light and dark, male and female, life and death. With confident precision we are told: "It is only a matter of fixing one's thinking on the point which lies exactly between the two eyes. This light is extremely mobile. When one fixes the thought on the mid-point between the two eyes, the light streams in of its own accord." It is a matter of directing the flow of attention, channeling and rechanneling the energies of attention. The aim is to open the gates of "seminal" consciousness, and mobilize the light that will stream into us of "its own accord."

The Secrets of Cultivating Nature and Eternal Life by Chao Pi Chen is a guidebook to experiencing the next world now. Like many spiritual practices, it combines breathing and visualization to help form "the immortal fetus." "Fetal breathing" is a gentle way to "practice" death; one slows and softens breathing, imitating the last faint inhalations before the last peaceful exhalation. By slowing the breath to the point of almost stopping, the light begins to stream of its own accord. By slowing and softening the breath, we can learn to sense our psychic "fetus" gaining in brightness and intensity.

Breathing techniques are combined with subtle sexual arousal. The texts recommend that we sublimate our "generative force" into a "golden elixir." This you can do by stirring up the libido but not dissipating it. In other traditions, this thermodynamics of ecstasy is known as male continence, maithuna, or Tantric sex. Concentrating on the "cavity of vitality," or lower abdomen, one is to "heat up consciousness." The practice is widespread. The Bushmen are renowned for what they call "boiling" during high spiritual states, as are Tibetan tummo-heat yogis and droves of hyperthermic Catholic saints. The intellectually refined Greeks discovered their own yoga of psychic heat: Erotic sublimation is the basis of Plato's theory of love, advocating self-control in service to ecstasy.

The more you work at it, say the instructions, the more you'll see signs that the "immortal fetus" is growing. You will, in short, experience your psyche, your self, as more of a piece, discords resolved and energies flowing in creative unison. And if by chance you reach a point where you start to see "flying snow" or "falling flowers," you will know that significant changes are at hand. Above all, you must be prepared to leave through the top of your head for a visit in the next dimension. Or so Liu Hai Shan assures us: "When the fetus is mature, you will leap over the mundane."

Color and Active Imagination

"The man of light in me has guided me; he has rejoiced and bubbled up in me as if wishing to emerge," says Mary Magdalene, in a cherished gnostic text. This sentence makes an important point. The light is a psychological reality with a life of its own, and it needs to express itself in our consciousness. There is a "light" within us—a deeper form of consciousness—that wants to "emerge." (Light, symbol of all discords resolved, all energies united.)

This brings us to one of Carl Jung's practical ideas: the power of active imagination. This is to use artistic and fantasy methods to activate and be guided by the unconscious mind. Also a concept of Henry Corbin's, it names our ability to contact the realm of "immaterial light."[24] Corbin and Jung think that active imagination can take us deep into the subconscious, where we can enlist aid to make ourselves receptive to the light.

From Zoroaster to the Sufis, the great Iranian thinkers have been devotees of the light that transforms. Thanks to near-death research, we know that talk of a transcendent light experience is based on solid empirical reality, and now we are discussing ways of experimentally evoking it.

The Iranian tradition is concerned with the spiritual power of imagery, especially the spiritual power of *color*.

Color plays a prominent part in the Myth of the True Earth in Plato's *Phaedo*. We do not live upon the True Earth, says Plato, but inside a darkened hollow full of obscuring fogs and vapors. When we die—we climb from the hollow onto the surface of the True Earth—and then for the first time we will see everything as it is, shining in the *aither*—Plato's symbol for a new consciousness. Every stone will blaze like a gem, and the world will dazzle us with divine beauty.

There is a place "ablaze with immaterial matter," says Henry Corbin who studied the Iranian traditions, ". . . a region without any coordinates on our maps: the paradise of Yima, the Earth of light. The ways of approach to it are pre-sensed in the splendor of a *visio smaragdina,* the outburst of green light characteristic of a specific degree of visionary apperception." An awakened sense of color is a sign of awakened spiritual consciousness: emerald green, ruby red, and a strange luminous black. Exact specifics aside, what counts is the spiritual significance of color.

Heightened color-sense is part of "visionary apperception." Many great painters saw in light and color the visible shadows of another world, and not just painters but master etchers like Rembrandt who revealed the mysteries of light by suggestive tone. Corbin coined the word *imaginal* to name this other world. One Iranian visionary Najm Kobra wrote: "The five senses are changed into *other senses.* "[25] Our ordinary senses are enriched, refined, even blended, as in synesthesia. Like Kobra, Blake said, cleanse the doors of perception, and see the infinite aspect of everything—the shining side of every nondescript thing. Sensory life would be transfigured.

Kobra suggests a sequence of meditations: first, concentrate on natural forms, then on circles and triangles, then on faces and archetypes. Begin with the mundane and the natural and graduate toward a kind of cosmic intimacy—*an archetype with a face*. Now here is where color comes in. When you start seeing shimmering colored lights, like gold, or ruby, or emerald green, it is a sign that your "visionary apperception" is awakening. What has color to do with spiritual reality? Color is less related to the struggle for existence than line. Line and shape help us identify things useful or dangerous, an obstacle to avoid or object to possess. Line is down to earth—horizon, curve of the road, shape of hammer and nail. Line engages our muscular sense; we use it to measure, weigh, compare; it orients us to the mundane, space and time. Color, less functional and utilitarian, is more soulful, more like a perfume for the eye. Color opens us to a subtler emotional scale.

The next world is made of "visionary apperceptions," according to Iranian tradition. For me this implies using active imagination. There's a strong sense in which we're actively imagining our lives, instinctively using whatever resources we have to shape our worldview. We experience what our imagination permits. Blake put this in language forged from his own visionary experience: "This world of Imagination is the world of Eternity," he wrote, "it is the divine bosom into which we shall all go after the death of the vegetated body."

I've been thinking about this remark of Blake's for a long time. Imagination has implications for eternity. If true, then I guess one way to anticipate our arrival in the Otherworld is to hone our image-making powers; train, develop, enrich our imaginal life. Just living our lives with imagination is a way of practicing for death—for entering eternity. The world, as Keats said, may be a "vale of tears," but it's also an opportunity for soulmaking, for shaping our vision of existence. In "the journey of a thousand years," as Plato called death, nothing could be more useful.

A Light Exercise

I conclude with some brief suggestions for experimenting with the light, and with a report from someone who tried it with interesting results.

The key to results is tenacity of intention.

So, on a regular basis, try to set aside some time; sit down, relax, and take a few deep breaths. Slowly deepen your breathing and turn your attention to your bodily sensations, to feelings, thoughts, and images, and let them drift and dissolve.

Intend now to experience the transcendent light. Trust that it is possible. Choose to be open and receptive to an extraordinary experience. Remember the experiences of untold numbers before you, and affirm with confidence that within you is a great power—as a great mystic once said— like a "Love Fire."

Imagine you feel this Love Fire warming everything near you, every cell of your body, every breath you inhale. Sense the burning power and embrace the luminous energy. Visualize the unvisualizable. Talk to your inner light self, step inside the sanctuary, and seek the unfailing bright friend within.

Repeat this in the morning and before falling asleep.

In one way or another, at one time or another, you will experience a response. It may come in a dream, as a sudden insight, or on the wave of some unexpected experience—but it will come.

It will come in exact proportion to the energy of active imagination that you put into the exercise.

Light on an Amtrak Train

A woman who attempted this experiment reported the following:

During my Thanksgiving Day vacation, I took a trip to Tarboro, North Carolina. As I was riding aboard the Amtrak train, I began reading about awakening the mystic light. Finding the information to be quite interesting, I became curious to know whether I could actually awaken this light inside me.

My experience began by focusing on a spot on the window. As the train moved along I became more and more focused on the spot, until I became absorbed in it. The state of mind I was in at the time was an emptiness of feeling. This lasted for about half an hour. I found being absorbed in the spot on the window refreshing to my mind. However, at this point, I didn't experience the light. What I recall was the feeling that something else was present. I began to imagine the spot was actually an eyeball, which after a while seemed alive, watching me. I became a little apprehensive.

It was hard for me to keep this up while I was in North Carolina, but as soon as I returned home I got back into it. At first I had a little difficulty, but after a few tries I began to focus on the image of the eyeball. The lights and television were off and everyone was asleep but me. While I continued to focus on the eyeball I began to imagine the eyeball was the light. I became a little frightened when I felt I was letting the light take over my body, so I stopped. I stopped and started about three or four times before I could surrender to the feeling of having something take me over. It was similar to what I felt when given anesthesia before surgery.

As I lay in my bed and let the light take over, it felt so good. It was like something was inside of me that was very light and lovely, something I didn't have to be afraid of. I guess the only way I can explain it is to say that it felt like the light was making soft, passionate love to my body.

I recall beginning to breathe heavily and feeling very light-hearted. The entire time this was happening, I was aware that my body seemed to be in one place while I (my soul, I guess) was in another place. I experienced this feeling twice since then, and each time it seems to get better and easier.

Coda

The experience of the light is more convincing than any proof. "I owed my deliverance," wrote Al-Ghazzali the Sufi philosopher, "not to concatenations of proofs and arguments, but to the Light that God caused to penetrate my heart." The same philosopher wrote in his book, *The Alchemy of Happiness:* "Men are asleep; when they die, they awake."

ⅹ CHAPTER 11 ⅹ

Changing Our Way of Life

The Doors named themselves after a poem by William Blake, and sang of breaking on through to the "other side." In the 1960s, drugs, sex, and rock 'n' roll were the preferred methods of breakthrough. Every age and culture has to invent its own ways of negotiating the unseen, tracking the transcendent. For two thousand years the ancient Greeks fasted and took psychedelics to induce a vision of Persephone, Goddess of the Underworld. Seeing her was the secret to a happy journey to Hades.

When the Catholic emperor Valentinian issued an edict ending these rites, the Crucifixion, the central Christian symbol of transcendence, filled the void. And it's a bloody symbol of the link between violence and religion, a fact I note because we can't afford to forget the violent side of spirituality today. The drive toward transcendence can get pretty grotesque, as we saw in the attack on the World Trade Center in 2001, and in the whole idea of spiritual martyrdom, which has a long history.

Spiritual violence takes many forms. Thirty-nine American members of a UFO cult called Heaven's Gate committed suicide in 1997, hoping to hitch a ride to the Otherworld on the tail of the Hale-Bopp comet. In their ascetic habits, eagerness for martyrdom, and apocalyptic fervor, they resembled the first Christian martyrs who often gladly embraced torture and death for the sake of their vision of paradise. Unfortunately, we shouldn't be surprised by how readily violence and spirituality intermix.

Tolly Burkan's book *Extreme Spirituality* (2001) explains how skydiving, firewalking, and treading barefoot on glass shards will open your eyes to the Infinite. One seeker used a technique of immersion in animal excrement. After a pit was dug and filled with dung, an American woman was buried in the pit; the shaman smeared the offal in her hair and stuffed it in her ears and mouth. This caused her to have a kind of near-death experience and to go out of her body. After the ordeal, she felt transformed.

A Better Way

I want to suggest a more subtle, humane, and socially useful type of spiritual experimentation—involving small but significant changes in ordinary life. The two examples I have in mind are the way we eat and the way we work. Both of these very basic human activities are bound to impact strongly on our inner life.

The reason for this seems simple. The more our brains are busy with basic survival problems, like food and shelter, the more restricted the scope of our spiritual life. When the brain relaxes, so to speak, and our immediate survival programs damp down, it's a whole lot easier to pick up signals from the outer reaches of consciousness. When the brain idles, as it were, there is more space for the play of intuition. My suggestion in this chapter is that by changing our eating and work habits it might be possible to open our psychic channels and perhaps experience intimations of the next world.

As things are today, much conspires against this happening. In plain words, we eat too much and we're too busy most of the time. There just isn't room in our lives for the unknown or the transcendent to break in. So the question is whether there are *ways of life* that might heighten our sensitivity to the unseen? Are there values and attitudes conducive to encounters with *another* existence?

Diet (the Enlarged View)

Diet is a multibillion-dollar business in America. The word is used rather narrowly to refer to losing weight for health and cosmetic reasons. But in ancient times, *diet* was about life itself, about one's "way of living, mode and rules of life." According to Liddell and Scott's *Greek Lexicon,* diet covered matters of food, but also dress, lodging, and general maintenance. Diet was the total philosophic regime, the conscious mechanics of one's lifestyle. It was about dealing with material needs—with one's consumer style—with how you take what you need from the world around you.

Food is only one aspect of consumer style, and diet for the ancients was a way to tune in to the spiritual world. Epicurus once said, "I could rival Zeus in happiness, if I had a barley biscuit and some fresh water." For some philosophers and religious ascetics fasting was a spiritual technique. Fasting is a proven and time-tested technique for cleansing the psyche—as well as the body—and opening the inner eye. Traditions worldwide agree on this.

Growing up Catholic, I remember fasting before receiving the sacrament at Sunday Mass. I bridled at this restraint, but I remember getting pleasantly clear in my head, and the experience left a taste in my memory of a certain lightness of being. After all, the Church had descended from the Eleusinian rites that sported nine-day fasts—capped by a potent entheogen. Tradition has always valued fasting. The Pythagoreans abstained from animal food and Porphyry wrote a treatise on vegetarianism. Robert Kirk, a seventeenth-century "second sight" researcher, author of *The Secret Commonwealth of Elves, Fauns & Fairies,* wrote of a clairvoyante who "took very little or no food for several years past, that she tarried in the fields overnight, saw and conversed with a people that she knew not, and . . . found herself transported to another place before day." Speaking of transportation, Saint Joseph of Copertino, star eighteenth-century levitator, fasted relentlessly.

The twentieth century saw an explosion of reports of visions of the Virgin Mary. Since the 1980s, appearances of the Blessed Virgin, seen by the children of Medjugorje, have been urging people to purify their consciousness by fasting on bread and water every Thursday. In 1987 I interviewed Father Bill Martin, formerly of Brooklyn, New York, in San Giovanni Rotundo, Italy. A convert to the faith, Martin's duty was to feed the ailing stigmatic, and recently canonized, Padre Pio, in his last years; Pio ate and drank almost nothing, joking that he got thin only when he overate. Catholic tradition is full of tales of God's athletes who fasted for months, even for years.[1] For the saints, fasting was a way of sharpening their appetite for God consciousness.

In Ghana, "most Africans who hope to be possessed on any given occasion are careful to fast. No doubt the low level of blood sugar induced dissociation."[2] Fasting facilitates spiritually useful forms of dissociation. In *The Doors of Perception,* Aldous Huxley echoes this: Enforced undereating during the Middle Ages affected collective brain chemistry, and this, Huxley believed, explains the high incidence of visionary experience in those times. Our rich modern diets might be making us opaque to such experiences. Without the right brain chemistry, the visionary potential suffers, and our conception of reality atrophies. Being victims of this decline explains the appeal of certain mind-altering drugs. For many people they're a way to circumvent the psychic evils of caloric excess.

Native American shamans went for days without eating or drinking, tiring themselves in order to become more receptive to sacred visions and hallucinations. The longest lasting pre-Christian mystery rite in the ancient world was designed to produce a vision of the Greek goddess of the underworld. For two thousand years it gave experimental proof of immortality. Celebrants at Eleusis prepared for the *epopteia*—the great vision—by fasting for nine days. At the climax of the fast, one drank a powerful entheogen. It was then that the Goddess is said to have appeared in a luminous form.

My main point here is not about fasting or psychoactive chemicals. It's about the consumer style that may be blunting our spiritual perceptiveness, our possible receptivity to the Invisibles. We used to take the deeply flawed notion of "IQ" so seriously; perhaps it's time to take the idea of spiritual "IQ" seriously.

Fasting—dread word in a culture of repast—should not be thought of in a narrow way. "Fasting" isn't just about food. We can increase our "spiritual IQ" by "fasting" in different ways: by abstaining from TV, radio, newspapers, movies, net-surfing—from *all* forms of psycho-clutter. The big point, I said, is to damp down the energetics of brain activity; open our mental space; make room for what's out there to edge its way in.

With all due respect, fasting from other people is an important part of the dietary regime I'm sketching. The monastic orders of the Middle Ages cultivated solitude—

essential, they thought, to spiritual life. This old spiritual virtue is not respected today, and may be on the verge of becoming extinct. Solitude has always been a virtue for the athletes of higher consciousness. Nowadays, it's a luxury we mostly enjoy in the sanctuary of the toilet. Technology has a way of encroaching on our ability to enjoy solitude. We're vulnerable to cell phones and telemarketers, for starters; solitude, like fasting, is hard to cultivate in our gadget-ridden world. Diet, in a broad way, is about uncluttering our minds, bodies, and lives. If we wish to open the pores of our mental existence, and if we want our psychic antennae to pick up signals from the Otherworld, diet is key.

The Way We Eat

Diet takes in many things: from solitude to abstaining from the media. But I do want to say something about eating. My point is that large issues are at stake in changing the way we eat. Consider, for example, the possibility of a vegetarian revolution. The Greek philosopher Porphyry was the author of *On Abstinence from Animal Food*. The main idea of this erudite book is that by abstaining from animal food we purify our souls and refine our spiritual vision. Certain foods, according to this disciple of Plotinus, "excite the passive part of our soul," and make it difficult to exercise spiritual energy or cultivate the contemplative life.

A contemporary philosopher, Peter Singer, has taken up the argument for vegetarianism.[3] Singer's viewpoint differs from Porphyry's. For Singer abstention from animal food should be based on concern for animal suffering, which did not concern Porphyry. Singer opposes "speciesism," the belief that humans are ethically privileged. The crucial fact is that animals, like humans, suffer and enjoy; that fact, not our verbal and rational superiority, is why we should be ethically responsible to animals.

Abstaining from animal food, according to one model, will enable us to be more conscious of the inner life of living creatures different from us. This would of course include other human beings who are different from us. Becoming vegetarians would push the ethical evolution of humanity, and expand our consciousness, so that we would be receptive to the inner life of animals, of other human beings, and spirits if they are out there.

The Metaphysics of Obesity

A recent report claimed that 14 million people are starving in Southern Africa. I heard this on the BBC. The same night I heard about the Obesity Prevention Act, instituted by New York Governor George Pataki. Something is wrong. In large parts of the world, millions are starving to death. In America, the government is trying to make overeating illegal. The problem of irrational obesity is a moral concern and a blight to health; it's also a metaphysical problem.

In traditional societies, diet was a way to exploit the physiology of higher consciousness, the spiritual value of fasting. In a time of epidemic obesity, the spiritual value of diet is easily forgotten. Eric Schlosser's *Fast Food Nation* shows in devastating detail how science, wealth, and power have joined hands in America to make it very hard to control our eating habits. The excesses aren't just bad for our health; more sinister, they cause metaphysical dis-ease—dangerous contractions of consciousness. The ancients tried to master appetite and open the eye of wisdom; today we are more concerned with stimulating appetite and distracting the eye of wisdom.

Not to equate spiritual keenness with thinness, Thomas Aquinas, who ended his life in a blaze of mystical vision, was a real tubby, weighing more than three hundred pounds. Still there seems to be a relationship between caloric reduction and heightened states of physical health *as well as* heightened states of consciousness. If so, we are presented with an opportunity for personal experiment.

A Renaissance writer, Luigi Cornaro, who lived till he was 103, wrote in his nineties: "I enjoy two lives at the same time: one, the earthly, which I possess in reality; the other, the heavenly, which I possess in thought." His vivid sense of another reality was due to the spare diet he methodically practiced, and the clarity of consciousness that entailed.

A Nigerian woman told me of her grandfather, David Uwubanmwen, who also died at the age of 103. "At the latter part of his life," she said, "he was living in two different worlds—the world of the dead and the world of the living. From time to time he was in contact with dead friends and relatives. He was always talking to them and inviting them to dine with him. I could remember two of his great friends that he constantly called, they were Osagie and Nosa. On the other hand, he was also able to communicate freely with us."

We know from accounts of deathbed visions that people on the verge of dying seem to catch glimpses of deceased relatives and otherworldly sights. They seem to slip back and forth between the two worlds. And we know of illustrious visionaries like Swedenborg and Blake, and great mediums like Gladys Leonard and Eleanora Piper, who were regular Otherworld visitors. All the indications are that intuitive glimpses of the next world are possible for most or at least for many of us, especially if we take care to change our diet.

Work and the Contemplative Life

We've talked about eating; now let's say a few words about work. The way we work, like the way we eat, is also part of our "diet." What we want to know is how our work style might influence our spiritual perception. How, if at all, can we adapt our work life to our spiritual needs? Is there a problem here? Is there a perception that *we work too much?* Working—working too much—can obliterate spiritual life. In the common frenzy to work, produce, and possess, it's easy to lose contemplative values. Clueless about contemplative life, we deprive ourselves of precious mental states, and remain locked in spiritual anesthesia.

Work: Ancient and Modern

In our work-driven world, there just isn't enough mental space to tune into the unseen spectrum; we're too frazzled to enjoy the contemplative life. We make things worse for ourselves by reinforcing unexamined assumptions. Traditionally, there are two ways of life: active and contemplative. The ancients seem to have valued the contemplative ideal of life more than the active—at least when they were not competing, or at war. The Greeks preferred the theoretical, the leisurely, to the busy *banausic,* or mechanical, life of labor. Work for the ancients was strictly for slaves—for machines, we'd say today.

Today of course we reject human slavery. But in some ways we have become a society of slaves to *work itself*—to an all-consuming ethics of productivity. So absorbed by work, so obsessed by the need to be productive, it's almost impossible to take seriously talk of the contemplative life. What? Smell the roses? Gaze at the stars? Isn't that time-consuming? And isn't time money? And isn't the world there for us to use and exploit, not contemplate? Why chase meta-physical mysteries?

In fact, for centuries in the Western world, the contem-plative vision of God was valued as the true goal of human life. Matthew's gospel (5:8) says: "Blessed are the pure of heart, for they shall see God." The great hope was to see God—a vision with heart. The supreme aim was achieved in "leisure time," a psychological place remote from the market and stock exchange. The beehive ideal of modern man, the work ethic that exalts performance above contemplation, was yet to see the light of historical day. There were fewer distractions, more opportunities for the play of higher con-sciousness.

The contemplative attitude has always been prized. "I loafe and invite my soul," said the American poet, Walt Whitman. "Consider the lilies of the field, they toil not," said Jesus, in the all-time put down of the work ethic. For the ancient Greeks and Hebrews, work was a curse. *Ponos,* Greek for work, meant "sorrow." Sinner Adam was evicted from paradise and condemned to work by the sweat of his brow. "Life," Pythagoras said, "is like a festival; some come to compete, some to ply their trade, the best people come as spectators." The Greek philosophers prized *theoria*—"see-ing," vision, the contemplative life—above the productive.

Receptivity to divine pleasure was more important than economic activity. Philo, an Alexandrian Jew, wrote about the "eye of the soul" that gives "the vision of peace." Peace, that elusive value, was a by-product of seeing, not of doing; of forming a relationship with a power beyond the worka-day world. Real hope lay not in doing, but in being, and there was no greater joy than "to see Him Who Is."[4] Egyptian mystic Macarius spoke with passion about being able "to behold and recognize the true Friend."[5] The con-templative life is a romantic quest for the sight of a True

Friend, as ancient philosophy implied a friendship with the Goddess of Wisdom.

Among ancient mystery religions, the supreme good was a visionary experience: whether of pure light, the dancing wine god, or the goddess of springtime and the underworld. In the wisdom of the ancients, human beings covet relief from the workaday mindset, and without the contemplative, the festive, we are deprived of our full humanness. Contemplative cognitive styles are essential to anyone looking to increase sensitivity to the subtle realms, the unseen—in short, Hades.

There are two ways we can know something, the active and the contemplative. The active way is focused, interested, aggressive, manipulative, and rational, suited for the highly focused business of survival in the material world. Contemplation is the opposite way: disinterested, receptive, cooperative, and intuitive. For next-world navigators, a contemplative cognitive style is needed: a way of knowing that's receptive to the *unknown,* more inclined to wonder than to dominate, open to the new and unexpected, sensitive enough to register exotic impressions and subtle presences. The active style of knowing is absorbed in mundane affairs, without much consciousness left over to register possible impressions of the Otherworld.

How We Became Obsessed by Work

How did the Western world get so obsessively busy? Scholars tell a fascinating if convoluted tale. It began through a strange piece of religious logic. During the Reformation, the Western mind shifted its allegiance—as an instrument of salvation—from the contemplative to the business life. The sociologist Max Weber has documented the Protestant invention of the work ethic. John Calvin, for example, a lawyer turned theologian (dangerous combination!) made capitalist acquisitiveness into a sacred duty and fostered the belief that successful business was the path to salvation. "What reason is there," he wrote, "why the income from business should not be larger than that from land-owning?" This attempt to validate the profit motive was anathema to medieval Christian theologians who likened it to wolves feeding off carrion. Calvin's ideas shaped the New England Puritans and pacesetters of early American life.

Profitable business is lauded to heaven and efficient productivity becomes surrogate grace. The new ideal of work led to the industrial revolution, the mechanization of life, and, as we know today, to a ruthless exploitation of nature. What did this imply for our spiritual IQ? Have there been any serious long-term effects? In 1525, Zwingili sounded the death knell of the contemplative ideal of life when he said: "In things of this life, the laborer is most like to God." This reverses Plato, Philo, and Aquinas for whom our likeness to God was best known in contemplative states, in hours of sacred idleness when we stop willing and stop thinking.

According to the new work ideal, if you want a foretaste of heaven, you have to roll up your sleeves, punch in a time card, and work your way to the Promised Land. Without denying the nobility of work, the new ideal went too far. With the industrial revolution, men acquired unheard of wealth, and the planet was overrun with work-obsessed humanity, overturning ecology and destroying indigenous cultures everywhere.

The modern ideal of work gradually won out, freed itself from Puritanical repression, and gave birth to a purely profane modern capitalism. The bottom line became the *summum bonum* and contemplative need was coopted by movies, television, DVDs, web surfing, and other voyeuristic technologies. Wealth became the new sacred power and celebrity conferred the intoxicating illusion of immortality.

During the rise to industrial power, fear of death grew in the Western world. The French historian, Philippe Aries, has chronicled the changes.[6] During the Middle Ages, and in ancient times, people accepted death; they died honestly, simply, without fanfare. As soon as they knew death was near, they arranged themselves for the event. With the rise of rationalistic capitalism, death lost its family ritual status, and became something technically managed. Acceptance changed to denial. Death has become increasingly forbidden, and, as much as possible, *invisible*. In the midst of this retreat, it's not surprising that fear of death is rising.

In an important psychological study by Charles Garfield, fear of death was found to diminish in people well practiced with altered states of consciousness.[7] Psychedelic users, for example, and Zen and Tibetan meditators, are less anxious about death than Western psychologists and theologians. Tests showed that high measures of death-anxiety correlated with the need for control and with excessive reliance on rationality. Needless to say, these two anxiety-producing virtues provide the moral backbone to the work ethic. The problem is that by practicing these virtues, which enable us so successfully to control and exploit nature, we also magnify our death-anxiety. As psychologist Edmund Jacobson has observed, the more effort we expend to exert control on the world, the more exposed we are to sensations of anxiety.

A release from the tyranny of effort is indicated, and exercises associated with the contemplative life take on new meaning. In Garfield's study, people accustomed to altered states of consciousness were more at ease with the idea of "nonbeing." Death became imaginable as a "trip" or journey or transformation. Among meditators and other aviators of altered states, death was interpreted to be another altered state. The implication of this study by Charles Garfield is that if we changed our attitude toward work, and spent more time in contemplative life, the prospect of death would generate less anxiety.

In the contemplative mode, in a lifestyle that cultivates radical openness of consciousness, we are more prone to having experiences suggestive of Otherworld realities. By contrast, in our work-driven world, consciousness cannot afford that kind of openness, and so is easily captured by the mundane, and contracted by anxious concerns. To tune into signals from the other side, we would need to reduce the noise and clutter of our lives. Rethinking, reframing our idea of work implies change in our *diet*—our way of life—change that would alleviate death-anxiety, and open the gates to Otherworld perception. What can we do to implement some of these possibilities?

A Neglected Evolutionary Potential

In most of our lives, there's a melancholy gap between our idea of what we may be and what we actually are. The solution lies in a neglected evolutionary potential we all possess. There is an inner resource we can use to change our lives and open ourselves to the inner forces of self-transformation. If we are looking for compelling intuitions of the next world, there is one common capacity, vastly underrated, that might pave the way. So let me conclude with a few remarks on this dark horse—this evolutionary sleeper.

"Now man is a creature of will, according to what his will is in the world, so will he be when he has departed from this life," writes the unknown author of the Upanishads. It is hard to predict what would happen if enough people became aware that a powerful and perfectly natural source of self-renewal was latent within them. For the most part, however, conscious voluntary activity is rare, as we are swept along by the twin tides of unconscious ideas and external events. This seems especially true in our age of information overload and corporate soul-snatching.

To combat this trend toward mind-control, we need to wake up to the unused potential of our voluntary intelligence. We are learning, thanks to psychologist Daniel Goleman, to recognize our emotional intelligence. We also need to recognize the value of our voluntary intelligence. For this is the basis of success in all the spiritual practices we talked about in the last chapter, as well as the basis of the lifestyle changes discussed in this chapter. We need to nurture awareness of this flickering inner power we call our will before taking up *any* spiritual practice.

Voluntary intelligence is key to the Yoga Sutras of Patanjali. This is indicated by the Hindu word, *yama,* meaning "restraint" or "inhibition." *Yama* is the royal road to the *siddhis,* or "attainments," and thus to the Otherworld. Or take a different example: Philosophy, according to Plato, is the practice of the soul freeing itself from the body—the practice of dying. This practice, or craft, of dying is based on the exercise of voluntary intelligence. The soul, to use Platonic language, must "drill" itself for "departure" to the Otherworld. The first step is to detach us from focusing too much on bodily pains and pleasures; one has to decide, marshal one's forces, fix or let go of attention. It is the sort of business we crudely refer to as "will power."

Unfortunately, the will is suspect nowadays, and for different reasons has acquired a bad name. People link strong wills to domineering personalities. And the musty Victorian, demented Hitlerian, connotations of "will power" are suspect. For some the words "will power" imply little more than "power trip." Doctrinaire materialism also adds to the animus against the will. Prozac, not Plato,[8] gene therapy not self-responsibility, are proffered as answers to all our problems. The spotlight today is on damaging childhood experiences, social injustice, genetic fatalism. Art critic Robert Hughes castigates us for being a "culture of complaint," for dwelling on ourselves as victims of bad luck, prejudice and circumstance. Talk of personal responsibility is construed as old-fashioned existentialism or anal Republicanism. With such bad press it's easy to underrate the importance of our voluntary intelligence and its central role in our lives.

Part of the problem is our narrow conception of will. The "strong will" is our main association, but strong will is just part of what we need, if we hope to whittle away the partition between this and the next world. The will needs muscle but it also needs skill. The skillful will is more like an impresario than a drill sergeant, a musical conductor than a prison guard. And let's not forget the idea of good will, another trait of our voluntary intelligence, more dormant in most of us than active. Good will implies being impartially well disposed toward all sentient beings. The spirit of good will lifts us beyond personal interests toward larger purposes, as the founder of psychosynthesis, Roberto Assagioli, remarks.[9] The great mystics have built their practical psychology on the premise of a higher will. "If we could stop willing for one hour," said the shoemaker mystic Jacob Boehme, "we would see God."

Fixing attention on something is all the will accomplishes, according to a famous essay by William James. James points out that we become "weak-willed" when our heads are crowded with competing ideas. In a market-driven culture, attention is a precious commodity, and the market vies for our attention, bombards us with options, makes us dizzy with possibilities. The more confused by a culture suffering from attention deficit disorder, the harder to marshal the will to be open to transcendent experience. In general, the spiritual teachers—Christian mystics, Hindu yogis, Greek philosophers—agree that enlightenment now is possible. Invaluable insights into deeper recesses of reality are open to us all. Gaining the wisdom that reconciles us to our mortality, and frees us for a fuller life, is possible now. But to achieve this is impossible without an alert voluntary intelligence.

Everything depends on how we deploy our attention. The busy conditions of external life work against our inner life. Still, the fullness of conscious experience is possible, and the openings to transcendence can always be explored. With "right effort," we can dehypnotize ourselves and break the mental habits that bind us to the treadmill of our everyday selves.

Epilogue

"*I* want out," said Mrs. James, prompting nurse Osborn to call for Dr. Yessod. Mrs. James was causing a ruckus, demanding that she be released from her body without further ado. It was getting to be a common sight in transitoriums all over the country: Dying patients cheerfully egging the nurses on to pull the plug and let them die. "I want out," repeated Mrs. James, "straight out through my crown chakra!"

Her voice barely rose to a soft cry, and it would have been comical if it weren't so serious. The records showed that Mrs. James was an accomplished meditator and out-of-body traveler, had worked for years in the psychomanteum, and was successful with the Arizona group mediumship project. She was more than ready for transit, but medication and painkillers were slowing things up. She was becoming unmanageable, very headstrong and very inconsiderate—forgetting that her son and daughter were en route, one flying from the West coast and the other from Paris—anxious to join her in her last hours. Dr. Yessod stepped out of the elevator and took the sharp turn to Mrs. James's room. He *smiled at the impatient lady. It was indeed becoming a problem—restraining dying people from wanting to rush prematurely into transition.*

Needless to say, this is not a tale of time present but a picture of how people may one day experience the end of their lives. In my opinion, the picture isn't that fantastic. We've presented real evidence that death may indeed be transitional, not terminal. And as we saw, there are skills we can learn to facilitate the transition. My bet is that the Transitorium—the hospice of the future—will turn out to be more than a science fiction fantasy.

Afterlife research promises eventually to create a much-needed revolution in medicine. In the present culture of medical materialism, death is the ultimate failure, and marks the moment the doctor throws up his hands in helpless resignation. All that may one day change.

Modern medicine is fine with technologies that postpone the inevitable, but the results are not always conducive to a "good" death. For one thing, in prolonging life at all costs, we prolong suffering and consume inordinate economic resources. In a brave book, *Reinventing Medicine,*[1] physician Larry Dossey describes what he calls "our war on death" and quotes a statement from Harvard physician Rodney H. Falk on the indignities we suffer in our death-denying culture, "where patients, regardless of mental status or the irreversibility of disease, are treated until the bitter end when they lie bloated, bleeding, and crushed after the final flurry of infusions and cardiac massage."

But suppose medical professionals learned to reframe the concept of death, and transform the hospice into a transitorium. Suppose medical science concluded there *is* reason to believe in an afterlife. No longer would we see death as a terrible enemy or accept without question the current "war against death." Much expense and emotional distress would be avoided. The idea of a "good death" would acquire a clear meaning. A good death would imply *being ready for the transition*—like our imaginary Mrs. James. By then, of course, medicine will require new kinds of skills and we will need new next-world guides and guidebooks.

Today, what we call "end of life care" is anything but optimal. "Alleviating the problems faced by dying persons and their families has drawn substantial public attention," begins a 1997 report in the *Annals of Internal Medicine*. Technological intervention can go only so far; we need new ways of assisting dying patients. Research has recently focused on the therapeutic value of religion and spirituality, and the idea of a "quality comfortable death" has been broached. That means "attending to the social, psychological, and the now recognized spiritual and religious dimensions of care." Hopelessness and depression aren't caused by the pain of dying, we are told, but by a "pessimistic cognitive style," by being overwhelmed by the negativity of dying. For most dying people, death implies the end of meaning. This, however, would change, once it became possible to realistically imagine a life after the present one.

The shock I described in the Introduction to this book— of discovering my mortality—forced me to explore things I would have otherwise ignored. Never, for example, did I suspect there was real evidence for life after death, or that it came in so many forms. Hauntings, for example, are as commonplace today as they were in early times. Out-of-body experiences continue to be widely reported. Mediumship seems to be making a comeback. And who knows how many rebirth cases have eluded the nets of Dr. Stevenson and his colleagues?

People experience themselves as temporarily separate from their bodies in states of ecstasy, during so-called out-of-body experiences. Ecstasy may be the most powerful antidote to metaphysical depression. The objective truth of the out-of-body experience has been proven; people "leave" their bodies and interact with distant objects. From a separate room, Alex Tanous identified visual targets correctly, and caused localized physical effects.

Apparitions and hauntings support the view that *something* becomes objectively present, that *something* is localized in public space. Especially interesting are collectively and reciprocally observed apparitions. These may be simultaneous, as when seven people and a dog reacted to Andre's ghost, or successive, in the case of Rose Morton's frequently observed phantasm. Elusive and taciturn, ghosts seem to pop briefly into public space. Temperature drops reported around them have been measured, and some revenants impart information unknown to any living person.

The best evidence from mediumship shows survival of the full personality. George Pellew, for example, kept a promise, pursued a goal with tenacity, remembered his intimate friends and family, and behaved like the man he was when he was kicking about in his body. George, speaking through Leonora Piper, flawlessly identified, and talked intimately with just the people he knew in life, and no others. This performance was nothing fly by night but went on for several years.

Is the surviving spirit a person? If by person we mean a conscious agent with memories, a being that acts freely and with purpose, the answer is yes. So, for example, the dead James Chaffin Sr. had to straighten out unfinished business; the Rumanian phantom was piqued over the fate of his corpse. Cross-correspondence cases reveal purpose, high intelligence, and retention of complex memories. Uninvited spirits show up during séances and manifest for reasons of their own. In line with many traditions, survival occurs through reincarnation, enlarging our view of human selfhood and adding new dimensions to depth psychology.

Perhaps the biggest obstacle to belief in survival is not lack of evidence but a timid view of human personality. For me the evidence destroys any cocksureness I might have had about the mind-matter riddle. Mind is no impotent by-product of the brain—far from it.

Our evidence—and this is the practical point—has implications for the art of living. Out-of-body experiences speak to our ecstatic potential; apparitional experiences to our latent visionary talents. Mediumship proves the polycentric nature of personal consciousness; the "I" we cling to so fiercely is somewhat of a sham, a delusion, and very superficial. There are other "I's," deeper and more interesting than the little I that rides the rickety wagon of my surface consciousness. Tapping into the deeper self is part of our creative endowment.

For myself, the often highly suggestive evidence is not quite enough. Reincarnation studies reveal the temporal depth of the human personality, its "eternal" aspect. In the course of my search I came to feel the need to experience the larger self, the timeless aspect of my personality. Without personal experience, all the evidence in the world isn't enough. Our afterlife research paradigm must be more practical, and I have tried to show in what sense experiencing the next world is possible.

One way is to recreate certain practices from shamanic and mystical traditions. Seeing the spirits, leaving the body, experiencing the light, all describe ways of making ourselves more open, more sensitive and transparent to the Otherworld. A dream, a memory, a moment of inspired imagination, an act of the will—such may grant any one of us a glimpse, a taste, an echo of transcendence. When we measure these private flashes of insight against our rich database, even small experiences, rightly honored, gain authority and inspire us to pursue our explorations.

Another way is to tweak some of the variables of our daily lifestyle. The habits of everyday life make us opaque to the Otherworld. I invoked the ancient meaning of the word *diet*. We can change our diet—our way of life—so that our minds and bodies become more sensitive instruments for detecting signals of the transcendent. How we eat, how we work, whether we meditate and value silence and stillness, whether we honor solitude, can slow the working pace of our existence—these, and other facets of practical life, need to become part of our changed "diet" and general lifestyle.

We prefer not to admit that fear of death subtly pervades our lives. No matter how successful repression may be, it always lurks in the background, and threatens to leap like a black cat into our consciousness. And, in fact, consciousness sometimes seems, as Dostoyevsky once said, to be a kind of sickness, an evolutionary mistake. It knows too much.

"A man should be able to say he has done his best to form a conception of life after death," said Carl Jung, "or to create some image of it—even if he must confess his failure. Not to have done so is a vital loss." I hope I've provided some materials for re-creating the reader's image of life after death. I have for myself, but first I had to put aside useless religious dogmas, and I refused to be bullied by dogmatic materialist science. Above all, I was inspired by countless stories people have told me, stories that continually suggest that much more is going on behind the familiar everyday façade of existence. Just as the physicists have long persuaded us that our senses conceal a wonderland of cosmic forces and micro-particles in nature, so should an expanded psychology enable us to imagine a hidden multiverse of mind.

"The wretched consciousness shrinks from its own death," wrote Miguel de Unamuno in the *Tragic Sense of Life*. Fame, history, achievement are all methods we use in the struggle to deal with the fear of death. The struggle never stops for most of us. "Animals let death be a part of life," wrote Norman O. Brown in *Life Against Death*, whereas, "man aggressively builds immortal cultures and makes history in order to fight death." We see proof of Brown's insight everywhere around us. Brown concludes that the way to restore the peaceful unity of life and death is to "eroticize" our consciousness, in other words, learn to enjoy life, quit the fruitless struggle to conquer death by being high achievers. Psychical research invites us to face death with tranquility, by keeping open the door to meaning beyond this life, and by taking the teeth out of our death-anxiety. And it promises to help us live more fully in the present.

In his Pulitzer Prize–winning book, *The Denial of Death*, Ernest Becker wrote that "the idea of death, the fear of it, haunts the human animal like nothing else; it is the mainspring of human activity—activity designed largely to avoid the fatality of death, to overcome it by denying in some way that it is the final destiny for man." Becker describes in detail how this denial shapes and misshapes our lives. Whether by grasping for power, trying to make up for our feelings of impotence, or by renouncing our own power, the result is always a diminished quality of life. The word for this diminishment is *neurosis*. "The ironic thing about the narrowing-down of neurosis is that the person seeks to avoid death, but he does it by killing off so much of himself . . ."

Unless we question the assumptions of the modern view, there is no way out of the battle against death, which so distorts and diminishes us. If we question the assumptions, especially in light of the data of this book, we will be able to think about life and death in new ways. A new affirmation of life would be possible, and new channels for repressed energies would open up.

What is this "self" we're so deeply attached to in the first place? Are we molecules of matter or monads of consciousness? What really is consciousness? Consciousness that results from stimulating nervous tissue, according to the great Darwinian Thomas Huxley, "is just as magical as the appearance of Djin when Aladdin rubbed his lamp." In 1991, scientific philosopher Daniel Dennett wrote: "Consciousness stands alone today as a topic that often leaves even the most sophisticated thinkers tongue-tied and confused." According to philosopher Colin McGinn, it's an insoluble mystery "how technicolor phenomenology can arise from gray soggy matter."

So consciousness is the last frontier of scientific research. The pattern of evidence we have collected suggests that we survive the death of our brains. If so, this fact alone is enough to revolutionize consciousness research, for it implies that our strange and poignant capacity to be self-aware is not just a puzzling outgrowth on the fringes of biological nature, but something original and elemental.

This exploration of the afterlife riddle has forced us to go deeper into ourselves. A great deal of evidence points to a profound mental life below the threshold of ordinary self-awareness. Drop the threshold and experiences of the next world become possible. The floodgates open and no one can predict what will emerge.

So the solution to the enigma of death must be in our reach, a question of changing, of freeing and mobilizing our consciousness. For the Otherworld is nearby—a sudden turn of the corner, an unexpected clearing. Perceiving the truth should be no stranger, no harder than waking from a dream. A thin veil prevents us from beholding it face-to-face.

Notes

Introduction

1. Michael Grosso, *Soulmaking* (Charlottesville: Hampton Roads Publishing, 1997).
2. Charles Fort, *The Complete Books of Charles Fort* (New York: Dover, 1974), p. 3.
3. Frederic Myers, *Fragments of Prose and Poetry* (London: Longmans, Green, and Co., 1904), p. 33.
4. Alan Gauld, *The Founders of Psychical Research* (London: Routledge & Kegan Paul, 1968).
5. Charles Boer, *Marsilio Ficino: The Book of Life* (Dallas, Texas: Spring Publications, 1980), p. xiii.

Chapter 1

1. John G. Neihardt, *Black Elk Speaks* (New York: Pocket Books, 1972).
2. Mircea Eliade, *Shamanism: Archaic Techniques of Ecstasy* (Princeton, N.J.: Princeton University Press, 1964).
3. D. Sheils, "A Cross-Cultural Survey of Beliefs in Out-of-Body Experiences," *Journal of the Society for Psychical Research* 49 (1978), pp. 697–741.
4. Charles Tart, ed., "My Search for the Soul," *Body Mind Spirit* (Charlottesville, Va.: Hampton Roads, 1997), pp. 50–67.

5. See Celia Green, *Out-of-the-Body Experiences* (New York: Ballantine Books, 1968: Carlos Alvarado, "Out-of-Body Experiences," in *Varieties of Anomalous Experience,* Etzel, Cardena et al, eds., (Washington, D.C.: American Psychological Association, 2002), pp. 183–218.
6. Augustine of Hippo, *The City of God* (New York: Penguin Books, 1980), pp. 783–784.
7. J. H. M. Whiteman, *The Mystical Life* (London: Faber and Faber, 1961), p. 57.
8. Frederic Myers, *Human Personality and Its Survival of Death* (London: Longmans, Green, and Co., 1903).
9. Green, ibid., pp.142–143
10. Charles Tart, "A Psychophysiological Study of Out-of-Body Experiences," *Journal of the American Society for Psychical Research* 62 (1968), pp. 3–27.
11. Karlis Osis and Donna McCormick, "Kinetic Effects at the Ostensible Location of an Out-of-Body Projection During Perceptual Testing," *Journal of the American Society for Psychical Research* 74 (1980), pp. 319–330.

Chapter 2

1. Grosso, *Soulmaking,* ibid, pp. 175–176.
2. Zoe Richmond, *Evidence of Purpose* (London: G. Bell & Sons, 1938), p. 33.
3. Henry Sidgwick and Committee, "Report on Census of Hallucinations" *English Proceedings of Psychical Research,* X (1894), pp. 5–422.
4. Raymond Marcel, *Marsile Ficin* (Paris: Societé d'Édition, 1958), p. 579.
5. Ibid., Census of Hallucinations, p. 227.
6. Camille Flammarion, *Haunted Houses* (London: Fisher Unwin, 1924), p. 56.
7. Ibid., Census pp. 383–385.
8. Ibid., pp. 371–373.
9. Ernesto Bozzano, "Apparitions of Deceased Persons at Deathbeds," *The Annals of Psychical Science* 3 (1906), pp. 67–100.
10. William Barrett, *Deathbed Visions* (London: Methuen, 1926), p. 2.

11. Barrett, ibid., p. 25.

12. George Gallup Jr. with William Proctor, *Adventures in Immortality* (New York: McGraw Hill, 1985), p. 85.

13. Barrett, ibid., pp. 72–74.

14. Karlis Osis, *Deathbed Observations by Physicians and Nurses* (New York: Parapsychology Foundation, 1961).

15. Ibid., p. 23.

16. Karlis Osis and Erlendur Haraldsson, *At The Hour of Death* (New York: Avon, 1977).

17. Walter Cannon, "'Voodoo' Death," *American Anthropologist* 44, no. 2 (1942), pp. 169–181.

18. Paul Edwards, *Immortality* (New York: Prometheus Books, 1997).

19. Brierre de Boisement, *On Hallucinations* (London: Henry Renshaw, 1859).

20. Emily Williams Cook, Bruce Greyson, and Ian Stevenson, "Do Any Near-Death Experiences Provide Evidence for the Survival of Human Personality After Death?" *Journal of Scientific Explanation* 12, no. 3, pp. 377–406.

21. Michael Sabom, *Recollections of Death* (New York: Harper & Row, 1981).

22. Michael Sabom, *Light and Death* (New York: Zondervan, 1998).

23. Kenneth Ring and Sharon Cooper, *Mindsight: Near-Death and Out-of-Body Experiences in the Blind* (Palo Alto, Calif.: William James Center for Consciousness Studies, 1999).

24. Henri Ellenberger, *The Discovery of the Unconscious* (New York: Basic Books, 1970), p. 74.

25. Herbert Thurston, *The Physical Phenomena of Mysticism* (London: Burns Oates, 1954), pp. 294–325; see also Anthony Walsh, "Mollie Fancher: Psychological Marvel of the 19th century," *Newport, the Magazine of the Newport College* 1 (1978), p. 2.

26. See Thurston, ibid., who quotes a Dr. Ormiston on page 300: "It seems incredible, but from everything I can learn, Mollie Fancher never eats."

27. Thurston, ibid., p. 302.

28. Arthur Varagnac, "The Problem of Prehistoric Religions" in *Larousse World Mythology,* Pierre Grimal, ed. (Secaucus, N.J.: Chartwell Books, 1976).

29. Zoe Richmond, *Evidence of Purpose* (London: G. Bell & Sons, 1938), p.43.

30. Ibid., pp. 33–34.

31. Ibid., pp. 28–32.

32. Robert Almeder, *Death and Personal Survival* (Lanham, Md.: Rowman & Littlefield Publishers, 1992), pp. 100–102, 121–124.

33. Janet and Colin Bord, *Unexplained Mysteries of the 20th Century* (Chicago: Contemporary Books, 1989), p. 90.

34. Rose Morton, "Record of a Haunted House," *Proceedings of the Society for Psychical Research* 7 (1892), pp. 311–332.

35. Frederic Myers, "The Subliminal Self," *Proceedings of the Society for Psychical Research* (1895), pp. 547–559.

Chapter 3

1. Stanley Krippner and Susan Marie Powers, *Broken Images, Broken Selves: Dissociative Narratives in Clinical Practice* (Washington, D.C.: Brunner/Mazel,1997), p. 8.

2. Nea Walker, *The Bridge: A Case for Survival* (London: Cassell, 1927).

3. D. Dewi Rees, "The Hallucinations of Widowhood," *British Medical Journal* 4, 1971, pp. 37–41.

4. James H. Hyslop, "The Thompson-Gifford Case," *International Journal of Parapsychology* 9 (1967), pp. 108–124.

5. Richard Hodgson, "A Further Record of Observations of Certain Phenomena of Trance," *Proceedings of the Society for Psychical Research* 33 1898 pp. 284–582.

6. Alan Gauld, *Mediumship and Survival* (London: Heineman, 1982), p. 61.

7. Erlendur Haraldsson and Ian Stevenson, "A Communicator of the 'Drop-In' Type in Iceland," *Journal of the American Society for Psychical Research.* 69 (1975).

8. Eleanor Sidgwick, "An Examination of Book Tests Obtained in Sittings with Mrs. Leonard," *Proceedings of the Society for Psychical Research* 31 (1921), pp. 253–260.

9. Peter Glenconner, *The Earthen Vessel* (London: John Lane, 1921), p. 33.

10. H. F. Saltmarsh, *Evidence for Personal Survival From Cross-Correspondences* (London: Bell & Sons, 1938).

11. Gardner Murphy, *The Challenge of Psychical Research* (New York: Harper, 1961), p. 273.

Notes

285

12. See C. Drayton Thomas, "A Proxy Experiment of Significant Success," *Proceedings of the Society for Psychical Research* 44 (1936–37), p. 295.

Chapter 4

1. Curt Ducasse, *A Critical Examination of the Belief in a Life After Death* (Springfield, Ill.: Charles C. Thomas, 1961), Part V.
2. Morey Bernstein, *The Search for Bridey Murphy* (New York: Pocket Books, 1956).
3. Tom Schroder, *Old Souls: The Scientific Evidence for Past Lives* (New York: Simon & Schuster, 1999).
4. Satwant K. Pasricha, "Cases of the Reincarnation Type in South India," *Journal of Scientific Exploration* 15, no. 2, pp. 211–221.
5. James B. Tucker, "A Scale to Measure the Strength of Children's Claims of Previous Lives: Methodology and Initial Findings," *Journal of Scientific Exploration* 14, pp. 571–581.
6. Antonia Mills and Richard Slobodin, eds., *Amerindian Rebirth: Reincarnation Belief Among North American Indians and Inuit* (Toronto University Press, 1994).
7. Paul Edwards, *Immortality* (Amherst, New York: Prometheus Books, 1997). For a general critique of the survival hypothesis, pp. 1–70.
8. Ian Stevenson, *Children Who Remember Previous Lives* (Charlottesville: University Press of Virginia, 1987).
9. Ibid., p. 113.
10. Ian Stevenson, *Where Biology and Reincarnation Intersect* (Westport, Conn.: Praeger Publications, 1997); Ian Stevenson, *Reincarnation and Biology* (Westport, Conn.: Praeger, 1997). Two volumes.
11. Marilyn Schlitz and William Braud, "Distant Intentionality and Healing: Assessing the Evidence," *Alternative Therapies* 3, no. 6 (1997) pp. 62–73.
12. Ian Stevenson, *Twenty Cases Suggestive of Reincarnation* (Charlotttesville: University Press of Virginia, 1974), pp. 111–149.
13. Stevenson, ibid., p. 155
14. Ellenberger, ibid., pp. 331–417.
15. Stanislav Grof, *Realms of the Human Unconscious* (New York: Viking Press, 1975).

Chapter 5

1. J. Munves, "Richard Hodgson, Mrs. Piper and 'George Pelham': A Centennial Reassessment," *Journal of the Society for Psychical Research,* Oct. V. 62, no. 849 (1997), pp. 138–154.

2. Richard Hodgson, "The Possibilities of Mal-observation and Lapse of Memory," *Proceedings of the Society for Psychical Research* 7 (1886), pp. 381–493.

3. Ian Stevenson, "Cryptomnesia and Parapsychology," *The Journal of the American Society for Psychical Research* 52 (1983), p. 1-30.

4. Daryl Treffert, *Extraordinary People* (New York: Harper & Row, 1989).

5. Hereford Carrington, *Eusapia Palladino and Her Phenomena* (New York: Dodge, 1909).

6. Anita Muhl, *Automatic Writing* (New York: Helix Press, 1963).

7. Gardner Murphy, *Three Papers on the Survival Problem* (New York: Society for Psychical Research, 1945), p. 76.

8. S. G. Soal, "A Report on Some Communications Received Through Mrs. Blanche Cooper, *Proceedings of the Society for Psychical Research* 35 (1925), pp. 471–594.

9. Otto Rank, *The Double* (New York: New American Library, 1971).

10. Stephen Braude, "Dissociation and Survival: A Reappraisal of the Evidence. In *Parapsychology and Thanatology,* Lisette Coly and Joan McMahon, eds. (New York: Parapsychology Foundation, 1993), pp. 208–237.

11. Ian Stevenson, *Xenoglossy: A Review and a Report of a Case* (Bristol: Wright, 1974).

12. David Griffin, *Parapsychology, Philosophy, and Spirituality* (New York: State University of New York Press, 1997).

Chapter 6

1. H. H. Price, "Survival and the Idea of Another World," *Proceedings of the Society for Psychical Research* 50 (1953), p. 123.

2. Keith Campbell, *Body and Mind* (New York: Anchor Books, 1970), pp. 91–92.

3. John Godbey Jr., "Parapsychology and Central-State Materialism,"

Antony Flew, ed., *Readings in the Philosophical Problems of Parapsychology* (New York: Prometheus Books, 1987), pp. 65–70.

Chapter 7

1. Frederic Myers, *Human Personality and Its Survival of Bodily Death* (London: Longmans, Green, 1903).
2. Julian Huxley, *Evolution in Action* (New York: Harper & Row, 1953), p. 34.
3. Ibid., p. 149.
4. Ray Kurzweil, *The Age of Spiritual Machines* (New York: Penguin, 2000).
5. Timothy Leary, *Design for Dying* (San Francisco: HarperEdge, 1997), pp. 167–178.
6. Alfred Russel Wallace, *Miracles and Modern Spiritualism* (London: Spiritualist Press, 1878).
7. Colm Kelleher, "Retrotransposons as Engines of Human Bodily Transformation," *Journal of Scientific Exploration* 13.1 (1999), pp. 9–24.
8. Henri Bergson, *Creative Evolution* (New York: Modern Library, 1944), p. 295.
9. Michael Murphy, *The Future of the Body* (San Francisco: Tarcher, 1992).
10. Rupert Sheldrake, *Dogs That Know When Their Owners Are Coming Home* (New York: Crown Publishers, 1999).

Chapter 8

1. Wilder Penfield, *The Excitable Cortex in Conscious Man* (Liverpool: Liverpool University Press, 1958).
2. Darold Treffert, *Extraordinary People* (New York: Doubleday, 1989).
3. H. Relinger, "Hypnotic Hypernesia," *American Journal of Clinical Hypnosis* (1984).
4. Claire Sylvia and William Novak, *A Change of Heart* (New York: Little Brown & Company, 1997).
5. Swami Nikhilananda, *The Upanishads* (New York: Torchbooks, 1963).

6. R. H. Thouless and B. P. Wiesner, "The Psi Process in Normal and Paranormal Psychology," *Proceedings of the Society for Psychical Research* (1947), pp. 177–196.

7. Robert Van de Castle, *Our Dreaming Mind* (New York: Ballantine, 1994). All the references to dreams from here to page 178 may be found in this text.

8. Stanley Krippner, Montague Ullman, and Alan Vaughan, *Dream Telepathy* (New York: Macmillan, 1973).

9. Carl Jung, *Man and His Symbols* (Garden City, N. J.: Doubleday, 1964).

10. Gordon Globus, *Dream Life, Wake Life* (Albany, N.Y.: State University of New York Press, 1987).

11. Marie-Louise von Franz, *On Dreams and Death* (Boston: Shambhala, 1987).

12. Antonia Mills, "Nightmares in Western Children: An Alternative Interpretation Suggested by Data in Three Cases," *Journal of the American Society for Psychical Research* 9 88, no. 4 (1994), pp. 309–326.

13. J. R. Harris, *Egyptian Art* (New York: Spring Books, 1966).

14. James Hyslop, *Psychical Research and the Resurrection* (Boston: Maynard & Company, 1908).

15. Suzi Gablik, *Living the Magical Life* (Grand Rapids, Mich.: Phanes Press, 2002).

Chapter 9

1. A. P. Elkin, *Aboriginal Men of High Degree* (New York: St. Martin's Press, 1977).

2. Dannion Brinkley, *Saved by the Light* (New York: Villard Books, 1994).

3. Ernst Arbman, *Ecstasy or Religious Trance* (Scandinavian University Books, 1968), p. 190.

4. Mircea Eliade, *Yoga: Immortality and Freedom* (New York: Pantheon Books, 1958).

5. Erlendur Haraldsson, *Miracles Are My Calling Cards: An Investigative Report on the Psychic Phenomena Associated with Sathya Sai Baba* (London: Century Paperbacks, 1987).

6. Herbert Thurston, *The Physical Phenomena of Mysticism* (London: Burns-Oates, 1952).

7. Joan Cruz, *The Incorruptibles* (Rockford, Ill: Tan Books, 1977).

8. Carl Jung, *"Flying Saucers: A Modern Myth of Things Seen in the Sky.* In Civilization in Transition (New York: Random House, 1964), pp. 307–436.

9. Ken Ring, *The Omega Project* (New York: William Morrow, 1984).

10. John Mack, *Passport to the Cosmos* (New York: Crown Publishers, 1999).

11. Karlis Osis and Donna McCormick, "A Poltergeist Case Without an Identifiable Living Agent," *Journal of the American Society for Psychical Research* 74 (1982), pp. 23–51.

12. David Fontana, "A Responsive Poltergeist," *Journal of the Society for Psychical Research* 57 (1991), pp. 385–402.

13. David Hufford, *The Terror That Comes in the Night* (Philadelphia: University of Pennsylvania Press, 1982).

14. Alexander Imich, ed, *Incredible Tales of the Paranormal* (New York: Bramble Books, 1995), pp. 47–95.

15. R. G. Medhurst, *Crookes and the Spirit World* (New York: Taplinger, 1972).

16. Jean Burton, *Heyday of a Wizard* (London: Harrap, 1948).

17. Alexander Imich, ed., *Incredible Tales of the Paranormal: Documented Accounts of Poltergeist, Levitations, Phantoms, and Other Phenomena.* (New York: Bramble Books, 1995), pp. 123–157.

18. Kenneth Batcheldor, "Macro-PK in Group Sittings: Theoretical and Practical Aspects." Unpublished, 1968.

19. John Klimo, *Channeling* (Los Angeles: Tarcher, 1987). The material discussed on this page was based on an email communication from the author.

20. Charles Permutt, *Photographing the Spirits* (Wellingborough: Aquarian Press, 1983).

21. Jule Eisenbud, *The World of Ted Serios* (New York: William Morrow, 1967).

Chapter 10

1. Peter Freuchen, *Book of the Eskimos* (Greenwich, Conn.: Fawcett, 1961).

2. John Lame Deer, *Seeker of Visions* (New York: Simon & Schuster, 1972).

3. Theodore Bestermann, *Crystal-Gazing* (New Hyde Park: University Books, 1965).

4. Goodrich-Freer, "Recent Experiments in Crystal Vision," *Proceedings of the Society for Psychical Research* 5 (1889), p. 508.

5. Arthur Hastings, and others, "Psychomanteum Research: Experiential Phenomena and Effects on Feelings About Deceased Friends and Relatives." Presented at 42nd Annual Convention of the Parapsychological Association. 1999.

6. Raymond Moody, "Family Reunions: Visionary Encounters With the Departed in a Modern-Day Psychomanteum," *Journal of Near-Death Studies* (1992) Winter, pp. 83–121.

7. Charles Honorton, "Psi and Internal States," *Handbook of Parapsychology*, Benjamin Wolman, ed. (New York: Van Nostrand, (1977), pp. 459–465

8. D. Scott Rogo, *Leaving the Body* (Englewood Cliffs, N.J.: Prentice Hall, 1983).

9. Robert Peterson, *Out of Body Experiences* (Charlottesville: Hampton Roads Publishing, 1997).

10. Van de Castle, ibid., pp. 444–448.

11. Stephen LaBerge, *Lucid Dreaming* (New York: Ballantine, 1986).

12. Evans-Wentz, *Tibetan Yoga and Secret Doctrines* (London: Oxford University Press, 1958).

13. Melvin Morse, with P. Perry, *Transformed by the Light* (New York: Ivy Books, 1992).

14. Richard Bucke, *Cosmic Consciousness* (New York: E. P. Dutton, 1969).

15. Kenneth Ring, *Heading Toward Omega* (New York: William Morrow, 1984).

16. Michael Grosso, *Soulmaking* (Charlottesville: Hampton Roads Publishing, 1997).

17. Mircea Eliade, *The Two and the One* (New York: Harper Torchbooks, 1965).

18. Nikhilananda, *The Upanishads* (New York: Harper Torchbooks, 1963).

19. Eliade, ibid., p. 77.

20. Eliade, ibid., p. 64.

21. Thurston, ibid., p. 218.

22. Garma Chang, *Teachings of Tibetan Yoga* (New York: University Books, 1963).

23. Ibid.
24. Henry Corbin, *The Man of Light in Iranian Sufism* (Lebanon, N.Y.: Omega Publications, 1971).
25. Ibid., p. 80.

Chapter 11

1. Thurston, ibid., p. 341–348.
2. Frank Field, *Spirit Mediumship and Society in Africa* (New York: Africana Publishing, 1969).
3. Peter Singer, *Animal Liberation* (New York: Avon Books, 1975).
4. Kenneth E. Kirk, *The Vision of God,* (New York: Harper Torchbooks, 1966), p. 39.
5. Ibid., p. 193.
6. Philippe Aries, *Western Attitudes Toward Death* (Baltimore: John Hopkins University Press, 1974).
7. Charles Garfield, "Consciousness Alteration and Fear of Death," *The Journal of Transpersonal Psychology* (1975), p. 7.
8. See the book by Lou Marinoff, *Plato Not Prozac* (New York: HarperCollins, 1999).
9. Roberto Assagioli, *The Act of Will* (New York: The Viking Press, 1973).

Epilogue

1. Larry Dossey, *Reinventing Medicine* (1999), p. 203.

Acknowledgments

Many people have helped me in writing this book, and I want to express my warm thanks to them. To Marilyn Schlitz, and the Institute for Noetic Sciences, who first invited me to write a status report on survival research, out of which the present book evolved. Again, to Rafael Collado who never failed to rescue me from computer problems. Several people have read parts of the book and provided useful feedback, or furnished comments I have been able to weave into the text: among them, John Cleese, Suzi Gablik, Stephen Grosso, Colm Kellehar, Don Keys, Jon Klimo, John Mack, Michaeleen Maher, Antonia Mills, Ruth Reinsel. Special thanks to my editor, Patrick Huyghe, for his expert assistance and to my wife, Louise Northcutt, for our many helpful conversations and for her uncanny knack to come up with useful books.

Index

active imagination, 249
afterlife, *see* life after death
aliens, 201–05
Almeder, Robert, 54–55, 108
American Society for Psychical
    Research, 36
animals, 56, 166–67
Annals of Internal Medicine, 275
Antigone (Sophocles), 52
apparitions, 2, 23–62, 276
  anomalous deathbed recoveries,
    41–43
  as boring, 56–58
  crisis, 27–32
  deathbed visions, 32–41
  haunting remains, 55–56
  meeting the spirits, 226–28
  motivation and, 26, 27
  with multiple witnesses, 53–55
  near-death experiences, 43–47
  seeking forgiveness, 58–62
  verified, long after death, 50–53
Aquinas, Thomas, 12, 229, 266
Arbman, Ernst, 193
Aries, Philippe, 267
artistic imagination, 182–87

Aserinsky, Eugene, 179
Augustine, Saint, 13
Augustín-François, 193
automatism, 63, 96, 135–36

Baggally, W. W., 213
Bander, Peter, 214–15
Barrett, Lady Florence, 34
Barrett, William, xv, 34
Battisti, Cesare, 212
Bayless, Raymond, 214
Beals, Bessie, case of, 136
Becker, Ernest, 279
Bergson, Henri, 162, 164
Bernstein, Morey, 106
Bestermann, Theodore, 228
Bhagavad Gita, 124
Bhagchandani, Deepak, 197
Bjnornsson, Hafstein, 87
Black Elk, 7–8
Blake, William, 61, 79, 183, 184,
    185, 187, 219, 250, 251, 255,
    262
Blavatsky, Madam, 64, 81, 129
blind, near-death vision in the,
    47–50

bodily elongation, 199–200
Boer, Charles, 6
Bozzano, Ernesto, 33
brain, the, 171–72
    as seat of consciousness,
        questioning, 41–43, 45–50,
        150, 151, 280
Braud, William, 115, 142
Braude, Ann, 65
Braude, Stephen, 140
Breton, André, 184, 233
Bridge, The (Walker), 69, 74–75
Brinkley, Dannion, 192
Brown, Norman O., 279
Bucke, Richard, 236, 237, 245
Buddha, 222–23, 227
Bugaj, Roman, 213
Burkan, Tolly, 256

Cahagnet, Alphonse, 67
Calvin, John, 265–66
Campbell, Keith, 150
Cannon, Walter, 39
Carington, Whately, 143, 189
Castaneda, Carlos, 233
Catholic Church, 198, 221, 243,
    257–58
Catholic mystics, 193, 194,
    198–99
Chaffin, James L., 52–53, 138–39,
    276
Chandogya Upanishad, 174, 175,
    176
changing our way of life, 255–71,
    278
channeling, 68
Chao Pi Chen, 248
Chattopa, Arpana, 197
Children Who Remember Previous
    Lives (Stevenson), 108
Christianity, 104, 193, 243
Clarke, Edward H., 32
Cobbe, Frances, 34–35
color, 249–51

connections, 153–218
consciousness, 148, 150, 164, 280
    death as change of, 222
    light as symbol of, 179
    in out-of-body experiences, 11,
        22
    questioning the brain as seat of,
        41–43, 45–50, 150, 151, 280
Contributions to the Theory of
    Natural Selection (Wallace),
    161–62
Cooper, Blanche, 136, 142–43
Cooper, Sharon, 47, 48
Corbin, Henry, 148, 249, 250
creative genius, 184
Crookes, William, xv, 211–12
cross-correspondence cases,
    95–101, 276
Cruz, Joan Carroll, 200
cryptomnesia (hidden memory),
    131–32
Crystal-Gazing (Bestermann),
    228
Cummings, Rev. Abraham, 54
Curran, Pearl, 140–41

Dale, Laura, 183
Dante, 176, 200
Darkness Visible (Styron), 5
Darwin, Charles, xv, 129, 155–56,
    166–67
David-Neel, Alexandra, 186–87,
    219
Davis, Gordon, 136–37
Death and Eternal Life (Hick),
    168
deathbed visions, 32–41, 138
Dement, William, 19
Denial of Death, The (Becker),
    279
Denison, Flora Macdonald, 35–36
Denner, William, 179, 280
depression, 5–6, 8
depth psychology, 120–22, 276

Descent of Man, The (Darwin), 166

diet, changing our, 257–62, 278

"direct voice" mediumship, 214

Discovery of the Unconscious, The (Ellenberger), 64

dissociation, 64, 194, 258

"distant intentionality," 115

Dodds, E. R., 101–02

Dommeyer, Frederick, 54

Donne, John, 121

Dorr, George B., 98

Dossey, Larry, 274

Doyle, Arthur Conan, 64

Dream, The (Byron poem), 177

dreams, 277
  creativity of, 180
  imagining the next world in, 147, 148
  lucid, 232–34
  as mental bridges to the next world, 176–82
  nightmares, 181, 208–09
  precognitive and clairvoyant, 177–78
  recurrent, 181–82

Eastern philosophies, 3, 104

Edison, Thomas, 160, 214

Edmonds, John, 217

Edwards, Paul, 41, 108

Eisenbud, Jule, 217

Eliade, Mircea, 10, 191, 194

Elkin, A. P., 191

Ellenberger, Henri, 64

Emerson, Ralph Waldo, 75

English Society of Psychical Research, 27, 29, 206

ESP, 174

Evans-Wentz, 234

evolution, 155–69
  of ability to survive, 167–69
  Darwin and survival research, 155–56

life and afterlife, 158–59
our next world body, 161–66
the postmortem environment, 156–57
survival of other species, 166–67
technology and life after death, 159–61

explanations of reports of life after death, 128, 129–44
  automatism and mythmaking, 135–36
  fraud and fabrication, 133–35
  inability to falsify a claim and, 141–42
  mal-observation, 131
  retrocognition, 142–44
  special skills, 140–41
  super con artist within, 136–37
  superpsi, 137–44
  tricks and errors of memory, 131–33

Extreme Spirituality (Burkan), 256

Falk, Rodney H., 274

Fast Food Nation (Schlosser), 261

Feilding, Everard, 213

Ficino, Marsilio, xv, 27–28

Field Guide to Extraterrestrials, The (Huyghe), 202

Flammarion, Camille, xv, 212

flatliner models, 225–54

Flournoy, Gustave, xv

flying saucers, 201–05

Fontana, David, 206, 207

Forbes, Bryan, 134

Foulkes, David, 179

Fox, Kate and Maggie, 134

Fox, Oliver, 230

Franklin, Benjamin, 161

Freuchen, Peter, 226

Freud, Sigmund, xv, 121, 135, 148

Gablik, Suzi, 186

Gallup, George, Jr., 35

ganzfeld, 229–30
Garfield, Charles, 267–68
Gauld, Alan, 87
Geley, Gustave, 212
ghosts, *see* apparitions
Gleanings in Buddha Fields
    (Hearn), 106
Globus, Gordon, 180
Godbey, John, 150
Godmakers, The (Pratt), 105
Goleman, Daniel, 269
Goodrich-Freer, Ada, 228–29
Gould, Stephen, 159
Greek philosophers, xiii–ix
Green, Cecilia, 12, 15–16, 17–18
Griffin, David, 142
Guirhdom, Arthur, 106

Hall, Stanley, 136
Hamlet, 55, 93, 148, 176
Haraldsson, Erlendur, 39, 40, 44,
    88, 196
Hardinge, Emma, 65
Hardy, Sir Alister, 162, 164
Hatch, Cora, 65
Hearn, Lafcadio, 106
Hearne, Keith, 232
Heraclitus, 121
Hick, John, 168
Hinduism, 200, 238, 241
Hodgson, Richard, 17, 81, 85,
    129, 130, 131
Home, D. D., 210, 211, 212
Homer, 177
Houston, Jean, 42
Hufford, David, 208–09
Hughes, Robert, 270
Huxley, Julian, 158, 165, 258, 280
Huyghe, Patrick, 202
hypermnesia, 132–33
Hyslop, Joseph, 186

idiot-savants, 172–73
imagining the next world, 145–52

afterlife research in a culture of
    death, 151–52
artistic imagination, 182–87
paradigm paralysis, 149–51
*Immortality Proved by Testimony
    of Sense*, 53–54
Indian deathbed visions, 40
Indridason, Indridi, 210

Jacobsen, Edmund, 231
James, William, xv, 79, 85, 132,
    270
Jesus, 227
Johnson, Alice, 27, 97
Joseph, father of Jesus, 198–99
Journey to Ixtlan, The
    (Castenada), 233
Juergenson, Friedrich, 214
Jung, Carl, xv, 121, 178–79,
    201–02, 249, 278

Kandinsky, Wassily, 183
Keel, John, 202
Keen, Montague, 93
Kelleher, Colm, 163–64
King, Stephen, 55
Kirk, Robert, 258
Kleitman, Nathaniel, 179
Klimo, John, 215–16
Kluski, Franek (Teofil
    Modrzejewski), 212–13
Knight, J. Z., 68
Kobra, Najm, 250–51
Krippner, Stanley, 64
kundalini energy, 200, 241
Kurzweil, Ray, 160

LaBerge, Stephen, 232–33
Lamarck, Jean-Baptiste, 162
Lame Deer, John, 226–27
Lang, Andrew, 56, 58
Lavater, Lewes, 62
Leary, Timothy, 160
Leonard, Gladys, 91, 262

Lessing, Gotthold, 105
levitation, 198–99
life after death:
  evolution and, *see* evolution
  explanations for reports of, *see*
    explanations of reports of life
    after death
  mental bridges to, *see* mental
    bridges
  the Otherworld nearby, *see*
    Otherworld nearby
  types of difficulties in weighing
    the evidence for, 127–28
Life Against Death (Brown),
  279
ligature, 193, 194
light, 179, 200, 234–38, 239–54
Lincoln, Abraham, 177, 217
Living Stream, The, 162
Living the Magical Life (Gablik),
  186
Locke, John, 178
Lodge, Sir Oliver, xv, 85
Loftus, Elizabeth, 133
London, Jack, 11
Lyons, Arthur, 93

McCormick, Donna, 20, 205
McDougall, William, xv
McGinn, Colin, 280
machines as keyholes to the next
  world, 214–16
Mack, John, 203–04
Macy, Mark, 215
Mailer, Norman, 120
Marilyn (Mailer), 120
Martin, Father Bill, 258
Maslow, Abraham, 21–22
materialistic paradigm, 149–52
Maugham, Somerset, 105
mediums, 2, 63–102, 136, 277
  book-tests, 88–90
  case of G.P., 79–86, 129–30
  controls, 80

cross-correspondence tests,
  95–101, 276
drop-in communicators, 87–88
love and life after death, 69–75
newspaper tests, 90–93
obsession, afterlife, and
  creativity, 75–79
physical mediumship, 209–13
police investigations and, 93–95
"proxy" sittings, 67–68, 69–75,
  101–02
memory, 131–33, 171–74, 277
mental bridges, 170–87
  artistic imagination, 182–87
  dreams, 176–82
  memory, 171–74
  the will, 174–76
Mercato, Michael, 28
Michelangelo, 185, 219
Mills, Antonia, 108, 124, 181
"mindsight," 47–50
"miracles," 195–201
Moody, Raymond, 229
Morell, 11
Mormons, 105
Morris, Robert, 216
Morse, Melvin, 234–35, 237
Muhl, Anita, 135
Muldoon, Sylvan, 230
Mumler, William H., 217
Munves, James, 129, 130
Murphy, Gardner, 136
Murphy, Michael, 165
Myers, Frederic, ix, xv, 27, 58, 85,
  95–101, 129, 135, 156, 157,
  184, 233
"My Platonic Sweetheart," 181–82
mysticism, 21, 189, 192–94, 222,
  243, 277

Nature of Consciousness, The, 150
near-death experiences, 1, 45, 192,
  203, 234–35
  apparitions and, 43–47

nightmares, 181, 208–09
"no-consent" cases of deathbed
    visions, 39, 41

Odyssey, The (Homer), 177
"Old Hag," 208–09
organ transplant patients,
    memories of dead donors of,
    173
Origin of Species, The (Darwin),
    155
Osis, Karl, 20, 36–39, 40, 42, 44,
    205
Otherworld nearby, keyholes to,
    188–219
  machines, 214–16
  "miracles" and, 195–201
  the "Old Hag," 208–09
  photographing the spirits,
    216–18
  physical mediumship, 209–13
  poltergeists, 205–08
  traditional openings, 189–90
out-of-body experiences, xii, 2,
    6–22, 230, 277
  ecstatic separation, 7–8
  experimental studies, 18–22
  heightened self-awareness and,
    15–16
  otherbodied environments,
    11–12
  "subtle" body, 12–14
  traveler's inner state, 13–14
  verifiable, 16–18
  as widespread experience, 8–9,
    11

Palladino, Eusapia, 210, 213
Palmer, John, 12
Parkhurst, Henry, 49
Pasricha, Satwant, 108
past-life regressions, 124
"past-life therapy," 104
Pastrovicchi, Angelo, 198–99

Patanjali, 193–94, 199, 269
Paul of Tarsus (St. Paul), 7, 64, 65
Peak in Darien, The (Cobbe),
    34–35, 138
Pellew, George, case of (G.P.),
    79–86, 129–30, 276
Penfield, Wilder, 171
Peterson, Robert, 231–32
Phaedrus (Plato), 185
Philo, 264, 266
Phone Call from the Dead (Rogo
    and Raymond), 214
photographing the spirits, 216–18
phowa, 244
Pio, Padre, 200, 258
Piper, Eleanora, 98, 132, 262
Piper, Leonora, 79–86, 136
Plato, xvi–xvii, 21, 125, 185, 250,
    266, 269
Playfair, Guy, 93
Pliny the Younger, 56
Podmore, Frank, 27
poltergeists, 205–08
Pratt, Orson, 105
Price, H. H., 116, 147–48
Price, Harry, 134
Priestley, J. B., 161
progressive relaxation, 231
"promissory materialism," 150
prophecy, 189, 190–91, 194
psychical research, xiv–xv, 16, 65,
    153, 279
  founders of, ix, 129, 156
  see also specific research topics
psychic capacity ("psi"), 20
psychokinesis, 174–75
Pullman, Philip, 14
purgatory, 168
Pursel, Jach, 68

Radical Spirits (Braude), 65
Rank, Otto, 139
Rasmussen, Knud, 237
Raudive, Konstantin, 214–15

Ravi Shankar Gupta, 122
reincarnation, 2, 103–26, 172,
    276, 277
  announcing dreams, 110
  appeal of, 123–24
  behavioral memories, 113–14,
    117–20
  belief in, 104–06
  bodily marks connecting two
    lives, 114–16
  Ceylon case, 117–20
  characteristics of cases of,
    109–16
  expanded depth psychology,
    120–22
  explanatory value of, 122–23
  imaged memories, 110–13
  intimations of past lives, 124–25
  nightmares and, 181
  possibilities for personal
    experiment, 125–26
  prediction of rebirth, 109–10
  Stevenson's work, 106–08
Reinventing Medicine (Dossey),
    274
religious fundamentalists, 148
responsive xenoglossy, 140, 141
retrocognition, 142–44
"Retrotransposons as Engines of
    Human Bodily
    Transformation," 163
Reynolds, Pamela, 45–47
Richet, Charles, xv, 33–34, 102,
    212
Rimbaud, Arthur, 146
Ring, Kenneth, 47, 48, 203, 237
Rogo, D. Scott, 202, 214
Roll, William, 12
Rostan, J. J., 67
Ryall, Edward, 106

Sabom, Michael, 44–45
Sailing to Byzantium (Yeats), 184
Sathya Sai Baba, 195

Schlitz, Marilyn, 115
Schlosser, Eric, 261
Schroder, Tom, 107
science, ix, 10, 62, 221
  see also psychical research
scrying, 228–29
Séance on a Wet Afternoon
    (Forbes), 134
Secrets of Cultivating Nature and
    Eternal Life, The (Chao Pi
    Chen), 248
Serios, Ted, 217, 219
Shakespeare, William, 61, 93, 178
shamanism, 10–11, 189, 191–92,
    194, 222, 259, 277
Sheldrake, Rupert, 162, 166
Shelly, Percy Bysshe, 185
Sidgwick, Eleanor, 17, 27, 85
Sidgwick, Henry, ix, 27, 85, 129
Simpson, Anne, 25, 26
Singer, Peter, 260–61
Smythe, Colin, 215
Soal, S. G., 136–37
Society for Psychical Research,
    25
Sophocles, 52
"spectral aphasia," 56
Spetzler, Dr. Robert, 45
spirits, see apparitions
spiritualism, 64–66, 134
  social philosophy of, 65–66
spontaneous illuminations,
    235–38
Sprague, Achsa, 65
Star Rover (London), 11
Stevenson, Ian, 106–16, 121,
    122–23, 124, 181
Stevenson, Robert Louis, 75, 184
stigmata, 114, 199
strain-gauge sensor, 20–21
Styron, William, 5
Sufism, 193, 254
"superpsi," 67–68, 137–44
surrealism, 184, 233

Sylvia, Claire, 173
Symposium (Plato), xvi–xvii

Tanner, Amy, 136
Tanous, Alex, 20–21, 22, 276
Tantric Buddhism, 240, 243
Taoism, 245–49
Tart, Charles, 18
technology and life after death,
    159–61
telepathy, 69, 157, 162, 163
Thomas, Charles Drayton, 90–93
Thurston, Herbert, 196, 198, 200,
    201
Tibetan Buddhism, 163, 200
Tibetans, 241–45
Toynebee, Arnold, 160
Traubel, Horace, 35–36, 38
Treffert, Darold, 172
Truzzi, Marcello, 93
Tucker, James, 108
tummo yoga, 200, 240, 243, 248
Twain, Mark, 75, 79, 177–78,
    181–82, 184

UFOs, 201–05
Unamuno, Miguel de, 278
unconscious, 148, 178–79, 249
Urbanski, Thaddeus, 212

Vallee, Jacques, 202, 204
Van de Castle, Robert, 176–77

van Gogh, Vincent, 183
Varagnac, Arthur, 49–50
Vedanta Society, xii
Visions: A Study of False Sight
    (Clarke), 32
Voltaire, 156
von Franz, Marie-Louise, 181

Walker, Nea, 69–75
Wallace, Alfred Russel, xv, 34,
    156–57, 161–62, 162
Weber, Max, 265
Whiteman, J. H. M., 14–15, 46,
    230
Whitman, Walt, 35–36, 38, 236,
    237, 264
Wilhelm, Richard, 247
will, human, 174–76, 268–69
Wilson, Colin, 210
Wordsworth, William, 186
work, 263–68, 278

Yama, the Lord of Death,
    238–39
Yeats, William Butler, 79, 172,
    184, 185
yoga and yogis, 192–93, 200, 222,
    241, 243, 248
Yoga Sutras, 193–94, 269

Zoltowski, Adam, 212–13
Zwingili, 266